THE INTELLECTUALS SPEAK OUT ABOUT

GOD

A Handbook for the Christian
Student in a Secular Society

Edited by Roy Abraham Varghese

A GATEWAY EDITION ● REGNERY GATEWAY

Published by Regnery Gateway, Inc.
360 West Superior Street
Chicago, Illinois 60610

ISBN: 0-89526-827-2

Manufactured in the United States of America.

The following people were of vital assistance in compiling *THE INTELLECTUALS SPEAK OUT ABOUT GOD* and we wish to thank them most heartily for their kindness and dedication:

Mr. Bradley Anderson
Mrs. Josi Bellinger
Miss Cindy Brinker
Mrs. Mary Crowley
Miss Ann Dodson
Miss Gay Dodson
Dr. Norman L. Geisler
Dr. Loyal N. Gould
Mrs. Janet Gutman
Miss Pamela D. Hallett
Miss Janet R. Haney
Mr. Lyle Harris
Miss Melissa Helm
Miss Julie Hetherly
Miss Tamara Ketler
Mr. Danny Korem
Mr. Ronald Linam
Mr. John Schiwitz
Rev. Maurice Stanford
Mr. Barry C. Steger
Mr. Steven Stinson
Mr. Jeffrey Talburt
Jogy, Rani and Anil Thomas
Mr. Hale Umstattd
Mr. & Mrs. M. Abraham Varghese
Mr. & Mrs. M. M. Varghese
Rena, Mohan and Anila Varghese
Mrs. Mitzi Watts

Acknowledgements

"From Scientific Cosmology to a Created Universe" was first printed in *The Irish Astronomical Journal*, Vol. 15, No. 3, March 1982, pp. 253-262 and was kindly offered for this anthology by Professor Jaki. It is reprinted with the permission of the editor of *The Irish Astronomical Journal*.

"God's Will: Reflections on the Problem of Pain" first appeared in *The Living Church*, June 21, 1981. "Unisexism: Second Thoughts on Women's 'Liberation'" first appeared in *New Oxford Review*, Dec. 1981. The author, Mr. Sheldon Vanauken, modified them for inclusion in this collection and they are reprinted here with permission from the editors of *The Living Church* and *New Oxford Review*.

Table of Contents

PART III — *Apologetics and Theology*

INTRODUCTION

Dedication

The Intellectuals Speak Out About God: A Handbook for the Christian Student in a Secular Society **is dedicated to C.S. Lewis in the hope that his works will draw millions more to the word of God and to the Word-made-flesh.**

A Message From Dom Bede Griffiths

It would seem that we are entering on a new age in which religion will be much more respected, and the case for Christianity will be able to be argued with more persuasiveness. Roy Varghese has collected in this book essays in defense of Christianity from different points of view and has dedicated the book to the memory of C.S. Lewis. I was fortunate enough to have C.S. Lewis as my tutor at Oxford in the days when neither he nor I professed any religion, and we journeyed a long way together on the path that led us to Christian faith. Lewis was engaged in defending Christianity in the context of the old mechanistic science and skeptical philosophy which, of course, still prevails to a large extent. But he was a first-class scholar in his own field of English literature and though not a professional philosopher-theologian had profound insights into the major problems of philosophy and theology. His defense of Christianity, though necessarily dated in some respects (as all apologetics must be in the course of time), yet remains deeply impressive because of the personal conviction and the intellectual honesty with which he faced the fundamental problems of religion. The defense of religion and Christianity has to be renewed in every generation as new systems of science and philosophy continue to develop and the climate of thought in the world changes. It is to be hoped that this book will provide a stimulus to Christian thinking in the world today.

Foreword

THE WHITE HOUSE

WASHINGTON

June 23, 1982

On a recent May weekend I had the privilege and
pleasure of attending my 50th class reunion and
giving the commencement address at Eureka College.
During that very nostalgic weekend, I was reminded
of the differences between the challenges which
my class of '32 had to meet and the problems that
confront today's college students.

While we spent our college years in the midst of
a severe depression, our generation thrived in
the special spirit of sharing what little we did
have and that helped us to pull through those
difficult days. Today, as students, you prepare
to step forward into a world enduring another
economic crisis, which I hope and pray my Admin-
istration can resolve. But I believe that our
Nation is in the grip of another crisis that is
ultimately far more serious -- an era of moral
decline.

Through every public medium available, our young
people are bombarded daily with assaults on the
fundamental values which shaped and sustained
this Nation. It is difficult to turn on a radio
or television, read a newspaper, magazine or popular book, or see a movie in a neighborhood theater
and not find an attack on the ethics and moral
values we have been taught to cherish. Drug and
alcohol abuse have taken a terrible toll on our
youth.

Great courage is needed to live a Christian life
in today's society. We know that only God can
give us the courage and the guidance we so badly
need. Challenges to faith today are legion,
and you may find yourself faced with choices that
another generation could not have imagined --
and the right choice will not always be the
popular choice.

I am convinced, however, that hope is the essence
of belief. The struggle to maintain the faith
is arduous, but life's storms are over at the
last and faith finds the strong ship at anchor
in a calm sea. We must always remember that we
are created in God's image, that we will never
be abandoned if we seek our solace and optimism
in trust and in prayer.

I wish all of you success in your studies. I
wish you every happiness and good fortune in
the future. I wish you God's blessings today,
tomorrow and always.

Sincerely,

Ronald Reagan

Message From The Vatican
Cardinal Joseph Ratzinger

Prefect of the Sacred Congregation for the Doctrine of
the Faith

I am very glad that these great scientists present us
their convictions here as well-founded, as scientifically
founded. I think also that the existence of God is not
only a matter of faith; it is really reasonable too, because
an objective reason exists in the world which is visible to
the natural sciences, which signifies the presence of a
creative idea and which is also a permanent demonstration of creative reason.

I think that the natural sciences are possible only
because in all things reason is present and a reason
which is much greater than ours. I would say that explanations purely in terms of evolution are unreasonable.

The Basic Truths of Christianity

These begin with the word of the Holy Gospel
which speaks of Christ our Lord and reveals that Christ
is really the Son of God. And a consequence of Christ
being really the Son of God and really man is the reality
of the Holy Trinity. Again, we have received justification
and forgiveness of our sins from our Lord, and on the
Holy Cross He has given redemption for the world. In
faith and in participation in the Christian life we can
receive forgiveness, renewed life and, finally, expectations and hope of eternal life and of the reign of God. I
think these are the basic truths of Christianity, common
to those who really accept the New Testament.

On Contemporary Christology

Basically the great Christian denominations, the Catholic church, the Orthodox church and the great traditional Protestant communities accepted the common heritage of the early church. At the time of the Reformation it was common to accept the great creeds of the early church and in accepting the common heritage of the councils also accepted was the divinity of Christ. Only with the onset of liberal theology which begins in the time of the Enlightenment, after the Second World War and in our time, has there developed and spread a theological tendency which does not accept the common heritage of the early church. This tendency interprets the word of the Bible only with historical methods, distinguishes different levels of credibility in the Bible and does not accept the divinity of Christ. This tendency is a separation from all Christian tradition, not only the Catholic tradition but also the common tradition of all the great reformed denominations. And, I think, it must be the common task of all Christians and of the Christian community to defend this common heritage of our Christian tradition.

Preface

THE LAST HOPE FOR THE UNIVERSITY

J. Stanley Oakes, Jr.

I search in vain for any reference to the fact that character, personal integrity, spiritual depth, the highest moral standards, the wonderful living values of the great tradition, have anything to do with the business of the university or with the world of learning.

Dr. Charles H. Malik — President, General Assembly of the United Nations; Distinguished Ambassador to the United States from Lebanon; Holder of a Harvard Ph.D. in philosophy and 50 honorary doctorates. Initiator and signer of the 1948 United Nations Universal Declaration on Human Rights.

The university in America has grown over the three and a half centuries of its existence like the Mississippi River does over its 2348 mile course. Beginning in Minnesota at Lake Itasca, it emanates in a stream so humble in its origins that even a child can step across it. One could hardly imagine that the mighty mile-wide Mississippi River of the New Orleans delta could be one and the same. So it is with our universities.

They have come from educating a few fortunate souls to tutoring the leaders of America and the world and making knowledge available to the masses. Now, over sixty million Americans are involved in the educational process each year. There are fifty million public and private school students below college level. They are taught by 2.3 million teachers. The universities are molding the minds of thirteen million more, and six hundred thousand professors orchestrate the entire process.[1] The university is now the architect of our society.

Unfortunately, education has lost its moorings. Where once a student was confronted with a Christian view of the world in over seventy percent of his course work through such texts as the original *McGuffey's Reader* and *The New England Primer*, now it is less than one percent. The public schools in New York City at one time required a minimum standard of character for a student to graduate. This was discarded in the 1930s. Steven Muller, president of Johns Hopkins University, summarized the essence of the problem when he said, "The failure to rally around a set of values means that universities are turning out potentially highly skilled barbarians."[2] Franklin Delano Roosevelt flatly rejected such an educational philosophy by declaring that to train a man in mind and not in morals is to train a menace to society. This failure is in spite of the fact that education in America owes its very existence to Christianity.

Within forty years of the landing at Plymouth Rock, the Puritans turned to the task of educating a "learned clergy and a lettered people."[3] The outcome was the founding of Harvard College in 1636. Few people realize it, but Harvard started out as a Christian college, and was one hundred years old before there was even one professor who was not a minister.[4] Furthermore, Harvard's original charter contains the following educational mandate: "Everyone shall consider the main end of his life and studies to know Jesus Christ which is eternal life." When Harvard professors began to lose their zeal for the faith, Yale was founded. When Yale began to falter, others were established to take its place. Even so, the president of Yale in 1754, Thomas Clap, declared the early purpose of colleges as "societies of ministers for training up persons for the work of the ministry."[5]

Gradually, colleges began to spring up all over, and of the first one hundred and nineteen, one hundred and four were started by Christians to acquaint students with the knowledge of God — including Princeton, Dartmouth and Columbia (and, of course, Harvard and Yale).[6] Out of a graduating class of forty thousand in 1855, *ten thousand* went on to become ministers — over 25 percent![7]

All over America, people are lamenting the deterioration in traditional values, though they do not understand how it all happened. Some might say that it is due to a general lack of interest in religion today, but actually the opposite is true. A recent Gallup poll indicated that 67 percent of all Americans are members of an organized church, and two out of every three people are more interested in religion today than they were five years ago. An incredible *43 million persons* are actively involved in Bible study groups.[8]

The problem is that this country's leaders within education, as well as the media, government, and business, do not feel the same way. A recent study by Research and Forecasts, Inc. for the Connecticut Mutual Life Insurance Company clearly revealed that although religion is "the one factor that consistently and dramatically affects the values and behavior of Americans," America's leaders are out of touch with the public and do not represent them. They are more compromising on the moral issues and are "less religiously committed," the study said.[9]

The university is in a paradoxical situation. It is desperately in need of the enduring Christian values that gave rise to its founding but is unable to provide them. There are basically two reasons for this. First, its leaders have drifted into or have been pressured into adopting a policy of *neutrality* towards religion. Neutrality towards religion may be benign in concept, but it has radically altered the face of the university by spawning an irreligious and even anti-religious bias. Also, a spurious application of the doctrine of separation of church and state is gradually being litigated into acceptance by the American Civil Liberties Union. Instead of keeping the state out of religion as the Constitution originally intended, religion (along with its humanizing values and morals) is being barred from the university. Whereas 12,000 Marxists are free to teach in state universities,[10] any Christian influence of even the most innocuous kind is met by intimidation and threats of legal action.

Let me make it clear that I am not so much against letting the Marxists be there (although it seems as though we find a perverse pleasure in letting our enemies educate us), as I am advocating that the Christian view of reality be allowed presentation in all of its power and clarity — especially as it affects each discipline, from history and psychology to science and ethics. This is easily done on an individual basis and in a manner appropriate to the university setting.

Another guiding principle which is beset by this narrow view of God and the classroom is academic freedom. As it is now advanced by the American Association of University Professors, it is the freedom not only to *research* a discipline in whatever way one wants but to *teach* whatever one wants. Any attempts by concerned alumni to protect their children from indoctrination or from material inconsistent with traditional American values are met by cries of "Academic Freedom!" and "Censorship!" As an aside, let me say that I enthusiastically support academic freedom as the freedom to research, investigate, inquire, or pursue any vein of interest within generally accepted parameters of decency. This does not, however, confer the right to teach impressionable students whatever one pleases. A recent University of Texas report on academic freedom concurred and forbade professors from using their finely-honed cognitive skills to "shake up students beliefs" or "lead them to question their values."[11] And yet only the naive would fail to see that this is being conducted on a wholesale level.

It now appears that the first realm of thought to be unceremoniously removed from the confines of academic freedom is the Christian view of reality. In almost any field, to identify one's self as a Christian invites intimidation reminiscent of the Ku Klux Klan toward blacks in the rural South with the exception that it is done in the name of progress, tolerance and broad-minded eclecticism.

One must ask how a scholar can eliminate one whole view of the world, which just happens to be the majority view in America and the view responsible for education in our land and call it academic freedom? It is inconceivable, and yet the situation will probably worsen because the university is such an ingrown environment, and its leaders are not really accountable for their lack of fairness nor are they uncomfortable with it.

These are not the only changes in education in 350 years. The inaccurate perception that Christianity is somehow based on blind faith and should never, or worse, cannot, be subjected to scrutiny is another. Even many well-meaning Christians adhere to this view. This anti-intellectualism is totally contrary to history as well as to the Bible. Christianity is a reasonable faith as evidenced by Paul's presentation to the first century intellectuals on Mars Hill in Athens. Recall, also, that Paul was a scholar of the first order before his conversion. He came humbly into the kingdom of God as all must, but his skills of inquiry and teaching were still his most utilized gifts. King Agrippa, in the face of Paul's loving but convincing defense of the faith, flagged under his verbal parries with the reply, "In a short time you will *persuade* me to become a Christian."[12] In spite of what the current feeling is, then, thought, like a wayward adolescent, needs to be guided and not abandoned.

The abandoning of the arena of ideas has its roots in America as early as 1738 when John Winthrop, Harvard's first professor who was not a minister, discovered that earthquakes are of a natural origin. This bothered a great number of ministers at the time.[13] Evidently they felt that to say earthquakes were not directly from the hand of God somehow impugned God's sovereignty. As a result, they rejected this earth-shaking discovery thereby setting the precedent for a loss of Christian leadership in the pursuit of knowledge. These ministers failed to differentiate between *revealed truth*, that is, answers to life's questions which only God can illuminate, and *observational truth*, the realm of truth which God did not reveal but wants us to seek out for ourselves, for example, the origin of earthquakes. Ironically, what was once the error of the Christian thinker is now the error of the secularist, the mechanist, the positivist, the agnostic, and the atheist. These also assume that there is only one kind of knowledge — *observational truth*. To them there is no such thing as *revealed truth*. So now we are a high frontier society of geniuses producing moral pygmies who are confused and befuddled by the choices of a technological age.

The anti-intellectual spirit among Christians could not be more misguided because the university is now besieged by a one-party mentality. Consider the sexual revolution of the last 30 years. The rise in teenage pregnancies, abortion, divorce, homosexuality, the break-up of families, birth control, sex education. All of these topics are regularly and rigorously being addressed in the university, but only in light of a fluctuating moral relativism. The absolute view of morals is not even considered an option, nor is any time or thought given to presenting its case.

Another intriguing situation involves the Carnegie Foundation's invitation to Gunnar Myrdal, the Nobel prize-winning socialist economist from Sweden, in 1937, to study the black problem in America. Seven years later he published his treatise entitled *The American Dilemma*. Professor John Kenneth Galbraith called it a "powerful document on racial injustice" and a "vital early step up in the struggle for civil rights."[14] In fact, it served as the foundation for much of what we see as the government's solution to inequality. While I personally appreciate the motives of many civil rights advocates and do not respect anyone who is so heartless that he does not care about the poor, the handicapped and the less fortunate of the world, I believe it is open to discussion as to how one goes about helping them. Why must we spend billions of dollars and devastate millions of people before we realize perhaps we should have solicited second opinions? And where were those second opinions? Where was the conviction that to wage war against inequality is the church's responsibility and not a political ideology? Where were those farsighted believers who could offer a voice of reason and hope to the task? Where was the manpower and funding to carry out this visible love of Christ? Why do we always settle for hindsight instead of foresight, reproducing instead of originating, getting on the bandwagon instead of leading the charge? Because a spirit of anti-intellectualism keeps us uninformed we can only attack and not contribute.

Interestingly, the connection between a professor, a foundation and the government is a familiar scenario. A foundation with vast sums of money in need of dispersal provides funds to a compatible professor who is deemed to be an expert on an issue in crisis. The results of his research are institutionalized either because they become the content of some university textbook and catalyze the minds of our future leaders or because they become another government program. The media then popularizes these results.

In my opinion this is one of the main ways America's leaders are building their "brave new world." In the meantime, America wanders aimlessly, desperate for a national resolve and an heroic moral leadership because the Christian values of the fatherland have been squeezed out of the educational system. Content without character.

Fortunately, there is a bright spot. In the last twenty years, the "best and brightest" of those making the cutting edge contributions in thought and discovery have been returning to God. *The Intellectuals Speak Out About God: A Handbook for the Christian Student in a Secular Society* is a reflection of this movement.

My friend, Roy Varghese, is particularly aware of this movement through his acquaintance with nearly everyone in the book. And the interview format is particularly helpful because it allows them to comment in a very readable style on many of the key issues. This is also done because most of these men are not popularizers in the tradition of a Carl Sagan or an Isaac Asimov but are the world's foremost living scientists and philosophers. Writers like Sagan and Asimov create the false impression that there is a contradiction between Christian thought and science or philosophy. Their campaign of intimidation will lose much of its force when these intellectuals speak out.

Previously, in the *Humanist Manifesto I* of 1933 and *Humanist Manifesto II* of 1973, the atheistic signers saw themselves as setting the intellectual agenda for subsequent years. They "regard the universe as self-existing and not created." And declared,

We find insufficient evidence for the belief in the existence of a supernatural; it is either meaningless or irrelevant to the question of the survival and fulfillment of the human role. As non-theists, we begin with humans, not God, nature not deity. Nature may indeed be broader and deeper than we now know; any new discoveries, however, will but enlarge our knowledge of the natural. But we can discover no divine purpose or providence for the human species. While there is much that we do not know, humans are responsible for what we are or will become. No deity will save us, we must save ourselves.[15]

"It would be naive to think that the *Manifestos*, in themselves, are solely responsible for the contemporary situation in which it is taken for granted that belief in God is an amusing anachronism that threatens social progress and intellectual emancipation. On the natural plane, the roots of this rejection of the 'mysterium tremendum et fascinans' can be found in the intellectual history of the last few hundred years. David Hume and his disciples held that only the data of the senses (what could be perceived in test tubes and telescopes) were acceptable and all else (goodness, God and the rest) was meaningless. Immanuel Kant reduced God to a subjective sentiment. Friedrich Nietzsche declared him dead. Charles Darwin found chance a better explanation for the cosmos than a Creator. Karl Marx revealed that God was the 'opiate of the masses' invented by the ruling classes. Sigmund Freud insisted that he was merely a neurosis.

"These caricatures of the Creator became a new Bill of Rights that took over the thought processes of the twentieth century, a set of magical mantras that mesmerized all levels of society and the intellectual world.

In the United States these caricatures were expressed in such 'philosophies' as: Ayn Rand's objectionism which was a rerun of Neitzsche and many of the fiercer atheists who had ambitions to divinity; B.F. Skinner's Behaviorism which, by Skinner's own admission, was an ideal intellectual instrument for totalitarian regimes and which, through its contemptuous rejection of 'freedom and dignity,' doomed any society seeking to root itself in values sacred to civilized man; and process theology which 're-made' God in the image of man and which was grounded in modern man's refusal to accept either the significance of the transcendent in daily life or any deity which he could not comprehend without difficulty.

"The last two or three decades, however, have witnessed a phenomenal, if muted, revolution in the international intellectual community (particularly in Anglo-American academia) and unprecedented in the last several hundred years. In philosophy, physics and most of the different disciplines, noted thinkers who had labored under the dogmas and doctrines of militant scientism have reversed the accelerating thrust towards secularism at the highest levels of academic thought. This radical shift in perspective has not been highlighted as much as it could or should have been in the mass media, but it has been occasionally noted."[16]

For instance, not long ago, *Time* magazine broke the story in an April 7, 1980 article: "In a quiet revolution in thought and argument that hardly anyone would have foreseen only two decades ago, God is making a comeback. Most intriguingly this is happening ... in the crisp intellectual circles of academic philosophers."

The story is also told by the increasing dissatisfaction among those in the scientific community. The president of the American Association for the Advancement of Science revealed recently: "It is my impression that some time in the past, either the scientific community oversold or the public overbought science and technology. There are questions that science cannot address and things that science and technology cannot accomplish."[17]

In *The Intellectuals Speak Out About God: A Handbook for the Christian Student in a Secular Society*, we seek to formulate rather informally, a theistic manifesto. We let several of the best-known intellectuals of the day — a number of whom have, in fact, spearheaded the theistic revolution — speak for themselves and to present what they perceive to be the factors which precipitated their flight from atheism.

The *Handbook* is also a call to bold action for Christians everywhere. The university is no longer a forum for the pursuit of truth but rather an ideological battlefield where a great struggle is being waged for the minds and hearts of young men and women. Bertell Ollman, an avowed Marxist professor presently engaged at New York University, fired the first public salvo by asserting, "More and more students and professors are being introduced to Marx's interpretation ... It is a peaceful and democratic revolution fought chiefly with books and lectures."[18]

The hour is late and the world is desperate for a dramatic upsurge of conviction. It is the era for a *new believer* to galvanize his or her own generation into a force to restore a proper Christian dimension to the university, nay, to recapture our universities for Christ. To do so the following issues must be understood by Christians concerned about the future of our land: 1) Realize the great heritage that Christianity has afforded the university and Western civilization. 2) Admit that because of our own collective anti-intellectual spirit, an unfounded bias has arisen against analysis from a Christian perspective. 3) Acknowledge that the Bible does not teach us to abandon the world system but rather to saturate it with a Christian perspective. 4) Realize that education is now a battlefield and must be approached in terms of winning and losing conflicts before it can be returned to a forum for the discovery of truth. Classrooms, students, professors, committees, tenure, academic freedom, research, textbooks, and journals represent the fronts on which the struggle must be played out. 5) Categorically reject the notion of neutrality since it fosters the denial of any possibility for absolute truth and promotes irreligion or anti-religion as well as stifling appropriate inquiry by Christians in academia. 6) Develop an integrated Christian view of things because Jesus Christ and the Christian message are the solutions to mankind's heart problem. Ultimately it is the solution to all other problems also, as we investigate the implications of His commands and teachings upon our lives andour world.

What must be done? In my opinion the last hope for our colleges and universities are their alumni. Alumni, in general, because they control the boards and the purse strings. Also, they are concerned about the anti-capitalist bent of higher education which now seems to be all-pervasive. Joseph Epstein, the editor of *American Scholar*, in a candid reflection on his own personal experience, revealed that "apart from certain religious schools and certain colleges in the South and perhaps in Utah, the reigning ethos in American colleges and universities today is the anti-capitalist ethos." He even revealed that the more prestigious the school, "the more the ideas of anti-capitalism tended to hold sway."[19] Since most businessmen content themselves with watch-dogging the direction of the sports program or the business school of their alma mater, they are unaware of the disdain with which the rest of the university often portrays them. One might even say that it is the function of top administrators to keep alumni from becoming upset over what is being taught and at the same trying to mollify their unruly academic community. Money, however, does speak loudly, and alumni must be awakened to their responsibility to hold the university accountable.

The Christian alumni can play a more significant role, that of demanding content plus character. I suggest a two-pronged approach. First, I propose the establishment of an all-university alumni organization. The call is to one million Christian alumni — graduates of every college and university in America — to take leadership in an orchestrated effort to return a vibrant spiritual perspective to the entire university — school by school and course by course. This new and unprecedented organization will provide the influence and the resources which could transform the university in our lifetime. Called the Christian Leadership Alumni Association, it will generate enormous sums of money by means of dues, endowments and contributions, to enable positive and creative input to the university.

At the same time we must involve at least 80,000 professors who are thoroughly Christian and the ablest of our generation, to blaze a trail of research based on the Bible. Soon this will spring forth in solutions to the issues in crisis: the role of women, sex education, prison reform, war and peace, medical ethics, crime prevention, law and the insanity defense, the sanctity of human life, and many others.

This dual approach — faculty and alumni — will open new "Northwest Passages" traversing the wilderness of ideas and pioneered by our own generation of true and enduring heroes.

Notes

1 National Center for Education Statistics, *The Condition of Education: Statistical Report, 1980 Edition*

(Washington, D.C.: U.S. Government Printing Office), p.57, p.70, p. 103, p. 120.

2 Alvin Sanoff, "Universities Are Turning Out Highly Skilled Barbarians," *U.S. News and World Report*, November 10, 1980, p. 57.

3 Frederick Rudolph, *The American College and University*, (Random Press, 1965) p. 6.

4 Ibid., p. 28.

5 Donald G. Tewksbury, *The Founding of American Colleges and Universities Before the Civil War*, Arno Press and The New York Times, N.Y. 1969, p. 55.

6 Ibid., p. 32-46.

7 Ibid., p. 84.

8 James Kilpatrick, "Turn to Religion," *Dallas Times Herald*, October 24, 1983.

9 "Public More Concerned About Moral Values Than Leaders," *The Sun*, March 31, 1981, p. A-10.

10 David Richardson, "Marxism in U.S. Classrooms," *U.S. News and World Report*, January 25, 1982, p. 42.

11 Saralee Tiede, "Academic Freedom," *Dallas Times Herald*, June 14, 1981, p. B-3.

12 Acts 26:28, *The New American Standard Bible*, Thomas Nelson, Nashville, 1979, p. 1075.

13 Rudolph, *The American College and University*, p. 28.

14 John Kenneth Galbraith, *A Life in Our Times*, Boston Houghton Mifflin Co., 1981, p. 83.

15 Paul Kurtz, *Humanist Manifestos I and II* (Buffalo, New York: Prometheus Books, 1977).

16 Roy Abraham Varghese, Press release for "Modern Thought and the Turn to Theism" Conference, March 7-12, 1983.

17 Anna J. Harrison, "Reflections on·Current Issues in Science and Technology," *Science*, February 26, 1982, p. 1062.

18 Richardson, "Marxism," p. 43.

19 Joseph Epstein, "The Education of an Anti-Capitalist," *Commentary*, August, 1983, p. 58.

PART I

THE SCIENCES

INTRODUCTION
Charles B. Thaxton, Ph.D.

Marching armies have, on many occasions, changed the course of history. But more powerful than armies are the ideas that compel armies to march. Control ideas and you control the world! It is not surprising then, to see a powerful struggle in the arena of ideas. All complications aside, the history of human thought can be described as a tale of two cities, the City of God *vs.* the City of Man. In more recognizable terms it is the age-old conflict between theism and naturalism. Theism is the broad category of thought which has as its most fundamental idea an absolute Creator distinct from the creation. Naturalism is an equally broad category of thought which denies an absolute Creator/creature distinction.

In our contemporary world of learning the disciplines are so fragmented and the intellectual puzzles in each area so challenging and engrossing that it is easy to forget that more profound issues are at stake. Seldom in modern education do we discuss in terms of these cosmic issues. Weren't those types of discussions reserved for cloistered clerics in the Middle Ages? Today we are concerned with survival, not only of races and nations, but also of the world. Yet, there are indications from several quarters that this may be changing. As reflected in the interviews below, fundamental changes in thought at the scholarly level suggest the mental climate is now more conducive to acceptance of theism than at any time since the great shift from theism to naturalism following the birth of modern science in the 17th century. A brief discussion of how the modern world arose will help build a context for appreciating the significance of comments made in the interviews.

It is by now well documented that modern science was born in Europe in a theistic culture.[1] As much of this scholarship has shown, theistic belief in a Creator was not only a circumstance but a significant part of the cause of modern experimental science. The contribution of Stanley Jaki below is part of this scholarship. Actually Jaki has written several books presenting the case for theistic influence in the birth of science.[2]

Despite this theistic beginning for science scientists were acutely aware that authoritarian religious control can stifle inquiry, and they sought to be free of such influence. Their hope for insuring this freedom was the scientific method with its emphasis on observation and experiment rather than authority, whether religious authority or that of the philosophers. Early scientists sorely needed a way to legitimately handle the connection between their belief in a Creator and the new science, to avoid the charge that they were making science religious. Finding none at hand and fearing heavy entanglement with religion, many simply ignored the problem by acting as if science were entirely neutral in regards to philosophy and religion.[3] As history shows, however, it turned out badly. Imagine a boy backing up to avoid a cliff and being eaten by an unnoticed dragon. That is like early scientists ignoring (or never finding) the proper relation of theism to science and being swallowed by philosophical naturalism or materialism. Of course it happened almost imperceptibly over many years, and a large part of the reason was that naturalism was implicit in the very scientific method that was supposed to insure the neutrality of science. That method included explaining *all* phenomena by secondary causes only. The philosophical implications of this were not seen at first.

Early modern scientists were busy applying the scientific method to unlocking the secrets of how the universe works (call it *operation science*). They were so enamored with nature's many regularities they hardly noticed when philosophical naturalists inferred from these regularities absolute natural laws which even God (if He exists) must obey. In other words in an age (18th century) which had been used to thinking in terms of absolutes, nature replaced God. The external signs of religious orthodoxy remained, but a mental dislocation had occurred in the intellectual world, a radical shift from theism to naturalism. So for more than 200 years many were blinded by scientific success and failed to notice that the anti-God message that seemed to be coming from many areas of science was the result of expressing a naturalistic (materialistic) philosophy in scientific terms. It took a long time to discern that materialist philosophy was masquerading as science. We are not saying that all science is materialistic, only that as a people we have been slow to distinguish materialism from valid science.

It wasn't long after its origin that science, which had belief in a Creator as an important foundation stone, began to entertain speculation on how the world began. Still largely oblivious to the vital role philosophical thought has in science, (in fact more and more scientists began to consciously claim philosophical neutrality) scientists of a more naturalistic bent began to speculate on origin questions. This was a significant step away from doing what science has traditionally done in seeking out the regular patterns in the ongoing operation of the universe. In fact some naturalistic scientists had entered the domain of what can be called *origin science*. In origin science a modified method similar to that used in forensic science is used to address origin questions. In the early days such a step was recognized as a departure from traditional science and, at least in the astronomical area, was given a name commensurate with its activity, *cosmogony*, i.e., the origin of the cosmos. *Cosmology* dealt with the structure of the universe, and the laws that are observed to function in its operation. Descartes, Kant and Laplace were instrumental in forging the recognizably modern cosmogony. Unfortunately this method of distinguishing between *origin science* and *operation science* by giving a different name to the disciplines (i.e., cosmogony, cosmology) did not continue.[4] Today many use cosmogony and cosmology almost interchangeably, and an established terminology for making this distinction never developed in geology, biology, etc.

In the latter 19th century the view became nearly universal that science is philosophically neutral and thoroughly objective. Also a new generation of scientists had arisen, one which had not only forgotten that science had a theistic base, but one which had embraced, albeit unconsciously for many, philosophical naturalism. Implicit within naturalism is the denial of a creation distinct from its Creator. Therefore it logically developed that science sought to answer the great origin questions without reference to a Creator. A new intellectual regime (naturalism) was now in place even if it was not recognized by the majority for what it was. It had no clerical trappings, no shrines, no symbols, no places of worship reserved for it alone. It was fitting, therefore, that origin questions would be answered by appealing to the new deity, natural law.[5]

Darwin attempted to explain the origin of species in terms of natural law too. The revolutions first in biology and then in other disciplines have been much publicized. The myth has been perpetrated that Darwin did his research as a thoroughly objective scholar. In fact, he had a viewpoint prior to doing any investigation. Darwin was a child of his time, and his time was breathing deeply the invigorating air of philosophical naturalism. Putting the question of Darwin in perspective is George Grinnell, Professor of History of Science, McMaster University:

> I have done a great deal of work on Darwin
> and can say with some assurance that Darwin
> also did not derive his theory from nature but
> rather superimposed a certain philosophical
> world-view on nature and then spent 20 years
> trying to gather the facts to make it stick.[6]

It is time this news got around.

What has happened generally in all the scientific disciplines is rapid growth and success in the area of *operation science*, i.e., the explanation of the structure and operation of the universe where it is valid to appeal exclusively to secondary causes. Numerous problems for science, however, have occurred in the area of *origin science*, where the attempt to account for phenomena by secondary causes only has not been nearly so successful. In fact it is the restricting of inquiry to secondary cause exclusively that identifies this area of origin studies as philosophic naturalism.

It has often been stated that the theory of evolution is the one overarching concept that gives unity to the scientific enterprise. This idea was expressed by Julian Huxley's famous statement, "the whole of reality is evolution."[7] The quest for a unifying theme in science is a response to the fragmentation process into ever more narrow and specialized disciplines of learning with their specialized vocabularies which virtually assure a minimum of communication across disciplinary boundaries. As a result many scientists are expert in their own area and quite ignorant of what is happening in neighboring disciplines. This is not a pejorative statement about scientists but a comment on how rapidly knowledge is accumulating. What we find, as a result, is a tendency for scientists to accept the traditional evolutionary view in most areas, *but* (and this is significant!) often questioning this scientific orthodoxy in their own area of expertise.

A word of caution is necessary here. In our zeal to point out some significant developments in science and their possible implication for theism we do not mean to suggest that proponents of evolution see evolution in any danger of collapse. What many experts see is merely need for refurbishing, not a new house. Readers of the following contributions can decide for themselves which is needed. Having stated this, however, some today are saying evolution needs to be replaced, that it fails to do what it set out to do, namely, explain origins, from atoms to zebras.[8]

The interview with Robert Jastrow points up the abrupt beginning of the universe which is, of course, what a theist believes, but against all naturalistic expectation. Jastrow, in *God and the Astronomers*, discusses the emotional responses of many well known scientists to this scientific discovery, and traces it back to a kind of religious belief in the unalterable laws of nature where there is no First Cause.[9] At one place in the interview Jastrow says, "The cause of the universe cannot be investigated by the study of cause and effect *within* the universe." This is another way of saying that we cannot hope to understand the *origin* of the universe by studying its *operation* or how it works. This is a point worthy of reflection by scientists and others interested in the question of origins.

Professor Henry Margenau, philosopher of science from Yale,[10] underscores the abrupt beginning. To those who would use science as a basis for disbelief in a Creator, Margenau adds, "It is absolutely unreasonable to reject the notion of a Creator by appealing to science. Science has definitely shown the non-contradiction of Creation out of nothing."

Both Jastrow and Margenau address the Anthropic Principle, from the Greek *Anthropos*, man, an approach to thinking about the universe as a whole which notes that the physical constants must be what we find them to be or there could be no intelligent life in the universe. Hugh of St. Victor said something similar to this in the early Middle Ages, "The world was created for man's body."[11] It is interesting that what was once considered theological prejudice should find a place as a notion of contemporary science. Some have even used this principle to argue that there can be only *one* intelligent life-form in the universe; hence it is an argument against intelligent life elsewhere. Jastrow remarks that " ... the Anthropic Principle ... is the most theistic result ever to come out of science." Margenau adds, "The Anthropic Principle is absolutely convincing to me."

The notion of a primordial soup of chemicals giving rise to life has been considered a necessity if life began by naturalistic means on earth. But Chandra Wickramasinghe says this is entirely false. Wickramasinghe's interview shows the struggle of one brought up in an Eastern naturalistic tradition trying to come to grips with the data regarding life's origin and being unable to fit them into the standard mechanistic, materialistic explanation. Readers may find difficulty in going along with his view of an origin of life from space. But his criticism of primordial soup seems well-founded. My own analysis of the origin of life problem[12] agrees fairly well with Wickramasinghe's criticisms of the mechanistic and materialistic offerings. And like Wickramasinghe, I find the evidence supporting an intelligent origin quite convincing. Perhaps due to parental and cultural heritage Wickramasinghe[13] seems not to have entirely broken away from the influence of an Eastern philosophical tradition when it came time to identify the intelligence which he places *within* the cosmos.

Wickramasinghe makes the worthy point that "the universe doesn't respect the boundaries between different disciplines ... these are man-made artifacts of thinking." It is this problem, I suspect, which leads a scientist in one specialized area to break with evolutionary tradition there and yet support that tradition outside the area of expertise. For example, Jastrow indicates that apart from a sudden beginning, the rest of the story ranged from "plausible" in regards to the notion that life began in a warm pool of chemicals, to "fairly convincing" for the traditional evolutionary view that man developed by stages from the chemical soup over a period of 4 billion years. Jastrow confesses to being a scientific materialist, and in a refreshing gesture of humility adds, "The only difficulty is that I am not *certain* that man appeared in this way." Jastrow elaborates on this point by noting that "in contrast to many of my fellow scientists, I do not believe that science has a *unique* grasp on reality."

We see more of the results of fragmentation in learning when we consider portions of the interviews dealing with mind and brain. Jastrow, (an expert in astronomy) confesses he can find "no mind distinct from the neurons and circuits of the brain." On the other hand, Sir John Eccles, a Nobel laureate who has devoted a lifetime to investigating the brain, points out that in spite of every effort to reduce mind to brain, he and others have been unable to do so. In Eccles' view, it is not scientific results, but materialist philosophy which prevents people from seeing mind as separate from matter. Eccles laments "the long deep depression of materialistic monism which has spread over the intellectual world like a dark fog blanketing out all the brightness and illumination of the ideals and imagination of human beings." Eccles, however, in his *Human Mystery* accepts as valid the evolutionary story from primordial soup to man. Eccles' expertise in brain science, however, causes him to question evolutionary orthodoxy there.

Rupert Sheldrake is today considered a maverick in the field of biology and his book *A New Science of Life*[14] is certainly controversial. The prestigious British magazine, *Nature*, called it "the best candidate for burning there has been for many years."[15] The equally distinguished *New Scientist*, however, described Sheldrake's book as "an important scientific inquiry into the nature of biological and physical reality."[16] The question of biological origins is beyond the scope of Sheldrake's book, but it is still condemned in some quarters as a creationist treatise.

In the interview Sheldrake touches the origin question only obliquely by criticising the mechanistic and materialistic philosophies which have long dominated biology. He points out that mechanistic biology became accepted as orthodoxy because "it grew out of a general cultural context where the materialist philosophy was particularly influential." The obvious appeal in mechanistic biology was that it seemed to offer scientists a way to do science "without concerning themselves with theological and philosophical issues." This was largely illusory, however, as materialism merely replaced theism, and became all the more devastating and controlling because it remained unconscious for so long. Materialists (and others) were deceived into thinking their views were the hard-won results of objective science. In fact, they had merely used science as a tool to give expression to their materialistic philosophy.

Eventually the myth of neutral, totally objective science was exposed, interestingly by developments in science itself. The great revolution in physics in the opening decades of the 20th century, primarily in quantum and relativity physics, showed the mistake had been to eliminate man, the observer.

In the discipline of psychology we see a similar journey through mechanism and materialism until now in the latter half of the 20th century they are being rejected. Paul Vitz tells how psychologists eventually learned to reject determinism and materialism, but in the process "inadvertently backed into religion, including Christianity." But by the time psychology began to abandon determinism most psychologists were already naturalistic in mental outlook. As they began to enter the religion area it was logical to consider the more naturalistic religions. Eastern religions had the richest history and greatest attraction for stuffy Westerners chained in mechanism. So open embrace of Hinduism and Buddhism became widespread.

But, as Vitz makes clear, much progress has been made in the development of Christian psychology even though it "has yet to be articulated in any detail." Vitz makes the tragic point that the current economic crunch threatens to freeze these naturalistic psychologies in place in Christian Institutions for some time to come. Even though exciting things are happening in Christian psychology, and the deficiencies of naturalistic self-psychology are becoming known, economics makes it more difficult to hire new faculty members acquainted with these developments. Thus students in Christian colleges will be the losers if they continue to get instruction in naturalistic self-psychology.

Sociologist David Martin points out that mechanistic science influenced sociology by viewing man as "simply a creature of culture and not a creator of all culture." Like psychology, sociology today is more tolerant of religious ideas than in former years. This religious influence is both from theistic and naturalistic religions. The force that opened up sociology was the simple fact that hard as they tried sociologists could not make people behave as "social atoms" after the manner of mechanistic science. It had held out an allure that maybe we could by-pass the vagaries of human nature and personality and just treat men in social groups as simply a collection of social atoms. Future social behaviour could then be predicted and sociology could become truly "scientific." But it simply didn't work.

With this recognition of the failure of mechanism in sociology, the way is clear for a new sociology to emerge which allows man to be man. But where will the vision of man come from? There is surely plenty of work for the Christian sociologist.

In conclusion it is worth noting that there is plenty of work to be done in all the scientific disciplines. As a suggestion we might think in the direction of building on what theists did in the 16th and 17th century. As was pointed out earlier, theistic minds contributed significantly to the bold new venture of science. They dared to supply a new mind to old material and produced a new result. In short, they acted on their belief in the brute fact that nature was created, and developed an approach that was consistent with it. As a result modern experimental science was born. Those early scientists were interested in investigating nature as they found it, not origins which they presupposed to have been wrought by a Creator.

Some discussion above was given to naturalistic origin science, that is, the view of origins that flows out of and is consistent with philosophical naturalism. Even though early theistic scientists were not specifically interested in inquiring into origins, does it not seem compelling that we today, especially since operation science is already going, begin a concerted effort to develop *theistic* origin science? Why leave the question of origins to naturalistic minds? History shows that naturalism was never able to produce operation science, having been "stillborn" in every naturalistic culture. If theism was a key ingredient for starting proper investigation of nature, then is it not reasonable that theism would have something of value to offer in the investigation of origins? Who will take up the challenge?

Notes

1 A.N. Whitehead, 1967 (originally published 1925). *Science and the Modern World*. New York: The Free Press, chapter 1.; Melvin Calvin, 1969. *Chemical Evolution*. New York: Oxford University Press, p.258.; M.B. Foster, 1934. *Mind* 43, 446.; R. Hooykaas, 1972. *Religion and the Rise of Modern Science*. Grand Rapids, Michigan: Wm. B. Erdmans.; Loren Eisley, 1961. *Darwin's Century: Evolution and the Men Who Discovered It*. Garden City, New York: Doubleday, Anchor, p.62.; C.F. von Weizsacker, 1964. *The Relevance of Physics*. New York: Harper and Row, p.163.; J. Robert Oppenheimer. *Encounter*, October, 1962.; Langdon Gilkey, 1959. *Maker of Heaven and Earth*. Garden City, New York: Doubleday, Anchor, p.9, 125, 129ff.

2 Stanley Jaki, 1974. *Science and Creation*. Edinburgh and London: Scottish Academic Press.; Stanley Jaki, 1982. *Cosmos and Creator*. Chicago, Illinois: Regnery Gateway.; Stanley Jaki, 1978. *Roads of Science and the Ways to God*, Chicago, Illinois: University of Chicago Press.

3 Often scientists paid their respects to deity in the preface of a book and promptly bid Him adieu.

4 For a fuller discussion of origin science and operation science, see reference 12; and the chapter "Theism, Naturalism and the Origin of Life," in *Modern Thought and the Turn to Theism*.

5 By the 1820s and 1830s in England there is no end of praise to the Creator, but there is a new verse to the song, i.e., 'God creates through natural law.'

6 George Grinnell, "Reexamination of the Foundations," an interview in Pensee, May, 1972, p.44. The authenticity of this quotation has been confirmed by telephone conversation with the author on May 11, 1983.

7 Julian Huxley, 1955. "Evolution and Genetics," Chapter 8 in *What is Science?* (Ed., J.R. Newman, New York: Simon and Schuster), p.278.

8 For a non-technical introduction to arguments challenging Darwinism, see Norman Macbeth, 1971. *Darwin Retried*. Boston: Gambit, Incorporated; Francis Hitching, 1982. *The Neck of the Giraffe*. New Haven and New York: Ticknor & Fields; and Jeremy Rifkin, 1983. "The Darwinian Sunset," Part Four in *Algeny*. New York: The Viking Press.

9 Robert Jastrow, 1978. *God and the Astronomers*. New York: W. W. Norton.

10 The genesis of my own interest in the philosophy of science dates back to 1960 when I purchased and read Professor Margenau's *The Nature of Physical Reality* (1950, New York: McGraw-Hill).

11 Hugh of St. Victor, cited by H.O. Taylor, 1938. "Medieval Mind," in Bk. 2, *Early Middle Ages*. London: Macmillan. The full quotation is: "The world was created for man's body, man's body for his spirit, and man's spirit for God: the spirit that it might be brought into subjection unto God, the body unto the spirit, and the world unto the body."

12 C. Thaxton, W. Bradley and R. Olsen, 1984. *The Mystery of Life's Origin*. New York: Philosophical Library.

13 F. Hoyle and N.C. Wickramasinghe, 1981. *Evolution from Space*. New York: Simon and Schuster.

14 Rupert Sheldrake, 1981. *A New Science of Life*. Los Angeles: J.P. Tarcher.

15 Anonymous, 1981. Nature 293, 245.

16 Brian Goodwin, 1981. New Scientist (16 July), 164.

1
THE ASTRONOMER AND GOD
Professor Robert Jastrow

Can you recapitulate the astronomical evidence for the beginning of the universe?

Discoveries in astronomy in recent decades provide evidence that the Universe came into existence abruptly. The evidence lies in the fact that all the galaxies — the great clusters of stars that populate the heavens — are moving away from us and one another at enormous speeds, as if they were recoiling from the scene of a great explosion. If the motions of the outward-moving galaxies are traced backward in time, we find that they all come together, so to speak, about twenty billion years ago. At that time all the matter in the Universe was packed into one dense mass under enormous pressure, and with temperatures ranging up to trillions of degrees. The picture suggests the explosion of a cosmic hydrogen bomb. The instant in which the cosmic bomb exploded marked the birth of the Universe.

This picture of the beginning of the Universe has been confirmed by the discovery of the remnants of the primordial fireball — the flash of light and heat that filled the Universe in its first moments. The two scientists who made this discovery — Arno Penzias and Robert Wilson — received the Nobel Prize in 1978 in recognition of their momentous finding.

The seed of everything that has happened since was planted in that first instant; every star, every planet, and every living creature in the cosmos has come into being as a result of events that were set in motion in the moment of the cosmic explosion. It was the moment of creation.

How can we explain the existence of matter at the time of the "Big Bang"?

Science cannot tell whether matter existed in the Universe *before* the Big Bang. It cannot tell whether the Universe was created *ex nihilo*, or instead the cosmic explosion — the so-called "Big Bang" occurred in pre-existing matter.

Normally the physicist or astronomer would try to answer this question by reconstructing a chain of events that led up to the moment of the Big Bang. This would be accomplished by searching for relics of the early Universe — pieces of matter that existed in the Universe just before the Big Bang or shortly thereafter. Such relics could be discovered by looking very far out into space with large telescopes, since, because of the finite speed of light, the astronomer who looks out into space also looks back in time. However, the properties of the Universe in its early moments — an infinite or nearly infinite pressure, temperature and density — must necessarily have melted down and eradicated any material evidence left over from a pre-existing Universe.

As a consequence, the astronomer can never hope to discover the evidence that might tell him the cause of the Universe's beginning; *he cannot hope to discover whether the Universe even existed prior to that first moment.*

Would the existence of matter at or before the time of the Big Bang discount the necessity of postulating a creator?

I do not believe it is a central question in theology as to whether or not the Creation occurred *ex nihilo*. In any case, whatever the answer is, that answer is not discoverable by the methods of science.

Isaac Asimov says that while scientists cannot explain the Big Bang today they may be able to explain it tomorrow, because scientific knowledge advances continually with the receipt of new data.

I hold fast to the view that science will not be able to decipher the cause of the cosmic explosion as long as it appears that the Universe was infinitely hot and dense in its first moments. This conclusion seems to me to be one of the hard facts of science, like the quantization of the charge and mass of the electron, or the double-helix structure of the DNA molecule. In my view the situation can change only if the Big Bang theory is overthrown by new information, but in the light of the discovery of the primordial fireball radiation by Penzias and Wilson, that development seems unlikely.

How should a theist respond to the possibility that the Big Bang cosmology could be overthrown by new scientific advances?

As noted above, the discovery of the primordial fireball radiation makes this possibility seem very remote. Anything can happen, in science as well as in other fields, but it seems to me that one should confine one's serious attention to possibilities that have a reasonable chance of being realized.

Is it reasonable to say that science cannot shed light on the creation because this question goes beyond the empirical?

I think this is a reasonable way of looking at the matter, if by the "empirical" one means the investigation of a chain of cause and effect. That is, science is of no help in matters of teleology (the study of the evidences of design in nature). To put it another way, the cause *of* the Universe cannot be investigated by the study of cause and effect *within* the Universe; or, quoting my friend Steven Katz, Professor of Religion at Dartmouth College, "The radicalism of modern science resides in its denial of teleological causation; but we must, however, recognize that teleology is a metaphysical concept, *whose ultimate reality cannot be affirmed or denied on the basis of empirical or scientific evidence."*

What is your comment on the various responses to *God and the Astronomers*, especially the misinterpretations?

The misinterpretations have been mainly of two kinds. First, there is the kind of rebuttal Dr. Asimov gave in his recent article in the *Skeptical Enquirer*, in which he took me to task for suggesting that, as he put it, "The Bible has all the answers." Dr. Asimov wrote, "(Let Jastrow) pour over the Bible until he finds out what a quasar is ... and whether the Universe is open or closed ..."

I think this criticism is frivolous because I clearly state that science and religion only agree on the necessity of a Beginning; science disagrees with the Bible about most other things that occurred in the history of the Universe after the Beginning.

In particular, scientists have a rather satisfactory explanation for the condensation of galaxies, stars and planets, the formation of the sun and the earth, and finally, the appearance of man on the earth.

It is only in the discovery — so peculiar from a scientific point of view — that the Universe came into being suddenly and abruptly, as a result of forces that are beyond the reach of scientific inquiry, that scientists find themselves in agreement with Western religious thought. However, I think this single point of agreement to be quite extraordinary.

The second misinterpretation relates to the proof of the existence of God. Some critics expressed the view that I am suggesting science has provided this proof. This is not correct. In the book I very clearly state that we cannot tell by scientific methods whether the birth of the Universe is the work of a Creator or some force outside the domain of science, or is instead the product of physical forces, that is, a part of natural law. As noted above, it is in the very nature of the events of the first moment that those events conspired to prevent a scientific resolution of the question of causation.

There is a third matter that might be called a point of misunderstanding. Many people, either with approval or with disapproval, depending on their views, say that I am expressing in a concealed way my own personal belief in the existence of the Creator. In a review of my latest book, Stephen Jay Gould asks, "Do I detect a theological bottom line?"

This is also not correct. On the one hand, it seems to me astronomy has proven that forces are at work in the world that are beyond the present power of scientific description; these are literally *supernatural forces*, because they are outside the body of natural law. On the other hand, my readings in the literature of science have led me to a reductionist philosophy and a position of *scientific materialism* — a view that the whole is *not* greater than the sum of its parts, that there is no "elan vital," no essence of life apart from the molecules of the body, no mind distinct from the neurons and circuits of the brain.

Furthermore, I believe it to be plausible that life arose in a warm pool of water and chemicals on the surface of the earth four billion years ago; and I find the evidence fairly convincing for the belief that man has evolved out of those first organisms by a succession of minute changes during the intervening four billion years.

The only difficulty is that I am not *certain* that man appeared in this way; I am not *certain* that all these events took place without the agency of some larger force, expressing a larger purpose of direction in the Universe. When I contemplate the nature of man, with his marvelous faculties of intellect and creativity, the emergence of this extraordinary being out of chemicals dissolved in a pool of warm water seems as much a miracle as the Biblical account of his origin. This is why I remain an agnostic in religious matters at the present time.

However, in contrast to many of my fellow scientists, I do not believe that science has a *unique* grasp of reality; I think there may be more than one avenue to the truth. By some circumstance of birth or scientific training, I happen not to be sensitive to revealed truth, but only to experienced truth. As a consequence, my mental and spiritual life is impoverished to some degree, because I must depend on scientific truth — on experience — for whatever insights I can hope to gain into the nature of man and his place in the Universe. But I am always very interested in a dialogue with people who may have a greater awareness of other avenues to the truth, or see the other faces of reality more clearly. This is my position at the present time, which experience and circumstances may change later.

Do you see any other results in science that have a bearing on the religious view of reality?

Yes, there is another aspect of modern astronomical discoveries that is, in my view, as remarkable as the evidence for the abrupt birth of the Universe. According to the picture of the evolution of the Universe developed by the astronomer and his fellow scientists, the smallest change in any of the circumstances of the natural world, such as the relative strengths of the forces of nature, or the properties of the elementary particles, would have led to a Universe in which there could be no life and no man.

For example, if the nuclear force were increased in strength by a few percent, all the hydrogen nuclei in the Universe would have been gobbled up to form helium nuclei in the first half hour of the Universe's existence, and the stars that formed subsequently would thus have been made almost entirely of helium. Stars that are made of helium live a much shorter time than stars made of hydrogen; as consequence there would have been no time for life, intelligence and man to evolve in this Universe.

On the other hand, if the nuclear forces were decreased by a few percent, the particles of the Universe would not have come together in nuclear reactions to make the ingredients, such as carbon atoms, of which life must be constructed; the Universe would be composed solely of hydrogen plus a little helium; and again, life, in any form remotely resembling that we know, could not have come into being.

It is possible to make the same argument about changes in the strengths of the electromagnetic force, the force of gravity, or any other constants of the material Universe, and so come to the conclusion that in a slightly changed Universe there could be no life, and no man.

Thus, according to the physicist and the astronomer, it appears that the Universe was constructed within very narrow limits, in such a way that man could dwell in it. This result is called the *anthropic principle*. It is the most theistic result ever to come out of science, in my view.

Some scientists suggest, in an effort to avoid a theistic or teleological implication in their findings, that there must be an infinite number of universes, representing all possible combinations of basic forces and conditions, and that our Universe is one of an infinitely small fraction, in this great plentitude of universes, in which life exists. Perhaps it is the *only* Universe within this infinite multitude in which life exists. But I find this to be a rather formal solution to the philosophical dilemma created for scientists by the anthropic principle — a typical theorist's solution. In any case, it is an untestable proposition, because all these other universes are forever beyond the range of our observations; they are outside the borders of the visible universe, and can never be seen. What is forever unobservable and unverifiable, seems to me to be scientifically uninteresting. I really do not know what to make of this result — the Anthropic Principle.

2
SCIENCE AND THE DIVINE ORIGIN OF LIFE

Professor Chandra Wickramasinghe

Could you give a brief account of the work you did along with Sir Fred Hoyle on the 'Origin of Life' and of the main conclusions you reached in your work?

This work really began some twenty years ago when we had set out to understand the composition and the chemical make-up of tiny dust grains that are known to be present in space in really vast quantities. At the time that we started research into this matter, the general belief was that these dust particles which show up as patches of obscuration in the Milky Way, are made up of tiny ice grains, rather similar to the ice grains that one sees in the cumulus clouds in the atmosphere of the Earth. But it was clear from the start of our investigation that this particular theory of the grains could not be right. It did not fit the data. And we found, on the other hand, that particles of carbonaceous character came much nearer for producing all the observed effects. So that was the first step: unravelling the nature of the dust particles. We found that they were not ice as astronomers had felt them to be, but particles that had a large carbon content. The research work from that time on had been to focus on the nature of the carbonaceous material in the dust grains. This was a long tedious process lasting many years. It was only about five years ago that we realized that the dust had to be not merely carbon, not simply carbonaceous, but it had to be biological in character. There was no other way to explain a whole lot of astronomical data except to say that the dust grains in space had essentially to be connected with life. And the marvelous agreement that we obtained with the astronomical data on how starlight is blacked out by dust clouds and so on gave us great confidence that this had to be correct.

Then we next looked at the conventional story of how life originated on the earth. This had been around for a good many years, the general belief, that life has to originate on the surface of our planet from some kind of primordial soup which developed in the very early days of the earth's history. Now, if you think about this proposition, there is no logic that demands this to be so. We know that the universe is very much older than the earth and there is no absolute requirement to have life start on the earth.

But even assuming that one had some reason to limit one's scope and to say that life had to start on the earth, then it was possible to look into the usual arguments. We did this rather carefully, and we found that all the conditions were wrong for life to start on the earth. The atmosphere of the earth was supposed to be of a character that permitted the formation of complex organic materials, according to the conventional story, and our investigations revealed to us that the earth's atmosphere could not have had this character. In technical language, a necessary requirement for organic soups to form on the earth, is that the early earth's atmosphere has to be reducing, that is to say it has to have a deficit of oxygen, of free oxygen atoms. If we look at the earth's atmosphere right at the present moment it's certainly not reducing. It's full of oxygen. Anything that lies around essentially rusts, iron rusts. Dead organic materials lying around no more than a few weeks, a few months, become essentially converted to carbon dioxide; it's very rapidly oxidized. One of the earliest questions that was raised in connection with the primordial soup was deciding whether at any early stage in the earth's history, if there was a situation when the earth's atmosphere was not of its present character, that is, it was reducing rather than oxidizing. We looked at this rather carefully, and we decided that the earth's atmosphere was never of the right character to form an organic soup. This was about 3 or 4 years ago that we came to this conclusion, and we published this in a book under the title of *Lifecloud*.

At the time that this book was published, the idea that the earth did not have the right atmosphere offended lots of people. But, at the moment, in 1983, it's almost taken for granted in the scientific community that the earth's atmosphere could not have been reducing. Geochemists and geologists have now come round; they now go on to say that the primordial soup had to be imported from outside. The comets and meteorites, and so on, landing on the earth had to bring the organic soup and so that's going part of the way. In *Lifecloud*, we said that the organic soup (theory) could not be right. There's no way it could have developed upon the Earth. Comets and astronomical objects do have organic material in large quantities. That's what we said in the first book. The general belief now is that at least part of that has to be true. The earth could not have produced an organic soup on its own. The organic soup itself is not such a marvelous thing. It is a pre-requisite for any biological activity to start; that's certainly true. But it doesn't follow that if you have an organic soup it could get life started. It doesn't follow logically that one can start from an organic soup and end up with a living system. There's no logic that drives you to that conclusion at all. And when we looked at the probabilities of the assembly of organic materials into a living system, it turns out that the improbabilities are really horrendous, horrific in extent and I concluded along with my colleague that (this) could not have happened spontaneously on the earth.

There's not enough time, there's not enough resources and there's no way in which that could have happened on the earth. If it could have happened easily, then I think it's also fair to say that scientists who've been bashing away at laboratory experiments for twenty or thirty years would have come somewhere close to a complex organization; such may not be exactly life but would have appeared to converge towards life. They conducted experiments in the lab with test-tubes, with flasks and organic soups contrived in the labs. If there was any truth in the statement that life can start in this way, then I think one could make a very strong case for saying that it should have happened in the lab already. The fact that the lab experiment, the flask, is only one part in 10^{15} or 10^{20} of the earth's oceans is not a very important consideration. Given the enormous information content that you need for life, the scaling down factor is unimportant. If you say this business happened on the earth in a billion years and that you have only done this for three years in the lab, then you can perhaps have another factor of a billion that might appear to be a credible way out of this dilemma. This is the usual (stance) scientists have adopted, to say give us more time, not a billion years, maybe 10 years. That's the usual story, but again, if you look at the extent of information that needs to be put together, a factor of a billion in time or a factor of a trillion in spatial volume, in the volume of the oceans relative to the volume of the flask is completely immaterial. Because what one has to really develop is an information content that is measured in ten followed by 40,000 zeros, $10^{40,000}$. So if you divide that ten to the power 40,000 by a factor of 10 to the power of nine for a billion and further 10 to the 15th, 10 to the 16th for the size of the oceans you still end up with an enormous factor, an enormous number. If you divide $10^{40,000}$ you still end up with $10^{39,000}$ (or more), a vast number. So, in one year, in a single test tube we should be generating a system that approaches life. That's a very hard fact that one has to face. If there's any way that one could justify the usual claims, every time you spark a test-tube with organic nutrients, you will be seeing, I mean not exactly life, you would be seeing a progression towards a living system or a quasi-living system and that has not been found to be true at all. What you get is an absolute mess of polymers, of uninteresting polymers and some of the polymers do contain nucleic acids, residues, amino acids and so on, but that's beside the point. It doesn't come anywhere near the structure of life here. So that's the main point.

To recapitulate, from the point of view of an astronomer, looking at the evidence of astronomy, life is everywhere around us, at the level of microscopic life (micro-organisms and genetic fragments around us in vast quantities throughout the universe). And from the point of view of geo-chemistry and terrestrial experiments, if you look at the early earth as a possible site for manufacturing life, it turns out that the case is non-existent, I would say, for such a thing happening on the earth. The next point that one has to worry about is to consider where the cosmic life arose from. Having seen it around on the earth in the form of large creatures and on the universe in the form of microscopic particles, one has naturally to ask the further question when and where this complex organization of happenings arose. And I think, at that point, I would give in to the theological answer in the sense that I cannot claim that I have an answer. All that I am sure about is that life could not have happened on the earth spontaneously.

Then the further investigation that we did over the past two to three years is to decide whether evolution of life on the earth could have proceeded in the way that biologists told us it happened, and the way it's happened, for a couple of generations now. And it's again a rather amazing conclusion that we reached. We found that there's just no way it could happen. If you start with a simple micro-organism no matter how it arose on the earth, primordial soup or otherwise, then if you just have that single organizational, informational unit and you said that you copied this sequentially time and time again, the question is does that accumulate enough copying errors, enough mistakes in copying, and do these accumulations of copying errors lead to the diversity of living forms that one sees on the earth. That's the general usual formulation of the Theory of Evolution. In making copies either sexually or asexually you pile up errors in copying. And the natural environment selects the best fitted for survival out of the very many genotypes that have developed to the accumulation of mistakes. It's been claimed that the combination of the mistakes and the selection leads to the steady evolution of life. We looked at this quite systematically, quite carefully, in numerical terms. Checking all the numbers, rates of mutation and so on, we decided that there is no way in which that could even marginally approach the truth. On the contrary, any organized living system that developed or emerged say in the form of a microbe, 4 billion years ago, if it was allowed to copy itself time and time again, it would have destroyed itself essentially. The pile up of copying errors could have two effects: 1) It could improve the genotype for survival or 2) it could decrease the survival characteristics of this particular living form. If you consider the balance between the two effects it turns out that it's always the destructive component that wins. For every favorable mutation there will be hundreds of unfavorable mutations. So it has to be a steady downward procedure. If we start with a highly organized system of a lot of information and if you are copying, it has to ultimately decline and degenerate. The way out of this is to suppose that Natural Selection operates, not in relation to the copying errors, but in relation to continual inputs of new information that organisms could imbibe from the outside world. Now, we know that viruses and fragments of viruses could get into cells of all creatures, of all plants and animals. Viral components could add on to the genomes of existing animals and we argued that this is the only way in which one could keep the evolution going essentially — that is, where the new information for new creatures, for new life forms, for new attributes, must be injected from the general pool of cosmic life around us.

Could you be a little more specific on what exactly you mean by that?

If you look at the fossil record, then you see instantly that the present day living forms have a whole range of structures and types, from matter organisms all the way up to human beings and, later on, if you get back in time, if you go deeper and deeper into the geological strata, there appears to be a progressive decline of the more complicated and more sophisticated life forms. The human eye, monkeys and apes are fairly recent in the geological deposits compared to dinosaurs. The whole range of living forms becomes progressively less complicated, as you go down in the geological strata. So there is a very strong indication of a sort of evolution, that has occurred. The earliest life forms are simple and the later life forms become more varied, more complicated, more complex. How is this pattern to be explained in the face of the arguments that I have outlined to you where any tendency is for mutations to accumulate in a closed system. If biology is a closed system, then it seems to me that the mutations degenerate in the life forms that exist at any given time. I think the way out of it is to suppose that instructions for more sophisticated life forms, for the continual evolution of life, has to be supplied from outside of the earth.

By some higher intelligence?

Yes.

Would this in some way solve the problem of the missing link, of the missing transitional forms, which I have understood to be one of the major flaws in most evolutionary theories?

Yes, transitional forms have never been discovered. Between the most important groups of creatures with major differences in attributes, transitional forms have never been discovered in the fossil records. I think that is a major defect in the conventional theories because the transitional forms, likely to be the most important, should have been sufficiently long-lived. If things move very slowly then there should have been some record.

It surprises me that many notable scientists have not paid sufficient attention to this problem. What was their response to your work?

I don't really know. I think they turned a blind eye to anything that doesn't tie up with their (essentially) theology. There's no evidence for any of the basic tenets of Darwinian evolution. I don't believe that there ever was any evidence for it. It was a social force that took over the world in 1860, and I think it has been a disaster for science ever since.

This is a sociological question, but do you see it as still prevalent in the academic world?

I think it's prevalent in the scientific, academic community (to this extent); it's very similar to the situation before Copernicus, when a very complicated system, the Ptolemaic system, was maintained as being the correct one.

And they tried to explain all the new discoveries within the framework of the old system?

It's exactly what one sees in modern evolutionary biology; there's an exact parallel. There is very considerable competence in the use of electron microscopes and very competent DNA techniques. And there's very powerful, experimental back-up for modern biology. But they have the wrong theory. [With extremely sophisticated equipment they have] discovered a lot of fine details in biology, that they try to force into a wrong theory and whenever there is a mismatch, they introduce new hypotheses. It's like the Ptolemaic system, cycles and epicycles.

You have encountered some of the most prominent evolutionists today like Stephen Jay Gould. How would you assess them?

They're all very arrogant, dogmatic people (I'm not referring to any one particular person); they hold absolutely tenaciously to a point of view which has become a theological issue. Whenever there's a clash between a theological attitude and a scientific attitude then the theological attitude takes precedence because it has a lot of social or sociological back up.

How did Gould respond to the problems you pointed out?

He just shrugs his shoulders and says that there's a lot of things we don't understand. There's a vagueness everywhere. They are deeply uncomfortable. They are deeply threatened by the weight of evidence.

There's another problem that one faces in modern science. It's so highly compartmentalized. Evolutionary biologists don't understand physics, they don't understand anything but evolutionary biology. But the universe doesn't respect the boundaries between different disciplines. The differences between biology and astronomy and chemistry and so on, these are manmade artifacts of thinking. I think the whole system is doomed unless one decides that all these barriers are cleared. And I will go further to say that even the interface between theology and the other disciplines is necessary.

Could the universe be infinite in terms of space and time?

Well, I think that the astronomical evidence now is against that. There doesn't seem to be such a universe that has an extended open time-scale. So under those circumstances, I think one is driven again to postulate an intelligence. The logically easiest way of beating the improbability is to say that an intelligence intervened. If you see that life or patterns of anything are too complicated for emergence in a random way, like the arrangement of items in this house, then the obvious conclusion that one is led to draw from this datum is that there has been an intelligence behind the design of the house. In a similar way, one could make the same statement for the living system.

If the universe is not infinite in size and time-scale, then is one forced to conclude there is a higher intelligence, not merely as a possible option, since this would rule out the possibility of an accident?

I would go along with that. I think if you look at the structure of our living system, micro-organisms or ourselves under the microscope, as it were (not literally), if you investigate a living system that is before us, that is accessible to us, one is driven to the conclusion, inescapably, that living systems could not have been generated by random processes, within a finite time-scale, in a finite universe. I think the evidence from life is very hard, a hard fact, from the nature of a living system as you study it in the lab. The information content in the living system that we have on the earth is perhaps the hardest cosmological fact. You can't get away from that, in the sense that the Universe has to in some way discover this arrangement. I would put that datum above the cosmological datum in quality of information.

Has your work led you to a position that strongly favors the theistic view?

I would say so. Yes.

What do you think of the position taken by someone like Jacques Monod who says that life is an accident, a chance occurrence?

I think it's not borne out by the facts at all. There's not a shred of evidence for it.

And it's more a metaphysical principle or judgment? It's not scientific in nature?

It is worse than that. It's a defiance of science. The scientific method should lead to quite the opposite result: that some miraculous property of life that's either explained in terms of a statistical miracle or in terms of an Intelligence intervening. It's one or the other.

Sir John Eccles said that Monod is increasingly sounding like a prophet.

But all these people do that. They have the general property of doing that. The people who work on the theories of the origin of life meet about 2 or 3 times a year and go around the world preaching their doctrine. They feel the need for doing this because their position is so insecure in terms of factual knowledge.

What do you think of all these reports of life being created in the lab?

I think it's totally to be discounted. Whenever they say that there's any evidence for evolution in the lab, what seems to be involved is that they start with a living system, make very small changes to it, and recover a living system, that has either those changes or some other changes. They start with the desired result essentially. It's cheating.

Would your work be fatal for the mechanistic view of things, the view that the whole thing is just matter rearranging itself?

Yes, matter rearranging itself without any intelligent purpose could not be proved, is not compatible with my work.

Have there been any notable responses to your work?

I haven't come across any biologist who's been convinced by the argument. But then I wouldn't have expected it. But I find that many of the astronomers I've been working with are gradually turning around to belief that there is life everywhere in the universe. That's a very slow transformation, but that's happening. And I also feel that I've succeeded in converting a lot of the medical profession to believe that viruses have an external origin or may have an external origin.

But that they are definitely not just a product of the evolutionary process?

Yes.

What do you think of the work of people like Carl Sagan, who propagate the Positivist point of view?

I think, from the couple of his lectures that I heard and the few things I've read of his, he has nothing original to say at all. He's just peddling the old mechanistic world view in relation to astronomy: the primordial soup that he starts all his expositions with, the non-existent mythical primordial soup. I think these people have no respect for facts at all. The facts are too disturbing. They consider it irrelevant.

Would you say the primordial soup account is fairly dominant or taken for granted by most of these evolutionists?

Yes, that is the starting point of their thinking — to say that it had to happen on the earth. And as I pointed out earlier, there's no logic that drives you to that conclusion at all. It's like saying, when you come to Wales here and discover that in certain parts of Wales they speak the Celtic language, that the Celtic language must have evolved from here. This is essentially what they're saying in terms of the life system. Whereas we know for sure that the Celtic language is imported from mainland Europe some couple of thousand years ago. In a very similar way the organizational pattern of life could have been imported from outside, could have been extraneous input to the earth.

How do you find the Anthropic Principle?

I think it is certainly, objectively true that the number of carbon atoms and oxygen atoms and nitrogen atoms in the universe have an appropriate proportion for life to start on a planet like the earth. That is certainly true. Whether that means anything much deeper than that those proportions have been controlled by an Intelligence, I don't know. I tend to think that they are, that they have been.

You would say that your work shows Darwinism to be fatally flawed?

Yes.

How would you evaluate the arguments of the Creationists?

You mean the arguments that are justifications of their position? I think they have a very good case by and large.

A minority among them insist on the "young earth" theory which is by no means essential to traditional Christian theism.

I would say that could kill them. It really would.

But in general how do you find their methodology?

It is highly commendable. I can't say it's in any way faulty. The greatest scientists of the 19th century were Creationists. Even the man who really drove home the Darwinian Theory of Evolution, not Darwin, but Alfred Russell Wallace never departed from the Creationist point of view. He believed that the small effects in biology, from the differences of one terrain to the other in the same kind of animal, could be explained in terms of natural selection. But he never went to the extreme and said that everything happened (through natural selection) and human beings evolved. He left out man. There are some marvelous quotes in Wallace. He couldn't believe that human attributes could have developed to the level of great mathematicians and musicians in response to natural selection.

3
MODERN PHYSICS AND THE TURN TO BELIEF IN GOD
Professor Henry Margenau

What relevance do you think modern science has for the religious view of reality, in general, and for theism, in particular?

Well, I'll try to present them. Modern science has changed in many ways and in a manner which makes religious beliefs much more tolerable than any kind of science did before. The novelties in modern science are, first of all, neglect of the materialistic aspects of the world. We can no longer say that an electron is a particle or that it is a wave. You have to say that it's quite different from any of these. It cannot be described as a particle, as a thing. It can only be described as a probability field and so forth. In other words, science has now taken on many characteristics of the mind. Reality has become as abstract as anything else in the world. So some of the notions of science are certainly no more contradictory to old-style materialism than is the notion of God. That might be one way of putting it.

Mechanism is dead except in a very limited domain.

What would you say were the most significant developments in modern science that led to the death of Mechanism?

Quantum Mechanics and Relativity Theory. In Relativity Theory materialistic things change their size even with motion. The mechanists would never have believed that. In Quantum Mechanics there is no mechanism at all. We don't even speak of mechanisms any more. Heisenberg's principle had an enormous effect on this and Heisenberg, of course, was one man who acknowledged this. I knew him very well.

How far do you see Einstein's work as having effected this transition from Mechanism to a more open view?

Well, they've opened our eyes immensely. They've shown us that what we believed to be a fact, an incontrovertible fact, namely the existence of three-dimensional space which can never change and so forth, to be false. We need four-dimensional space now in order to explain what's happening, transformations all need four co-ordinates not three. That has nothing to do with religion directly. But it certainly looses the grip which the materialistic, mechanistic view had upon us.

Many of the popular science-writers today seem to be Positivists. How accurate do you think is their approach?

There are many Positivists. They have made no contribution to science directly. So therefore I would suppose that their knowledge of what is going on in modern science is insufficient for them to see the whole.

How much more plausible is belief in a Creator of the universe in the light of the advancement of modern science?

May be there are two points I should make. In the first

place, if there was no Creator, how did the universe come into being? I don't believe, I could simply not get myself to think that it all happened by accident. One of the most explicit writers on Creation was St. Thomas. St. Thomas said that the universe was created by God out of nothing. It sprang into being out of nothing. He was ignored for many years because that was an impossibility from the point of view of physics. After all, the Creation of the universe had to obey the Law of the Conservation of Energy, of Mass, and so forth. That was St. Thomas. Now, some people have said that St. Thomas was right because God can violate the laws of Nature, which I don't believe. God made two creations: one of the world and one of the Laws of Nature. He presented the laws of Nature through Noah after the Flood, as you read in the fourth chapter of Genesis. Henceforth there should be seed-time and harvest, summer and winter, day and night, and so forth and I promise by the rainbow that I shall keep this promise.

It now happens, and this is not known to many people, that the Creation of the universe out of nothing does not contradict the laws of Nature. If you write down the equation for the total energy of the mass of all matter, of radius, let's say, R and Mass M, you find the following. The energy, according to Einstein, is Mass times C^2, MC^2. This ball of matter also has gravitational energy. Gravitational forces are attractive. Therefore the gravitational energy has a negative sign, it's a negative energy. The total energy consists of two parts: MC^2 and the second one happens to be Newton's constant of universal gravitation, G, times the square of M divided by R plus MC^2 minus the latter term. Now if this difference was zero, the ball could spring into existence out of nothing and not violate the principle of conservation of energy. Well, it turns out that if you put the equation, the first term minus the second term equals zero, you get almost exactly the condition of the black hole. Therefore the Creation of the universe out of nothing is by no means contradictory to modern science; Relativity and Quantum Mechanics have shown us that it isn't.

And it would be highly unreasonable for someone to reject the notion of a Creator by appealing to science?

Oh yes. It is absolutely unreasonable.

Modern science has definitively shown the non-contradiction of Creation out of nothing?

Yes, it has definitively shown it. This is not widely known.

What about the Anthropic Principle?

Yes. It is absolutely convincing to me.

Do you see Purpose in the universe and, if so, what is its relation to the Creator?

There my argument is extremely simple. What is the difference between cause and purpose? Cause is determination of future events by the past. Purpose is determination of future events by a vision of the future. You can't have a purpose unless you visualize what you want to do. Therefore, purpose requires a mind. As soon as you speak of purpose, the mind must be involved somehow. Eccles gives some very clear evidence that cause alone, physical processes alone, don't do the trick. Eccles actually shows that the state of mind can precede a certain muscular action. In some instances (it's not his experiment, but he refers to it) the motion of the finger comes first and the state of knowledge of it afterwards. And sometimes the mental state comes first and the physical action afterwards. So he claims that the mind can affect the body just as the body can affect the mind. In my latest book, called *Einstein's Space and Van Gogh's Sky* I make that point.

Does your approach of seeing purpose in the universe as an indication of a Creator differ from William Paley's Watchmaker Argument?

It doesn't.

And you say that this argument is validated by modern science?

Yes, science is much more tolerant nowadays to religious ideas than it ever has been before.

But there still is a lot of hostility to religion among certain scientists in the scientific community?

Well, this is a common belief. And, if you ask scientists who have a mild training in science, especially high school teachers and so forth, you do get the impression that there is a conflict between science and religion. But if you ask really good scientists, I mean men who have made contributions, I'm thinking of people here like Eccles, like Wigner, who is a good friend of mine, Heisenberg, whom I personally knew, Schroedinger, who visited me personally at home ... Einstein was less explicit about his religious views but he had it. The leading scientists, the people who have made the contributions which has made science grow so vastly in the last fifty years, are, so far as I know, all religious in their beliefs. None of these men had any objection to religion. They didn't write about religion much — Heisenberg did occasionally — but they were certainly not atheists. So what I'm saying is that, if you take the top-notch scientists, you find very few atheists among them.

[On another occasion, Professor Margenau added the following.]

It is often said, and widely believed, that scientists on the whole are anti-religious or, at least, are not interested in religion. I believed that for a long time too. But no longer. Perhaps I shouldn't say this, but as I perceive it, the fact is, the scientists, the physicists at least, who have been most active, most successful in developing the quantum theory and further innovations in physics, are very interested in religion. If you consider scientists of the type of high school teachers or grade school teachers or Carl Sagan, you find that, yes, there is a lack of interest. Quite a few of them are anti-religious. But, if you take the outstanding physicists, the ones who have done the most to advance modern physics, especially Heisenberg, Schroedinger, Dirac (a Nobel Prize winner) you find them all interested in religion. All these men were intensely interested in religion.

Could you comment on Einstein's religious beliefs?

He did not like to talk about religion very much. But, of course, he did say, "God does not play dice," which is, of course, a well known fact by now. Everybody would agree with that. He was not religious in the sense of going to church. He did not go to church very often. But he certainly did not disdain religion or speak against it. Never.

In fact, he once remarked, "Everyone who is seriously involved in the pursuit of science becomes convinced

that a spirit is manifest in the laws of the universe — a spirit vastly superior to that of man, and one in the face of which we with our modest powers must feel humble" (*Albert Einstein: The Human Side*).

That is quite correct. Precisely. We should be humble before the inspiration. We should humbly accept the kind of inspiration which comes when we make the kind of discoveries that he made. I think, if you would have pinned him down on this, he would have regarded a discovery like the Relativity Theory as an inspiration, divine inspiration. In fact, many scientists do. Especially the ones who have discovered new, wholly new, abstract theories of physics.

Is the idea of a beginning of the universe now accepted in science?

Oh yes. That's clearly accepted by almost everybody.

But you do have some in astronomy, like Carl Sagan, who are almost vehemently anti-religious.

Another man who is working in the same field, Robert Jastrow, is not, and Jastrow is a better man than Sagan, as a scientist, as a physicist. Sagan is a popularizer, Jastrow is a physicist who has done research in the field in which he speaks. And Jastrow is a religious man.

I might tell you a story, of my last meeting with a very famous chemist, Laars Onsager, a Nobel Laureate. He was a neighbor of ours. They have a farm in New Hampshire. We have a summer place not far from there. And in New Haven we were neighbors. So we saw a good deal of each other. As a matter of fact, I was in the hospital with a very desperate sort of illness ... and I needed a blood transfusion. Within half an hour he was there and gave his blood and so forth. He was a wonderful person. I don't know of anybody whom I would respect more highly. We were at his farm in Fall. We stayed there a few days. He showed me a paper which he had just written and he was about to publish it. It dealt with some of the chemical phases in the process of evolution. It dealt only with the chemistry of it. He analyzed the action which led from one stage to the other in a most remarkable and convincing way. He showed me the paper and I said I would like to read it. So I kept it that night and read it. The next morning we got together, we walked through the woods. This was September. The woods were beautiful, lots of maple trees. He asked me, what do you think of my paper? I said, I think it was wonderful; you explain this particular result in an incontrovertible way. He said, I'm glad you liked it. Then I said, What is your opinion of the process of evolution? Are you a Darwinist? Well, he said, yes, I think so. Do you think that evolution takes place by chance? He said, I haven't really thought about it very much from a philosophical point of view, but, yes. I picked up a maple leaf which was lying on the ground. It was red with golden edges, perfectly symmetrical. I showed it to him. I said, Do you think that this just results from survival of the fittest? Why should it survive, it's going to lie on the ground? Don't you see the beauty in the thing? Doesn't that mean that elements like beauty, and possibly purpose, are also involved in the process of evolution? Why should a maple leaf, which is going to rot on the ground, survive? He said, You have a point there. Yes, I think there is more to evolution than just survival of the fittest and random mutation. That was the last time I saw him. Two days later he died.

4
MODERN BIOLOGY AND THE TURN TO BELIEF IN GOD
Sir John Eccles

Do you see any shift away from Mechanism in the sciences and what comments do you have about the future of Mechanism?

Let's put it this way. I think the physical sciences are more likely to be religious than the biological sciences because they have, as it were, perhaps, a simpler concept of the universe and they are not so involved in minutae as the biological sciences. In *The Human Mystery* I deal with findings that are relevant for the theistic view, the Big Bang theory, the anthropic principle.

What Heisenberg called the First Principle, the principle of order — I don't know whether by that he meant God — as long as we carry on the tradition of this, which was derived from the Christian religion ... some dim theistic view that goes on guiding us; if that should go, he said, that will be quite terrible, worse than concentration camps. I can see that very much today still. What you have is a scientistic view, science as a kind of religion. Jacques Monod is an arch-priest of this, or arch-prophet, but there are quite a lot of others in the same way in other movements like sociobiology denying anything human, value-systems which animals don't have. The situation I regard as quite serious, and I don't think that in the seminaries training Protestant and Catholic clergymen, I don't think they are really training them properly to face the modern world, to go out into a world where the average man in the street says that science has disproved religion. This is what you're up against.

I think it is very important indeed to be examining the whole mental outlook, from time to time, that is governing our lives and that is developing into the future. I hope very much that we are recovering from the long deep depression of materialistic monism which has spread over the intellectual world like a dark fog blanketing out all of the brightness and illumination of the ideals and imaginations of human beings. I hope very much that we can be restored to some sanity in relationship to the mystery of existence and become more and more freed from this domination by the dogmatic assertions of materialists that can only lead to despair and nihilism. I would like to see a turn back towards hope and value and a higher meaning of life, and eventually a divine view of human existence.

What evidence is there for the existence of the mind and for its distinctness from the body?

There is the evidence for dualism which is presented in *The Self and Its Brain*, the book I wrote with Sir Karl Popper and in my more recent books, *The Human Mystery* and *The Human Psyche*. The existence of the mind is something I think you must simply accept because it is the whole of your mental experience, from moment to moment. There is no argument about that, that you are conscious. Having a mind means that you are conscious. That's fair enough. The mind as an entity distinct from the brain is what you are asking. You may ask what "distinct from the brain" means. It means that these exist in two different orders. The brain is in the

material world and the mind is in the world of subjective experience (this is the World 2 of Popper). You are
asking for the evidence for the independence of these
two worlds. What is your alternative? The alternative is
some monism which means either a spiritual monism of
the Kantian type or a material, mechanistic monism or
there is also the neutral monism, for example, of Russell. We've discussed all that in *The Self and Its Brain*.
One has to have the idea that thoughts exist. Thinking is
what I am doing now trying to answer your questions.
And I live in this world of many other mental events
besides thoughts. But that might be one to start with,
the existence of thought. Thoughts, of course, do eventually find expression in language, that is what one does
in the ordinary business of talking, thoughts converted
into language. So that part of the story is fairly clear:
that we do have mental events before they are converted
into brain events. The monist materialist thinks that the
mental events are simply derivative of aspects of the
nerve endings. But there is no evidence for this whatsoever. It's part of a hypothesis. But they think that,
therefore, they are escaping from the difficulties of
physics. But they just create a worse difficulty in physics, namely there is no such thing in physics as mental
events, mental happenings. The world of the mind is
not recognized by the physicist at all. They invented
something which they superimposed upon physics simply to escape from the difficulties of having mental
events as distinct from material events.

**What do you think of the work of Jacques Monod and
of Francis Crick and of the general claims of
materialism?**

Monod, of course wrote *Chance and Necessity*. I knew
him very well. He was a materialist. But he was different
from most materialists. He believed he was God. He
had this kind of divine obsession. In the last chapter of

his book, "The Kingdom and the Darkness," he is dictating there. This is, of course, not science at all. It is prophetic utterance. He's gone away from any rationality and has proceeded to deliver doctrine according to the dictates of Jacques Monod. "The Kingdom" is if you follow the beliefs of Monod and become one of his loving disciples. "The Darkness" is if you don't. About Francis Crick. He has a less developed philosophy of religion. He is, of course, a materialist but I don't think a very profound thinker in all these respects.

I think that promissory materialism is still a principal belief of the scientists. But it is promissory: that everything will be explained, even intimate forms of human experience in terms of nerve endings ... This is simply a religious belief, not even a religious belief; it is a superstition based upon no evidence worth considering at all. The longer we go on understanding the performance of the human brain, the more remarkable does it become, the more unique are we from anything else in the material world.

Do you think there is any conflict between science and religion and do you yourself accept a theistic view of reality? (Sir John's responses to this question came at a discussion sponsored by the Isthmus Institute in Dallas and at Modern Thought and the Turn to Theism, another discussion in March of 1983).

Science and religion are very much alike. Both are imaginative and creative aspects of the human mind. The appearance of conflict is a result of ignorance. We come to exist through a divine act. That divine guidance is a theme throughout our life; at our death the brain goes, but that divine guidance and love continues. Each of us is a unique, conscious being, a divine creation. It is the religious view. It is the only view consistent with all the evidence.

5
MODERN BIO-CHEMISTRY AND THE COLLAPSE OF MECHANISM
Dr. Rupert Sheldrake

Give a brief outline of Mechanism and summarize its defects.

The word "mechanism" is related to the word "machine" and obviously has the same root as words like mechanical. It comes from the view that the universe is a machine, which used to be called the mechanistic philosophy, an aspect of the materialists' philosophy. Of course it was associated with rather old-fashioned views of machinery in the 19th century, and now man uses machines which are more complicated and sophisticated. But, nonetheless, the mechanistic theory of nature, and the modern mechanistic theory of life, is still based on the idea that living organisms are machines.

The key thing about machines is that they are made up of parts which interact with each other, and that they work entirely in terms of the laws of physics and chemistry. The machine has no soul, no vital principle, no spiritual entity in it.

Machines carry out purposive activities but they themselves don't have souls, or spirits, or any mysterious vital factor. But machines are made by man to serve human purposes as a result of human creativity. So, in a sense, the psychic, the mental aspect of the machines is not inside themselves but outside themselves in the minds of their inventors and their makers. And actually, this machine analogy used by mechanistic biologists is the very same analogy which was used in traditional theology: because living organisms have a machine-like aspect, so they must have been designed and made by an intelligent creator.

The mechanistic theory of biology preserves the machine analogy but it denies that there is any inventor or maker of the machine. But in fact machines do imply inventors and makers. However, the point about the mechanistic theory of life that commends it most strongly to mechanists and materialists is the idea that living organisms obey only the laws of physics and chemistry and that there is nothing psychic, conscious, or mental, no vital factor, nor spirit which does anything or makes any difference to living organisms. They can be considered purely as physical and chemical entities.

Now the defects of this theory, I think, are several. One is that our own experiences of ourselves as conscious beings is not that of machines. We think of ourselves as beings with choice. We think of the things we say as having some meaning ... not simply as things such as result from our genetic and environmental programming. Even the view that we are machines, if we are to take the mechanists seriously, is something that they must believe has some meaning and truth. If they are simply saying it because they've been programmed to say it, or because their genetic factors combined with the environment they've been brought up in necessitated their saying it, then we've no reason why we should pay any more attention to that than to any other view.

Secondly, insofar as the mechanistic theory is taken to mean that living organisms obey only the *known* laws of physics and chemistry, then it could easily be wrong because we know so little about the way organisms develop, the processes of embryology, the way in which instincts are inherited, and so on. We're not in fact in a position to say we can explain it all in terms of physics and chemistry. There may be unknown factors involved ... and there probably are.

If we want to find out whether or not we already know all the laws of physics and chemistry which are involved in living organisms, we'd have to think out experiments to test whether or not they could be entirely explained in terms of the known laws of physics and chemistry. This is the way we could proceed in recognizing how to resolve this question. But the mechanist theory, as it is commonly understood, doesn't even ask the question. It denies that there is any validity in the question, and it seems to assume we already know the principles we need to know. Therefore it prevents us asking questions that could enable us to find out more about the true nature of living organisms ... and of nature in general.

What is the relevance of the revolution in physics for biology?

Well, there hasn't been just one revolution in physics, there have been several. But I don't think that the theory of relativity has a great deal of relevance. What has more importance is quantum theory and subatomic physics.

Two main points are relevant here. One is the principle of uncertainty. We now recognize that the universe is not entirely predictable. The subtle inherent unpredictability of things means that we can never really know what's going to happen next with any certainty. We can make informed guesses, but the course that the universe or a particular system takes is not fully predictable in physical terms. This I think is important for biology in several ways. One is that it shows that there could be a genuine element of chance in living organisms. This of course has been seized upon by the current theory of random mutation. Another is that, as far as physics is concerned, many different things *could* happen in cells, nerves, etc., but only some of them *do* happen. This leaves room for a new kind of causal factor. Not something that we already know about but some new thing in nature that we really haven't discovered yet.

Secondly, in quantum theory it's become clearly recognized that observations depend on observers, measurements depend on measuring instruments and people who are doing measurements. The human observer is a part of the process of observation. Of course this has been blindingly obvious to a number of thinkers for a long time. Schopenhauer, for example, pointed out that all observations require observers, thoughts require thinkers and theories require theorists. They presuppose the consciousness of the observer, the thinker, the scientist.

So our theories of physics and theories about how brains work, the minds of the observers, are theories that are produced by minds, and so all our theories, all our observations presuppose the minds of the observers who are doing the observations. There is an inevitable circularity here. Quantum theory, with its rigorous examination of conditions of observation and measurement, has made this general philosophical point very clear in the context of modern physics. This has relevance to biology because it undermines the mechanistic assumption that everything about life including the human mind can be understood in terms of physics.

The orthodoxy in biology you have said is Mechanism: could you explain why this is so?

I think the main reason is because it grew out of a general cultural context where the materialist's philosophy was particularily influential. Moreover it allows scientists to get on with the job of looking at the physical and chemical aspects of things, living organisms in particular, without concerning themselves with theological and philosophical issues. And I think they wanted to have a freedom to maneuver that could only be had if they cast off the spectres of philosophy and theology. This was particularily true in the 19th century. I think this is the background to this orthodoxy.

The persistence of the orthodoxy has been greatly reinforced by the advances in molecular biology. But although many things have been found at the molecular level, we still know very little about what makes living organisms living. The truly biological aspects of living organisms remain as mysterious as ever. I think that we have to recognize that the rather limited mechanistic approach has been valuable and perhaps it was a necessary phase for biology to pass through.

But, I think, that we have now reached the point where we have to try to get beyond it, if we want a deeper understanding of the nature of life.

Would you comment on the rather confused notion that it will soon be possible to create life in the lab?

Well, there are many people who seem to think that life has already been created in the lab. It's of course possible to synthesize nucleic acids and proteins and it's possible, no doubt, or it will be possible, to make viruses synthetically. It's conceivable that it may even be possible to make a cell synthetically, actually to make a living organism from non-living materials in the laboratory. But I don't think this would prove anything one way or another about the nature of life.

It's obviously indisputable that living organisms are made up of chemicals and contain numerous different kinds of protein, DNA, etc. Also many aspects of them work according to physical principles, electricity and so on. Now this doesn't prove there is nothing but physical-chemical systems and that we can understand them completely in terms of physics and chemistry. The best way to illustrate this is to consider the analogy of a transistor radio. Imagine that someone who didn't know anything about transistor radios, was shown one and he was amazed at the music that came from it and tried to understand it.

He might think that the music originates entirely within the set as a result of complicated interactions among its parts. If somebody suggested they were coming from outside through a transmission inside into the set from somewhere else, he might deny it on the grounds that he could see nothing coming in. Nor could he measure anything because the set weighed the same switched on and switched off, and although he couldn't understand the set in terms of its parts, and their interaction, he might think that as a result of further research, he would be able to do so. So, he might think he understood the set, or could understand the set in principle, even though, in fact, he knows nothing about radio waves, etc. He might even try to prove he understood it. He could take it to pieces. He could find out the things it was made of, silicon crystals, copper wires and so on. He might then think he could prove that he understood the set by making a replica. By getting copper, crystals and all that he could make a radio set which would work in the same way as the original. When switched on, music would come out of it. He could say, "Look I've fully understood this thing, I've synthesized one of these things entirely from known materials."

But still, you see, he wouldn't really understand how it worked. He still wouldn't understand about radio waves in spite of the fact he'd been able to make a radio set. I think that's just the position we're in in relation to life. I think the mechanists are like people who try to understand radio sets ignoring radio waves and concentrating only on copper wires, components and the way they're wired together. Those are important of course, and they're really there and if you destroy a component or take one away the radio won't work properly. But it's only part of the picture. What's wrong with the mechanistic view is that it's a limited view; like most errors, it is based on a half-truth.

Doesn't the advent of the computer make it possible to think of what is called the mind in purely physical terms?

I don't think so. A lot of nonsense is talked about computers, I don't want to go into this at length, as I find the whole subject so tedious. I think the most obvious thing is that computers are produced by human minds; they are the product of human minds. They couldn't possibly exist without human inventors, the people who make them and the people who program them. They mimic some of the aspects of the minds that give rise to them. Looking at them and saying they are a bit like the mind and can do some of the things that minds can do when they themselves are products of the mind, can really prove nothing about the physical nature of the mind. It seems to me a childish argument to say that because computers do things a bit like minds therefore minds must be like computers. It completely ignores the fact that computers are entirely dependent on human minds for their existence.

Do you have any comments on Jaques Monod on chance?

I think Monod elevates chance to some creative principle in the universe to account for the creativity of evolution. In fact, he propounds a metaphysical theory where chance is given the same role as God in certain traditional systems. It sounds as though it is a scientific concept, but it isn't really. If an organism does something new, even if there is a truly random mutation that blocks a normal process in the organism or prevents it from doing what it would normally do, the response of the organism to this mutation is not a matter of chance. It is a creative response of the whole organism. There is no one-to-one relationship between the accidental change in the DNA and the response of the organism to that change.

To make this clearer, think of a human analogy, (and, after all, according to the mechanistic theory people are just machines, so the same thing should apply there). Imagine that someone is blinded in a terrible accident by flying glass; we can understand in terms of physics the trajectory of the glass as it flies through the air, the impact as it hits the eye tissue, the damaging effects as it hits the retina and so on. That's easy to understand in terms of ordinary physics. No problem there. We've got a chain of physical causation that leads to blindness. That's easy to understand. But now what the man does as a result of being blind is quite unpredictable. He might, because he can no longer see properly, develop tremendously good hearing, he may take up music, he could even become a composer. Whereas, if he had gone on with his normal eyesight he might have continued in a perfectly routine way and never thought of composing music or any of the other things that blind people sometimes do. Now this creative response to the new necessities caused by this chance event doesn't bear a one-to-one relationship to the trajectory of the glass, etc., which can indeed be understood in purely physical terms.

This is true with everything to do with organisms. Anything that happens in an organism is not some isolated thing; it's something that happens within the context of the whole organism. And the response of the organism is sometimes creative. It's this creativity that can't be explained in a one-to-one way in terms of the chance event that gives rise to it. The materialists believe that chance can be the only source of creativity because they rule out the existence of any non-material creative factor. Therefore all creativity has to be attributed in the final analysis to chance. But this is nothing more than a metaphysical assumption; there is nothing scientific about it.

What implication does purpose in nature have for neo-Darwinism?

Again this is something that is often argued about and I don't want to spend a lot of time on it. The main argument of neo-Darwinism, is to try and show that purposiveness can be explained upon the basis of random mutation followed by natural selection. But you see, random mutation doesn't entirely account for purposiveness in nature. Random mutation imposes a new necessity upon the organism. For example, as a result of a mutation an organism may be born blind. But if it responds to that blindness in a new creative way by, for example, listening to echoes and developing an echo location system, this creativity cannot be explained by chance mutation. The organism is already purposive to start with and so the purpose of an organism's response to a mutation can't be explained in terms of chance and necessity. Monod's thesis is in reality the materialist's philosophy restated in scientific terms and we must see that it can't be tested as science. It is a metaphysical idea, which we can either accept or reject on philosophical grounds.

6
FROM SCIENTIFIC COSMOLOGY TO A CREATED UNIVERSE

Stanley L. Jaki

Almost exactly a hundred years ago, in 1885, Berthelot, a leading French scientist, declared that owing to the progress of science the world became free of mysteries. Then came a rash of unexpected discoveries: cathode-rays, X-rays, electrons, radioactivity and quanta. The world suddenly looked so mysterious that even politicians took note. On January 21, 1910, Jean Jaures, a leader of the French socialist party, told the Chambre des Députés: "The admirable scientist who once wrote that the world is without a mystery seems to me to have uttered a naiveté as great as his genius." Twenty years later there appeared the most successful high-level popularization of science published so far. *The Mysterious Universe* by James Jeans. The universe seemed to the famed British astronomer so mysterious that he was even willing to see beyond it a God, a sort of super-mathematician. A few years later Etienne Gilson wondered aloud why scientists should take any satisfaction in the apparent mysteriousness of the universe. Most Christian readers of the book seemed satisfied. Belief in God, the greatest mystery, often appeared safer when God's handiwork, the universe, also looked mysterious. Unfortunately, true mysteries were often seen in mere gaps of scientific knowledge, gaps which as a rule are rapidly filled as science progresses.

Even if by mysteries Berthelot meant such gaps, his really scientific bungle was not that he saw all mysteries, that is, gaps in scientific knowledge, being filled at least potentially, although this was enough of a bungle. In 1885 there was not even an inkling of the true explanation of spectral lines which by then had been measured by the tens of thousands and held the key to an atomic realm defying all scientific prognostication. Berthelot misread science most as he spoke of the universe without hinting at its scientifically problematic character. He should have known that in 1885 it was not yet possible to speak in a scientifically unobjectionable way about the universe, the totality of consistently interacting things.

Scientific cosmology was still to be born in spite of the fact that throughout the 19th century scientists spoke more and more often of the universe, a topic which had largely been the preserve of philosophers and of a few philosophically inclined scientists. That during the 19th century and before, scientists spoke of the universe in the sense of doing cosmology, was not in itself completely unscientific. One ought to speak of a problem one cannot solve if that problem is ever to be solved. The universe was for 19th-century science, or for Newtonian science, a huge problem, but, and this was scientifically reprehensible, scientists preferred not to speak of this, rather, they tried to talk away the problem.

The problem was the alleged Euclidean infinity of the universe. Such a universe was largely the product of 19th-century thinking. Newton himself believed the material universe to be finite in an infinite space. This idea was endorsed and propagated, as something most conformable to reason and to God, by no less publicists than Addison and Voltaire. But with the early 19th century there came a radical shift. Thus the astronomer Olbers declared in 1823, with a reference to Kant's authority, that the universe of stars had to be infinite. The context spoke for itself. Olbers wanted to save the infinity of the universe from the paradox of the darkness of the night sky. If the number of stars was infinite and homogeneously distributed, it followed, if one did not take into account the average lifespan of stars, that the intensity of starlight should be equal at any point to the brightness of the surface of a typical star, such as the Sun.

Whatever the loopholes in the optical paradox, which had already been discussed by Halley and intimated by Kepler, there were no loopholes in its gravitational counterpart. Here too the story goes back well before the 19th century. As early as 1692 Bentley called attention to the gravitational paradox in his famous Boyle lectures and also privately in his letters to Newton. After Green formulated in 1827 the theory of potential, the gravitational paradox could have been given a rigorous formulation. This did not happen until 1871 when Zöllner, professor of astrophysics in Leipzig, showed that in an infinite homogeneous universe any force obeying the inverse square law should produce an infinitely large potential at any point. At the same time Zöllner also suggested that Riemann's four-dimensional space-time manifold could provide a way out, provided the total mass of the universe was taken to be finite. Two years later, W.K. Clifford, professor of applied mathematics at University College in London, stated that Riemann's geometry made the universe a scientifically valid notion, the very basis of the possibility of a scientific cosmology.

Although both Zöllner and Clifford were prominent figures, scientists paid little if any attention. Some, like Seeliger in Munich, tried to change slightly the inverse square law to save the infinite homogeneous universe; others took the Milky Way for all the universe that was investigable. The infinitely large part beyond the Milky Way was declared by Kelvin, among others, to be forever beyond the reach of science. Such a solution was not science, but a schizophrenic thinking which split the universe into two parts: One finite (the Milky Way), the other infinite (everything beyond). Thus was the universe rid of its mysteries. So much in a way of commentary on the real scientific blunder which Berthelot made in speaking of the universe. Assuming as he did that the universe was infinite in the Euclidean sense, he had no right to speak of it as if it had no mysteries, that is, scientifically debilitating problems.

The first chapter in a scientifically rigorous cosmology came only in 1917 with Einstein's memoir on the cosmological consequences of General Relativity. There Einstein showed that the gravitational interaction of all material bodies could be given a formulation free from the gravitational paradox which plagued the so-called Newtonian universe. This was not, however, the most important aspect of that memoir which was the last in a series published by Einstein between 1915 and 1917 on General Relativity. The most important point was a formula which stated that from the values of the average density of matter and of the gravitational constant one could infer the value of the total mass of the universe and its overall radius of curvature produced by that mass. Such an inference was not a mere play with formulas. The inference was based on a broad theory, General Relativity, which already at that time provided three experimentally verifiable predictions, each independent of the other: the gravitational red-shift, the gravitational bending of light, and the advance of the perihelion of planetary orbits (readily observable in the case of Mercury). While the early verifications of these effects were not altogether convincing, today the margin of error in measuring them is too small to permit real doubt. During the last half a century several other predictions of General Relativity have been submitted to observational tests which further confirmed its reliability. No less valuable confirmation of General Relativity is the increasingly vaster field of study: scientific cosmology. All branches and further developments of that study are based on the conviction that it is scientifically meaningful to discuss the consistent interaction of the totality of matter, a totality which is the universe.

Such a conviction is further strengthened by the fact that in modern scientific cosmology the study of galaxies and other large-scale celestial objects is closely united with the atomic, nuclear, and subnuclear studies, that is, the study of the smallest material objects. That scientific cosmology deals with the totality of consistently interacting matter is strikingly shown by the expansion of the universe. This large-scale motion to which all matter is subject was first a mere prediction by Abbé Lemaître on the basis of General Relativity before it obtained observational proof in the red-shift of the spectrum of galaxies. That shift can be explained only if galaxies have a recessional velocity with respect to one another which is the greater the farther they are from one another. This, however, entitles one to follow the motion of galaxies backward in time to a moment where all matter was condensed within a relatively small space.

Scientific cosmology gives so far an account only of the gravitational interaction of matter. Other interactions, electromagnetic and nuclear, are incorporated only in part in that picture. A Unified Field Theory valid for all these forces (to say nothing of some forces still to be discovered) is still to be formulated. Such a theory is the most coveted prize for leading scientists today, in proof that in their eyes the notion of the universe is a truly valid and not merely a regulative idea. They are encouraged by the success achieved so far by General Relativity. Twentieth-century science provides indeed powerful support on behalf of the validity of the notion of the universe, a validity which since Kant's *Critique of Pure Reason* has been largely dismissed in philosophical circles (and even in some theological realms which should know better). Kant's ultimate purpose with the *Critique* was, it is well to recall, to provide a rigorous basis for man's autonomy or independence. In that strategy an all-important step was the presentation of the universe as a bastard product of the metaphysical cravings of the intellect. If the universe was not a valid notion, then it could no longer function as a reliable basis of inference to the existence of the Creator, the only Independent Being. In the absence of such trustworthy inference man's autonomy seemed to be fully secured.

The really dangerous part in Kant's strategy was that he largely succeeded in creating the impression that his reasoning was in the spirit of exact, that is, Newtonian science. Now, if he had been well informed and really perceptive in matters scientific, he should have realized that his antinomy about the finiteness versus infinity of the universe had no scientific merit. The so-called Newtonian infinity, which he had in mind, had no scientific validity and therefore could not be used as an alternative to the possible finiteness of the universe. Twentieth-century science or cosmology has shown that it is meaningful to speak about the infinity of the universe as well as about its finiteness, without being thrown back thereby into the hold of Kant's first antinomy. That modern scientific cosmology restores confidence in the validity of the notion of the universe should seem no small bonus for those who see the universe as a jumping board to its Creator. The same cosmology does something even more important in that respect. The universe as described in that cosmology strikes us as a truly existing thing. Scientific cosmology provides this impression not by philosophical arguments, however valid and precious they may be about existence. Rather, it does so by its portrayal of the universe as a most specific, most peculiar, most particular and at the same time fully consistent entity.

Here again a recall of the historical background against which this development should be seen may be very helpful. A hundred years ago Herbert Spencer rode the crest of the wave with his *First Principles*, a cosmic philosophy. Like Kant, Spencer too succeeded in presenting his philosophy as steeped in science. Spencer first made a name for himself with his account of Laplace's nebular hypothesis in which the solar system, and ultimately all solar systems and celestial bodies, were the products of an evolution which started with a nebulous, that is, most homogeneous state of matter and ended with a most specific or inhomogeneous form of it. The effort was a somersault both philosophically and scientifically, worthy of a philosopher who did not have proper scientific training and who prided himself that never in his life was he surprised by anything. Yet, because Spencer's scientific bungle was not perceived, his philosophical bungle, too, was readily overlooked. The scientific bungle was tied to the lack of any information about the nebulous state, the presumed starting point of cosmic evolution. The pale whiteness of nebulae was simply taken by scientists for a homogeneous fluid for no real reason whatsoever. Scientific unanimity based on wishful inference fully reassured Spencer that his starting point was correct and reliable. For all that, it remained thoroughly incorrect for him to assume that complete homogeneity would ultimately give rise to a high degree of inhomogeneity. As one would expect, Spencer assumed a "very slight imbalance" in that original state, but the significance of this proviso was largely lost on him and on his readers, among them Charles Darwin who naively took Spencer for one of the greatest intellects of all times. Spencer, as is well known, took that homogeneous, nondescript, unspecified entity for the starting point of the natural form of existence. It was a matching counterpart to the perceptual non-specificity of Euclidean infinity which in the eyes of many served as a natural frame of existence which needed no further, let alone metaphysical, explanation.

A hundred years after Spencer the farthest point in the past to which scientific cosmology carries us is the very opposite of non-specificity. With the discovery in 1965 of the 2.7° K cosmic background radiation, a proof was served on behalf of earlier theories about the genesis of chemical elements, at a time when the universe was in a highly condensed state. Chemical elements, as ranged in the Mendeleev table, are not only very specific in themselves (Mendeleev himself was so impressed by their specificity as to take all of them for irreducible primordial entities). Their relative abundances are no less specific. Such a compound specificity could arise from a cosmic soup comprising all matter in which for each proton, neutron, and electron there were almost exactly 40 million photons at a very specific temperature and pressure. Only under such conditions could the interaction between those particles yield hydrogen and helium in their actual and very specific proportion and make thereby the genesis of heavier elements possible.

On looking at a proportion of 1 versus 40 million, no sane mind would be tempted to take it as a natural or, rather, exclusive state of affairs. The same lesson is on hand when one follows modern scientific cosmology beyond the baryon state of the cosmos (described by Dr. Carr above*) to states which modern scientific cosmology calls lepton, hadron, and quantum states. Beyond those states is the matter-antimatter state where things appear dizzyingly specific. Nothing would be more natural than to see that state as comprising an equal amount of matter and antimatter. But interaction between equal amounts of matter and antimatter would yield only sheer radiation. In order that our ordinary matter and world may arise, scientific cosmology must resort to a most "unnatural" assumption, according to which there had to be an original imbalance of one part in 10 billion in favour of ordinary matter. Such is not a mere speculation. Its reasonability is implied in the finding by Fitch and Cronin of a slight asymmetry in the decay of K_2 mesons, a finding which earned them the Nobel Prize in 1980.

Clearly, there is an immense contrast between the primordial state of matter as described by Spencer and as described by scientific cosmology, a contrast which should provoke the utmost surprise. The difference is not merely a difference between studies vagueness and a study steeped in scientific precision. The real difference is that a most specific entity may strike even a philosophically desensitized mind with the fact of existence. While the queer specificity of everyday things can easily be lost on us, such is hardly the case when one is forced to face up to cosmic specificity, described and verified in all details by science. About the universe scientific cosmology states not only that it is a valid notion, but also powerfully suggests that it does exist — a most welcome contribution in an age in which philosophizing is stranded on the shallows of idealism and logicism, two skilful guides to solipsism and sheer willfulness.

To grasp all this requires no familiarity with that elaborate mathematics which is an integral part of scientific cosmology. Because of its mathematical aspect, scientific cosmology is subject to Gödel's incompleteness theorem, according to which no set of non-trivial arithmetical propositions can have its proof of consistency within itself. This means that all scientific efforts aimed at an account for the universe, which would show that the universe can only be what it is and cannot be anything else, are doomed to failure. Eddington was not the only major scientist in our century who seriously devoted himself to such an undertaking. Einstein himself would have loved to construct a Unified Theory such that, as he put it half seriously, "even the good Lord would not be able to improve on it." In the past two decades several Nobel laureates admitted that their work was motivated by some such aim. Of course, it is not absolutely beyond the realm of possibility that a scientist should be fortunate enough to hit upon a mathematical formalism which would fit the quantitative aspect of all material processes. In that case there would remain no mysteries or unsolved problems with respect to the physical universe where, let us not forget, God "disposed everything according to measure, number, and weight." Such a fortunate theory would account not only for all data on hand but also for data still to be gathered in the future, however distant.

Yet even such a theory could not claim to itself intrinsic consistency. Its proof of consistency would, in virtue of Gödel's theorem, lie in a set of considerations not included in it. In other words, scientific cosmology, because of Gödel's theorem, can never pose a threat to that cosmic contingency which is intimated in the scientific portrayal of the specificity of the universe. A universe which is contingent is the very opposite of cosmic necessitarianism, the age-old refuge of materialists, pantheists and atheists, all of whom, with Nietzsche in the lead, consider the dogma of creation as the most pernicious error man can espouse.

The final and most striking pointer of scientific cosmology to the createdness of the universe is a sequel to the contingency of the universe. The contingency meant here is not its confused sense equivalent to an undefined indeterminacy. Contingency here means the utter dependence of something on something else. The actual specificity of the universe is a striking reminder of such a dependence. Precisely because the actual cosmos is so specific, it should be easy to see the possibility of an immensely large number of other specificities. The actual specificity of the universe, which cannot be necessary, reveals therefore its dependence on a choice beyond the universe. Since the specificity of the universe is highly understandable, the choice underlying that specificity, a choice which also gives the universe its actual existence, must involve an intelligence and power which is supercosmic, that is, beyond that cosmos which for science is the totality of consistently interacting things. Things, even world, which do not interact consistently are, it is well to recall, irrelevant for science. Nor is relevant for science that spurious philosophy which is often equated with quantum mechanics, the probabilistic method to account for atomic and subatomic phenomena. The radical inconsistency or purely chance character which is attributed by that philosophy (Copenhagen theory) to atomic processes, is a consequence of the radical rejection by that philosophy of any question about being (ontology). Typically, such a philosophy is not consistent to the point of recognizing the fact that it therefore has no right to ask, let alone to answer, the question: What is chance?

Is it reasonable to assume that an Intelligence which produced a universe, a totality of consistently interacting things, is not consistent to the point of acting for a purpose? To speak of purpose may seem, since Darwin, the most reprehensible procedure before the tribunal of science. Bafflingly enough, it is science in its most advanced and comprehensive form — scientific cosmology — which reinstates today references to purpose into scientific discourse. Shortly after the discovery of the 2.7° K radiation cosmologists began to wonder at the extremely narrow margin allowed for cosmic evolution. The universe began to appear to them more and more as if placed on an extremely narrow track, a track laid down so that ultimately man may appear on the scene. For if that cosmic soup had been slightly different, not only the chemical elements, of which all organic bodies are made, would have failed to be formed. Inert matter would have also been subject to an interaction different from the one required for the coagulation of large lumps of matter, such as protostars and proto-solar systems.

Yet the solar system ultimately emerged and with it that curious planet, the Earth, which if placed at a slightly different distance from the Sun, would have undergone a very different evolutionary process on its surface. At any rate, the emergence of life on earth is, from the purely scientific viewpoint, an outcome of immense improbability. No wonder that in view of this quite a few cosmologists, who are unwilling to sacrifice forever at the altar of blind chance, began to speak of the anthropic principle. Recognition of that principle was prompted by the nagging suspicion that the universe may have after all been specifically tailored for the sake of man.

That scientific cosmologists were forced by their own findings to formulate the anthropic principle may please some philosophers and theologians. In Aquinas' philosophy it was a central tenet that the universe was created for the sake of man. It must not however be forgotten that such a tenet, or the anthropic principle, can never be a part of scientific cosmology. Science is about quantitative correlations, not about purpose. Not that science as such is not a purposeful activity. As all truly human actions, science too, is for a purpose and to a very high degree. This is true even of those scientists who devote their whole lives to the purpose of proving that there is no purpose. Such scientists, as Whitehead once put it, constitute an interesting subject for study. And yet, no matter how deeply is the actual implementation of scientific method steeped in purpose and therefore steeped in metaphysics, it is very important to keep in mind the self-imposed limitations of that method. Otherwise one will expect from that method something it cannot deliver. Scientific cosmology can reassure the philosopher that science poses no threat to the validity of such notions as universe, existence, and contingency. Actually, scientific cosmology powerfully suggests these notions and indeed makes use of them on a vast scale. But a suggestion, however powerful, is one thing, philosophical demonstration is another. While science or scientific cosmology can be a powerful prompting for considering the createdness of the cosmos, it can never become a discourse about creation as such.

The importance of this distinction becomes obvious when creation in time is considered. If there is a theological theme, it is creation in time, the theme or dogma which supports all other Christian themes and dogmas. Whenever the meaning of creation in time is weakened, let alone eliminated, the meaning of all other tenets of the Christian creed become weakened or eliminated. Those tenets — Fall, Incarnation, redemption, the growth of the Kingdom of God, eschatology, final judgment — presuppose not only creation but also a creation in time because all those tenets refer to events in time which alone can constitute that sequence which is salvation history. When in 1215 the Fourth Lateran Council solemnly defined creation out of nothing and in time as a dogma, it merely confirmed a long-standing tradition. The continued strength of that tradition, which, by the way, was again reasserted by Vatican I, is so great as to evidence itself far beyond Christian realms. A case in point is the widespread custom of scientists and science writers to refer to the dating by science of the age of the universe. Few customs can become more unscientific. While science can assure us that it can carry its investigations 12 billion years back into cosmic past, there is no science whatever which can date the birth of the universe. There is no scientific value whatsoever in statements, often seen nowadays in print, that through the launching in 1985 of the Space Telescope man will have a glimpse of the moment of creation, because his farthest view into the universe will be increased from 2 to 20 billion light years. The reason for the absence of science in such statements is simple. Physical science or scientific cosmology is absolutely powerless to show that any stage of material interactions is not reducible to a previous state, however hypothetical. If science is impotent in this purely scientific respect, it is even more impotent with respect to a far deeper problem, a problem of very different nature, namely, that a given physical state must owe its existence to a direct creative act, which brought that physical state into being out of nothing.

Scientific cosmology has, however, made a very important contribution with respect to the existence of time, the very basis for making meaningful the phrase, creation in time. Scientific cosmology shows all too well that the universe carries on itself the stamp of time. Such a stamp is the expansion of the universe. In a very real sense the universe is ageing. It clearly burns up energy and by doing so it shows the signs of transitoriness. The force of that sign can best be judged by the frantic efforts of some cosmologists to erase that stamp from the face of the universe. The enthusiasm with which the steady-state theory was hailed thirty years ago is a case in point. The real aim of that theory was to secure for the universe that infinity along the parameter of time which it already lost along the parameter of mass and space. That the theory was indeed markedly antitheological in character could easily be gathered from the emphatic insistence of its proponents. They claimed that the continued emergence of hydrogen atoms, whereby the density of matter is kept steady in an expanding space, should be conceived as a creation out of nothing though without a creator. For the atheistic candor of those proponents one ought to be appreciative. It is hardly to be expected that they would be appreciative of the remark already made about the impossibility of physics to see the nothing beyond any given state of matter.

An equally atheistic, or simply pagan, or at best agnostic, longing for the eternity of matter is beneath that jubilation which greets the periodic news about the finding of the so-called missing mass, a curiously countertheological counterpart of the still elusive missing link. If that extra mass should be found in cosmic spaces, then the present expansion would turn into a contraction, and possibly that contraction would be followed by another expansion. Yet, even in this case the process would not go on ad infinitum. There has not yet been found any physical process that would be exempt from the law of entropy. Indeed, more and more attention has been given recently to the rate at which subsequent cycles in an oscillating universe would be less and less energetic. It is indeed possible to calculate, however tentatively, the number of cycles which would bring us back in time to the point where the period of a cycle would be vanishingly small. To some sanguine souls and uninformed minds that vanishing point may appear the moment of creation which would then certainly vanish.

The idea of an oscillating universe presupposes the finiteness of matter. That finiteness, when cognizance was first taken of it in the early 1920s under the impact of Einstein's General Relativity, produced shock waves in scientific and philosophical circles in which the infinity of the universe had for some time played the role of a convenient ultimate entity, making God unnecessary. The shock waves were all the more telling because, as Einstein already pointed out in 1917, there were ways in which it is possible to assume the infinity of matter without running into contradictions. Yet, all those ways are such as to provide further evidence on behalf of the stunning specificity of the universe. A distribution of infinite matter which would give rise to paths of motion resembling a cylindrical helix is too specific to be taken for that natural and necessary form of existence for which Euclidean infinity could so readily pass. The same is true about a distribution of infinite matter which would permit motion only along the curving slopes of a saddle with no edges, corresponding to an infinite hyperbolic space. About none of these specific situations is it natural to say that they are such forms of existence which one would naturally expect to exist and exist necessarily at the necessary exclusion of all other possibilities.

So much, in broad strokes, about the contribution of scientific cosmology to the idea of a created universe. The suggestiveness of that contribution is anything but small. Long before the discovery of the 2.7° K cosmic background radiation filled the world of science with metaphysical puzzlement, there was plenty of it under the surface. Einstein indeed felt it necessary to reassure with the words, "I have not yet fallen in the hands of priests," a friend who worried that on account of his cosmology Einstein might become a believer.

Reluctance to face up to the fact that the universe has a message pointing beyond itself is an old story. All too often the reluctance issues in a patently antiscientific posture. John Stuart Mill, who saw in cosmology the stronghold of theists, did his utmost to discredit it. In the process he deprived the cosmos of its intrinsic rationality. He did so by peddling the idea that in some faraway regions two and two may not necessarily make four.

Since Mill the same story has been enriched with further and no less telling chapter. They are usually provided by those educated in a milieu in which "interest in the greatest problems that ever agitated man is successfully stifled." Such was Henry Adams' characterization of that intellectually high-powered milieux of Boston and Harvard where he was brought up. Bologna, Paris, Oxford, Cambridge, Bottingen, Uppsala, Basel, Leiden — to keep the historical order — and many other illustrious places of learning, would provide ample material for painting that milieu. What is stifled is not, however, extinguished. Henry Adams had to realize, fifty years after he left Harvard, that "if he were obliged to insist on a Universe, he seemed driven to the Church." So he opted for what he called the Multiverse. He did not suspect that his option for the counter-metaphysics of multiworlds demanded a renouncing of science at its best. The coming of scientific cosmology was less than a decade away from the moment when Henry Adams looked for salvation in multiworlds which, precisely because they could not interact consistently, could not form a universe and were therefore useless for science.

Science and Universe form indeed a seamless garment, a thesis not falsifiable unless the principle of falsifiability is turned into a *petitio principii*. That all science is cosmology has been an old truth long before K.R. Popper, hardly suspect of metaphysics, earned the aura of originality by voicing that truth to an unsuspecting generation which failed to notice its exemptness, implied by him, to the unrestricted sweep of falsifiability. Science, philosophically and historically, is an ally, not of the Academy of agnostics but of that Church which, unlike some of her theologians, knows all too well why her creed starts with the words: "I believe in God, the Father Almighty, Maker of Heaven and Earth." The effort which tries to resolve conficts between Christianity and science by stating that religion is about persons and not about the universe of things, should seem a very poor half truth. For God, at least the Christian God, is above all the Creator of the Universe. Thanks to science, that universe appears less and less mysterious, though at the same time more and more specific, and thereby an irrefragable pointer to God, the mysterious origin of all.

Notes

*In an article preceding this paper in *The Irish Astronomical Journal*.

For further details and documentation of the main topics of this paper, see my latest books, *Cosmos and Creator* (Edinburgh: Scottish Academic Press, 1981; Chicago: Regnery Gateway, 1982) and *Angels, Apes and Men* (La Salle, ILL.: Sherwood Sugden and Company, 1983). The history of the optical and gravitational paradoxes is given in my book, *The Paradox of Olbers' Paradox* (New York: Herder and Herder, 1969) with additional data in my article, "Das Gravitations-Paradoxon des unendlichen Universums," *Sudhoff's Archiv*, 63 (1979), pp. 105-22. The historical context of Gödel's theorem and its first application to physics and cosmology can be found in my book, *The Relevance of Physics* (Chicago: University of Chicago Press, 1966), pp. 127-31. On the half-a-century-old history of the antiontological meaning attributed to chance in the Copenhagen school, see my article, "Chance or Reality: Interaction in Nature versus Measurement in Physics," *Philosophia* (Athens), 10-11 (1980-81), pp. 85-105. The utterances of H. Adams are from *The Education of Henry Adams* (New York: The Modern Library, 1931), pp. 34 and 429.

7

MODERN PSYCHOLOGY AND THE TURN TO BELIEF IN GOD

Professor Paul C. Vitz

Professor Vitz, could you tell us of some of the main secularist prejudices which dominate psychology today? And do you see any trend away from these, as there is in philosophy and modern science? A trend away from the mechanistic world view towards a more open, theistic view of things?

Yes, there has been a very clear long-term trend in such a direction. The assumptions of psychology in the 1900s were extremely scientific in the old sense, that is restricted to physiological and mechanical models of explanation. By 1930, although there was still a very intensive positivist strain of psychology, clinical psychology under Freud and others had changed the subject matter so that now you could at least deal with human problems with concepts and language much closer to human experience. Of course, Freud claimed to be a materialist and determinist and that his work was fundamentally scientific in the old scientific sense. And if it had turned out to be that way, then, Freud would have been a contributor to a great materialist interpretation of the mind. What has happened, however, was much the opposite, namely clinical psychology and the theories of personality and counseling which developed out of the Freudian approach have become less and less scientific as time went on. Indeed, today there are very few claims made in the old sense. What they did was to decide to live with the new idea of science as much more "humanistic," much less deterministic, much less rigid. But, of course, when they did that they were introducing a major qualitative change. I don't believe at the time they really knew what they had done. By rejecting determinism and materialism, they inadvertently backed into religion, including Christianity. This occurred with the development of the humanistic psychologies of the 1940s — 1960s. Now this secular and humanistic psychology has caused a great deal of harm to Christianity, and I have written extensively on that (*Psychology as Religion: The Cult of Self-Worship*, Vitz, 1977). These psychologists rejected God, revelation, and morality in the absolute sense. They simply assumed that everything could be understood without such ideas. As for their general intellectual strategy, they made many of the assumptions that I mentioned in my paper here. But in the 1960s, a funny thing happened to the humanistic movement. They began to directly accept and incorporate religious ideas. Now these were secular psychologists and so when they moved into religious notions they moved into eastern religion; they moved into a vague mysticism; into transcendent experience. They did this because they thought they could understand transcendent experience in natural terms, for example, as an altered state of consciousness that could be explained psychologically. At the least, they assumed, such states were natural and not supernatural. They also accepted general notions from eastern religion because they wanted experiences that didn't have any clear or disturbing doctrines. They didn't want anything that would put a restraint on the self and its pride. They wanted transcendent experience without theology; they liked the emphasis on power for a transcendent or higher self. Finally, in recent years the transformed humanism of trans-personal psychology has explicitly accepted Eastern religions, e.g., Hinduism, Buddhism, without much qualification. They have transformed personality theory and psychotherapy so that it is in no sense a science. This development has opened the door for an explicit Christian psychology — a psychology that is spontaneously developing all over the country. So far, I would say the Protestants have been in the forefront of this movement, in part because they were so heavily involved in counseling. This Christian psychology is not coming from the mainline Protestants, but from evangelical Protestants: those who had a strong faith and just began to come into psychology in the '60s and '70s and refused to give up their faith. They have put the two together. Sometimes, of course, not successfully. But there are a number of these Christian psychologists who are formulating important Christian views of counseling. In some respects, I think I am also part of this, though what I'm doing is perhaps more theoretical than practical.

How could a Christian psychologist be most effective in the apologetic sense of molding a Christian world view in psychology?

Develop a Christian psychology out of hard earned experience with clients, both Christians and non-Christians, that's the best way. We have yet to understand how to grasp the powerful psychology contained in much Christian scripture and doctrine. This psychology has yet to be articulated in any detail. In this venture, we can often use the techniques of secular psychologists, e.g., Skinner's behavior modification or at times an understanding of the unconscious. So it can be very useful to know all the secular techniques and all the secular contributions, but the crucial thing is to place them in an integrative Christian framework. First, a framework of values which Christianity can provide and secular psychology cannot, but also a framework of an understanding of the spiritual life and the true purpose of life. When all of this is brought in, secular psychology is transformed. Furthermore such a Christian psychology has an enormously greater effectiveness than any secular psychology. A Christian psychology would have so much more. Why not have all of it and not just a little fragment. Each of the secular psychologies is a little fragment — without the synthetic power of a Christian psychology.

What would you say are the main fallacies of Freud and Jung?

Well, they're different and, of course, you asked a complicated question. I will have to simplify. Freud's philosophy was supposed to be biological, deterministic and materialist. But his contributions have really been incompatible with these philosophical assumptions. His understanding of religion as illusion I would say is one of the greatest errors in the Freudian system. He simply failed to understand spiritual life, as distinctively and qualitatively different. He has described the unconscious (his most important contribution); he understood much of the conscious mind. But his third notion, the super ego, is not really superior to the ego — it is not a "super" ego, like superman is superior to ordinary man. Instead, the super ego is part of the unconscious and part of the conscious. It's not qualitatively different. But religious experience is not the same thing as that of the id or the ego; it's not a primary process activity nor a secondary process activity. It's what I would call "tertiary" activity. It's a third qualitatively distinct realm of mental life. It is super-natural, truly above the ego. This is an ancient idea. But Freud denied it explicitly in theory and implicitly with his term super ego. So he overlooks the whole problem of spiritual life as a third kind of mental life.

Jung is also a complicated theorist.

Did he die a Christian as some people say?

There is some evidence that he might have, but he didn't begin as one, that's for sure. He was initially quite hostile to Christianity. He had a long intellectual career and he changed and developed and so forth, but the major problem of Jungian psychology is that you get so involved in your own psychology, your own subjectivity, that you forget the objectivity of God. You respond to your religious experience. Consider the following situation. Say you were in love with somebody, but all you really did was spend your time reflecting on your feelings of love and not on the person. It would be like someone who wants to have a love experience, not somebody who wants to love another person. You can imagine what would happen if you love your love experience instead of the other person. Well, the other person after a while would withdraw. The danger in Jungian psychology is that you analyze your dreams and the symbols and the archetypes, in short, yourself ... but ignore God as objective, as other, as transcendent and interpret Him as part of your psychology. This trap is what might be called the intrinsic narcissism of religious psychology.

And the third giant, B. F. Skinner ... giant in terms of influence?

Skinner, I wouldn't worry too much about — at least in these days. He was, of course, a complete determinist, influenced by his own religious background. He said (in the 1970s), "Don't you know that I am the new Calvin?" Isn't that incredible? Apparently he saw his behaviorism as a kind of secular religion. He turned the theology of predestination into a psychology of behavioral determinism. However, B. F. Skinner's position is narrow, and, along with positivistic theory of science, pretty well played out and rejected. Also, it's a kind of harsh and dreary determinism that even Skinner himself does not live by or consistently follow in his theory.

I think he had a destructive influence on American psychology. Does he still have it?

No, I don't think he still does. He did cause a lot of harm, along with others of his kind in the 1920 to 1950 period, but he's pretty much passe' now. I haven't met a real behaviorist in a long time. They're all going cognitive, and getting much more complicated in terms of their philosophy of science.

Do you still see a lot of emphasis on the cult of self-worship? In books like ... *Your Erroneous Zones* **and popular books of that kind?**

Yes, those are still around. But the influence is not so great as it was in the '60s and '70s. This, too, is declining. Let us hope it is a long term decline; but it is too early to tell. But a big problem remains. You have a lot of psychology departments in Christian colleges, especially in Catholic colleges, that are staffed entirely by psychologists who were trained in the self or humanistic psychology of the '50s and '60s. And now, since those colleges have financial troubles they are not hiring many new professors, and so they're going to freeze humanistic self-psychology into the curriculum for thirty years. That's the danger. But I do see a new Christian psychology in the making and obviously if you can get such an approach developed clearly and get the message out, things will improve.

How would you translate Jesus as being the true model of the person into psychology?

Well, in some ways you can approach it in terms of identification with Jesus, in terms of Jesus as a role-model. But, first, it is very important for Christians to know and insist on the fact that the *concept* person is an intrinsically Christian concept. Historically the concept of a person was first created by early Christian theologians developing the doctrine of the Trinity, that is, God as Three Persons, etc. From this we can note that a person involves committing yourself to others, it involves covenant relationships. A human being comes into existence *as a person* through commitment, through covenant and not by separating from others, not by becoming an individual. We're made in the image of God. And God is a Person, and Three Persons in particular, and all equally committed to each other. And Jesus is the model of a person whose commitment to the Father is our model of how to commit ourselves to God and how to commit ourselves in agape love to others. I would call a Christian theory of personality (a theory of a person) a "covenant theory" of personality. This understanding is in many respects the opposite of self-theory of Carl Rogers' approach. For example, his book, *On Becoming a Person*, is mis-titled. Rogers is presenting a theory of how one can become an individual — an autonomous, independent, self-actualized individual. The Greeks knew about this 2500 years ago. But a person, as mentioned, is a Christian concept (and also, of course, Jewish in many respects as well), and a person is formed not by breaking away and becoming autonomous, but by union, in love, with God and others. The individual and the person are essentially opposites — the individual is devoted to himself and sometimes through the self to others; the person is devoted to God and through God to others. Oh, and by the way, since the foundation of a person is agape love — first received from God, then returned by us to God and others — the foundational or deep down emotion of a person would be the emotion of love — namely, peace and joy. (A point which I believe you, Roy Varghese, have emphasized, as well.)

8
MODERN SOCIOLOGY AND THE TURN TO BELIEF IN GOD
Professor David Martin

It is often said that new insights and discoveries in modern science have made nonsense of the whole Mechanistic way of viewing things and that these findings have uprooted Mechanistic prejudices in different disciplines. So much so, it is said modern thought is more or less open to a theistic view of things. Do you see any such trend in sociology?

I don't know if there is a carryover from these other disciplines into sociology but there are certainly parallel movements, even in my own brief academic lifetime. That is to say, when I first went to the London School of Economics, I was regarded as a madman for paying any attention to religion at all. The L.S.E. was [then] dominated by a kind of Positivism and the sole interest was in the quantification of issues related to education, mobility, class distribution and this sort of thing. Religion was regarded as a kind of miasma. If it was real at all it was a kind of fog which obscured what was being said. And also, there was this view, in many areas of the discipline, of man as simply part of the social machine. Society programmed him to fill particular slots and he didn't have any individual creativity with which he could remould his own role. In other words, he played the role which was set up for him, but he couldn't use the role creatively.

There were several kinds of determinism. One was the stimulus and response determinism, the Skinnerian view, which was really not very important in sociology. There was another functionalist view in which all his roles were subsumed into the maintenance of the social fabric so that he was almost a walking copy of the social program. (It was very popular in America.) Man was simply a creature of culture and not a creator of all culture. All those views are very much under pressure now, so that we have recovered the idea of man ... Of course, he lives in culture; and of course he's constrained by culture and society; but also he is an active agent in constructing his own world. That means you can think of persons as both creators as well as creatures of society. That leaves open the possibility of a religious understanding and not simply some variety of Mechanistic interpretation.

Do you say, then, that there has been a shift from Positivist dogmatism in sociology?

Yes, I can give another example of the shift away from that dogmatism. When I first became an academic in sociological theory, it was believed that secularization was some kind of inevitable process. You move from point A, maybe, say that social situation which existed possibly in the 12th century and was the high point for religion. Then you moved downward stage by stage. First the Renaissance, and then the Enlightenment, and then modern science, until religion disappeared. It was just as if mankind were steadily walking away from religion to his own autonomy. This was an Evolutionary view which could be fitted to Marxism in that man would become de-alienated or it could be fitted to Positivism in that you would become a truly autonomous, scientific person with no accretion of superstition attached. Those were two views which were, what you might call, unilineal views, dogmatic views, about religion. They are very much less [prevalent] nowadays.

What exactly made these views less plausible?

A Norwegian political scientist said recently that anybody in the year 2000 who doesn't understand religion will not be able to understand politics. There are various phenomena such as, in a very obvious way, Iran, and the rise of Islamic fundamentalism as a political force. Similarly, the importance of the Moral Majority in America; it's certainly a powerful political force. Or, again, the ability of the Roman Catholic Church in Poland to mobilize the consciousness of the people against its own regime. This is ordinary empirical evidence that anyone who doesn't understand the role of religion in politics has simply missed a vital dimension.

Another source of evidence would be the appearance of new religions, various kinds of Eastern religion, and techniques of meditation. This indicates that if orthodox Christianity disappeared then some need of the depth and height of the soul would still remain.

Do you see a certain openness to theism in the academic sociological world?

There used to be a time when, if you wrote sociology as well as theology, you would be practically thrown out of the sociological community. I will say this, you still have to do some good sociology as well in order to be allowed a special dispensation to write theology. I really cannot talk about myself in that connection, but sometimes I am quite willing to write books that alternate between sociology and theology. And I just assume that people will have the intelligence to distinguish when I am making a sociological statement and when I am making a theological statement. But I am not drummed out of the sociological community, whereas my academic reputation would have been suspect had I [done] so even twenty years ago.

What do you think is responsible for this openness?

I think it's actually that social scientists have rediscovered the existence of human beings in sociology. You would think it odd that the science of persons in society is capable of forgetting that there are human beings. But it has been capable of doing that. So the rediscovery of human beings, and therefore of the range of human experience which includes religious experience, enables people to say why shouldn't the sociologist not only write about religion but himself think religiously.

Another thing is worth noting here. Although the classics of sociology were anti-religious they actually spent a great deal of their time on the subject of religion. Weber and Durkheim in particular centered their work around the issue of religion. But that was a kind of debunking exercise I think that people now regard [their findings] as useful insights but not as dogmatic scientific certainties. There were certain ways of looking at things provided by Weber and Durkheim which are very, very useful; they provided the perspectives. But one is not required to take on board the particular kind of sociological mysticism, for example, which Durkheim indulged in.

Among the present generation of sociologists, some of the most distinguished are not anti-religious at all. Daniel Bell, for example, is actually now writing a book on religion and also wrote a famous essay on "The Return of the Sacred." Talcott Parsons at Harvard, who was the single most powerful influence in sociology, was himself a believer, not simply just sympathetic. Actually, I talked to him once and he said that if you wanted to know the whole, the summary, of everything that was invoked in sociology, you should listen to Bach's *St. Matthew Passion*. All the themes of power and sacrifice, and of social cohesion, and of the individual confronting the authorities ... and how, out of this crucible could emerge a new faith. (This is not what he said but what lies behind his statement.)

All this I think has gradually altered the atmosphere.

What were the roots of the various forms of reductionism that dominated sociology?

I think the roots of this reductionism were in the transfer of old-fashioned notions in natural science to social science. The notion, for example, [that] the only things which matter are those things which can be quantified and which are susceptible to mathematical manipulation. That idea, which had been fruitful in natural science, when transferred to social science simply did not work. Also, there was the idea that you could only have science where you could have controlled experiments. That meant manipulation of variables. You treated groups of human beings as simply concatenations of variables which you played with. So you began to think of people not as persons but basically as social atoms, playing one into another. You took the superior view, the scientific priest looking in a superior way at these carefully programmed ants which were building their social anthills. You had this very high view. You stood back and were objective. It's not that I am a relativist because relativism also has its dangers. But the idea that you could be this superior, objective, scientific being, that has tended to disappear. The trouble is that, when it disappears, initially there is a tumble into sheer relativism, which simply means that there is no statement which you can make that is actually true. So the idea of truth disappears also.

On the one hand you had this crude Positivist view of quantifiable, mathematically manipulable truth and, on the other hand, you had this total cultural relativism in which there is no truth at all. So it's been quite a business fighting crass scientism [on one hand] and crass cultural relativism on the other. They are two equal and opposite errors.

Has Wittgenstein's language-game theory helped in liberating Sociology from Positivism?

Oh yes. In the wider cultural context many hold that there is a language specific to religion and that all languages cannot be boiled down to one single true scientific language. Not that there are strictly separate realms of reality but there are at least different forms of discourse and you have to understand the way in which they are separate and how they relate. I think the sociological view is that one cannot separate these realms of discourse entirely; otherwise we have a fragmented universe. But one has to find some way of understanding in what sense they are independent and in what sense they are interdependent. The importance of the Wittgensteinian viewpoint is that it establishes that one has to take seriously each realm of discourse on its own terms, not try to translate it *down* into something else, sociology into biology, biology into physics.

The generation of dogmatic atheism is now very much a past generation.

What do you think is the major task of the Christian thinker and how can he be most effective?

One way is to say to the humanist that it is a false humanism which wants to restrict the valid range of human experience to a particular level of experience, and to say that only this mundane experience is what counts. Human beings have explored the possibility of transcending not only their natural environment but their own nature: of restoring nature itself, the world without as well as the world within. So we have this transformative capacity, of which God is the ultimate point. It's really a false humanism to deny this and I would take the humanist ground and extend it. That would be one way. It would have to be balanced of course against the endemic nature of evil and destruction, and the need for grace.

I think that [you can also take] off from the point of divine discontent: Augustine's statement that "our hearts are restless till they find their rest in Thee," the curious restlessness and incapacity of the mind of man to find a resting-place. At each point where he seems to have found a niche suddenly he finds he cannot rest comfortably.

Another thing I would say is [this]. There is a very crude form of critique of religion which has to do with the evil caused by religions. One thing that is very interesting is that when you get rid of religion, all those evils that you thought were associated with religion reappear, just as strongly and sometimes even more forcefully. So they were inherent possibilities of social life as such, not characteristics specifically associated with religion.

PART II

PHILOSOPHY

INTRODUCTION
Stephen D. Schwarz

Is my existence as a person intended, or simply a chance occurrence, the result of blind impersonal physical forces? Is my death the absolute end of my existence, the annihilation of my being, or a new beginning, the gateway to a new level of being? Does my life have a meaning beyond what will be lost when I die and the earth ceases to be, or not? Does my life as a whole have a purpose, or not? Will sufferings, disappointments and frustrations be somehow redeemed and overcome, or are they the last word? If we are happy at being alive, can we be grateful for that, or not? Many people pray when a loved one is grievously ill, or a war threatens, or danger lurks; is this reasonable, do we reach God in our prayer, or do we remain within ourselves?

We feel that the good and valuable things of the world should *be*: love, beauty, moral goodness, individual persons. Yet they are fragile in their being. A child dies of leukemia, a mountain remains. Is not the child's life of greater value and importance than the mountain? Shouldn't it rather be the other way around: that the child continues to be, and the mountain ceases? The precious things are fragile, exposed to impersonal elements; many things of lesser importance are solid and resistant to destruction. Is this the final word? Or will love, beauty, moral goodness, individual persons, and other valuable things somehow continue to be, or acquire a new level, a higher level of being?

We have a deep longing to be fulfilled, to overcome

our limitations and faults, to be freed from suffering. We long for fulfillment in love, in goodness, in knowledge. We seem to be made for more, more than we will ever be or become in our present life. We seem to have an emptiness that "speaks" and "reaches for" fulfillment. We may ignore it, cover it over with a preoccupation with daily routine and life projects. But it remains, and is never totally silenced. "Is this all there is?" Or is there more? And if we are not made for "more" why do we have a longing for more?

All these questions point to God. Or rather they point to the great alternative: God is, and there is ultimate meaning — or God is not, and existence is ultimately absurd. Thus, either God is, and my existence was intended by Him; I can be grateful to Him; my prayers to Him really reach Him, they are heard by Him; my death is not my annihilation but a new beginning in union with Him; the precious things of existence are not ultimately destroyed by impersonal forces, but have their full being in Him — or, God is not, and existence is ultimately absurd.

Theism, the belief that God is, and atheism, the belief that God is not, are not simply two beliefs. They are two fundamental ways of seeing the whole of existence. The one, theism, sees existence as ultimately meaningful, as having a meaning beyond itself, the other sees existence as having no meaning beyond itself.

Theism means that existence is ultimately meaningful. But is theism *true*? All the promises of theism, that we are not alone, that there is a person who knows and understands us, above all who loves us, with whom we will be fully united in an eternal life; all these promises and more are empty and useless, if theism is not true. If religious faith is embraced merely because it gives life meaning, makes us happy, helps us to cope with the trials and difficulties of life, then it is a shame. If it is not true, it is nothing, or worse than nothing. We want meaning and happiness and fulfillment; but above all we must seek truth, for a meaning or a happiness or a fulfillment which is not grounded in truth is worthless.

The great French philosopher-scientist-mathematician, Pascal (1623-1662), in seeking to know the meaning of existence, or whether it had any meaning, found himself in darkness. "I look on all sides and see only darkness everywhere. Nature presents to me nothing which is not a matter of doubt and concern."[1] He bewails his fate, and seeks to escape from his darkness. But what he longs for is not primarily the "light" of meaning and purpose, but the light of *truth*. "My heart inclines wholly to know where is the true good, in order to follow it; nothing would be too dear to me for eternity."[2] Truth, that is the all important thing. Better to be unhappy in truth, than "happy" in error or illusion. Ultimately only truth, only what is truly good and beautiful and loving, can make us genuinely happy.

Theism means that existence is meaningful; but is it true? There is a tradition in Western thought that says that it is not true; that religious beliefs are false, that religious sentiments are illusory, that the religious life of a person has only a subjective existence, in him, and does not correspond to anything in reality. In science, according to this view we can reach objective reality, because we can get evidence; while in religious matters we lack evidence. Science, in this view, is seen as antithetical to religion, and this for two main reasons. First, it is thought that science has somehow shown that belief in God is irrational because it is superfluous, a relic of primitive times when people had no rational-scientific explanations for events in the world; it is believed that the picture of reality presented to us by science is one without God and the realm of the supernatural. And second, it is held that science, and inquiry modeled on scientific method, is virtually identical with rationality, while religion is dismissed as irrational.

The chapters that follow (in Part II and elsewhere) can be seen as direct challenges to this view. We may note in them two basic themes, corresponding to the two parts of the atheistic view above, and directly contradicting them. They are, first, the evidence from science itself that theism is rational; that the world as given to us by science points unmistakably beyond itself to a Higher Being. And second, the collapse of the view that would identify rationality with science and scientific method. This is an important development in philosophy that has opened the way to a turn to theism. Let us now briefly explore these two basic themes.

Until recently it was thought by many people that science supports atheism, that science is even the rational alternative to theism. It is now clear that science not only does not support atheism, but even lends rational support for theism. There is strong scientific evidence for God. Scientists, without presupposing God or creation, without trying to prove them, have come up with findings that strongly support God, His creation of the universe and man, and a supernatural purpose for the world we live in. Four of these important scientific findings are:

1. *The Second Law of Thermodynamics.* According to this law, the amount of usable energy in the universe is decreasing, hence there is continuing heat loss; in other words the universe is "running down." This shatters the idea of an eternal, "steady state" universe that always was, and always will be. For if the universe has always been running down, it must have started from a point of maximum energy, in other words, an absolute beginning. But then where did it come from, why did it begin to exist? It could hardly have "popped" into existence out of nothing. It must have been created out of nothing. And creation implies a Creator, God.

An atheist denying God and creation is virtually forced to hold that the universe has always been there. But if it started to exist, as the second law of thermodynamics implies, that hypothesis is shattered. Nor is the atheist's case rescued by supposing that the implications of the second law are overcome by the addition of new energy, to stabilize the universe. Where would that energy come from? Nothing? God?

2. *The Impossibility of Spontaneous Generation of Life from Non-life.* Even with the universe somehow there, the atheist faces another great challenge: how did life arise? If we picture the universe as totally devoid of life, a kind of "prebiotic soup," can we rationally suppose it possible for biological life to arise spontaneously: by itself, without a cause or design, purely by chance? The probability against this is 1 in $10^{40,000}$, a number so vast one can hardly begin to imagine it. But to give some indication of its vastness consider these facts. The number of atoms (tiny, tiny atoms!) in the universe (the entire universe, with billions of stars, distances of millions of light years) is only 3×10^{74}:[3] "only" merely by comparison. For each addition to the exponent (in our case 40,000) represents a mind boggling increase. For example, if 10^{74} is a huge number then 10^{82} is 100,000,000 times greater! And 10^{90} is 100,000,000 greater than that, or 10,000,000,000,000,000 greater than the original 10^{74}. Now continue this process until you reach, not $10^{1,000}$, or $10^{2,000}$ or $10^{3,000}$, each of them a mind boggling increase over the previous, but $10^{40,000}$! Thus the probability against life arising by chance amounts to a virtual impossibility.

3. *Information Theory and DNA.* Information theory shows that the information patterns of a written language can be expressed mathematically. When a study was made of the information patterns in living organisms, coded in DNA, it was found that the mathematical

patterns in language and in DNA were exactly the same. Now information cannot come about by chance. When you read something that gives you information — about the past, about far away places, about human behavior, about any other thing — you know that the source of that information is a mind, a being with intelligence. So if DNA codes are essentially information patterns, they too require intelligence as their source, that is, Intelligence, God. Thus, as Professor Geisler puts it, "it is scientifically necessary to point to intelligence as the cause of the first living cell."

4. *The Anthropic Principle*. Modern discoveries in astronomy show that if the universe had been only slightly different, life, including human life, could not have arisen in it. Professor Jastrow explains how a slight increase in nuclear forces would have resulted in stars made almost entirely of helium, stars which have a much shorter "life" span, resulting in insufficient time for life, and man, to arise in the universe. On the other hand, a slight decrease in nuclear forces would have prevented the formation of carbon atoms and other necessary ingredients of life. Again, life, and man, could not have arisen in the universe. The same applies, in addition to nuclear forces, to other factors as well, such as the strength of electro-magnetic forces, and the force of gravity.

The conclusion is "that the universe was constructed within very narrow limits, in such a way that man could dwell in it," as Professor Jastrow puts it. This is strong evidence for saying that the universe was designed for man. And of course design requires a Designer, God. Thus the atheistic materialistic picture of the universe as the accidental product of pure chance receives a devastating blow, from science itself.

These four scientific findings, diverse and independent of one another, form a logical and humanly significant pattern. The first points to the creation of the universe, the second to the creation of life, and the third to the creation of human life. All three refer to causation, to bringing something into existence. The fourth adds another essential dimension: purpose. The first three have to do with the fact *that* the universe, and life, and man exist; the fourth, with *why* the universe exists, namely so that life, including human life, could live in it.

Let us turn now to the second basic theme, the collapse of the view that would identify rationality with science and scientific method. This is an important development in philosophy that has opened the way to a turn to theism. A major factor here is the demise of a certain conception of philosophy as an inquiry modeled on natural science and mathematics. The principal impetus to this conception of philosophy was a movement dating back to the early 30's in Vienna, Logical Positivism. The proponents of this movement claimed that only statements describing the world (such as, "It is now snowing lightly"), and statements typical of the natural sciences, mathematics and logic were "cognitively meaningful"; that is, only such statements asserted anything that could be true or false. All other "statements" were said to be merely emotive, such as, "Would that everyone showed respect to others," but not "cognitively meaningful," since nothing was asserted. Cognitively meaningful statements were those that could, in principle at least, be verified or falsified. But typical philosophical statements such as, "God exists," "human consciousness is distinct from the body," "lying is morally wrong," were said to be cognitively meaningless since there was no way to verify them or falsify them by the methods of science, or ordinary observation of the world, or mathematical reasoning. Since all philosophical statements are in this category, positivism meant the death blow to all of philosophy — including itself, of course! For the claim that only what can be shown true or false by scientific or other empirical methods, or mathematical reasoning; that claim can itself not be shown to be true or false by these means. In addition, the theory suffered other defects, including its inability to formulate its criterion of cognitive meaningfulness in such a way as to do justice to science, which was a central part of its original aim.

The failure of the positivist program is instructive. Ever since the beginning of modern philosophy (Descartes), there has been a temptation to model philosophy on mathematics and natural science. Descartes proposed the method of mathematics, especially geometry, because of its precision and certainty. Hume's famous *Treatise of Human Nature* (London, 1739) had as a subtitle "An Attempt to Introduce the Experimental Method of Reasoning into Moral Subjects."

Logical Positivism was the culmination of this attempt, the most explicit and extreme form of it. The collapse of positivism made clear once again (what many philosophers of the past and present already saw clearly) that philosophy isn't science or mathematics, but an inquiry in its own right, with its own goals and methods.

The demise of positivism is not complete. There are still philosophers who aspire to its "ideals," who carry positivistic assumptions into their thinking, and who use positivistic-verificationist arguments. But to the extent that philosophy has freed itself from the positivist strait-jacket, it has moved in a direction where the question of God can be taken with the seriousness that it deserves. In this climate, traditional arguments for God's existence have been re-examined and vigorously discussed. A point made by several authors in Part II bears directly on this, namely that in order to be rational in holding a position, say God's existence, one need not have "proof" in a scientific or mathematical sense, but only good reasons, or a "ground" for one's belief. This too relates to the demise of positivism with its model of scientific or mathematical evidence for rationality.

Let me turn now to summaries of some of the chapters that follow (in Part II); to amplification of certain crucial points, especially arguments for God; and to a discussion of certain further important dimensions connected with the turn to theism, in particular the question of agnosticism, the non-parallel nature of the two risks, believing and not believing in God, and the role of gratitude in our existential situation. All these are united through the central theme of this book (of which the two basic themes just discussed are aspects), that we have good reasons to believe in God, that the turn to theism in modern thought has a solid rational foundation.

I begin with Professor Geisler's essay, which provides an excellent statement of many of these points. Professor Geisler details the collapse of some of the main intellectual grounds for holding an atheist position. He examines various alleged "proofs" for God's non-existence and shows why they fail. The most significant of these is the well-known "argument from evil," or suffering, which Professor Geisler discusses under the heading, "Moral Disproof of God." The core of this argument is the seeming incompatibility between, on the one hand, God who loves His creatures infinitely, and who has the power to do anything He wills, and, on the other hand, the terrible evil in the world, the sufferings of animals and human beings. If God really loves His creatures, why does He not save them from evil? Why, in other words, does God not defeat evil? A profound question, a deep mystery. But is it a proof that God does not exist? No, for all the argument shows is that God has *not yet* defeated evil, or not yet completed the task of defeating evil. If God exists, as the Infinite Being Who is All-Loving and All-Powerful, then He will defeat evil. And if this has not yet occurred, we can be sure that it will occur, which is precisely the content of the theist's hope.

Professor Geisler brings out another significant flaw in the argument from evil against God's existence. Does the person who uses this argument base his case on an absolute moral standard of good and evil? That is, a standard that holds objectively, that exists in its own right, independently of man? If he does not, he has no basis for his argument, for the argument rests on the reality of moral good and evil: evil and suffering should be defeated; not to defeat them if one can is morally evil. If an absolute moral standard is denied, there is no way of judging that God, if He exists, *ought* to defeat evil; or that since He ought to and therefore would do so if He existed, He cannot exist since evil is not defeated. In effect, the argument from suffering means that man is judging God, judging Him by an absolute standard, that applies universally (and not just to men, or groups of men). But if the argument rests essentially on a moral standard, and points to the reality of this standard, it actually points to God rather than away from Him. For God is the ultimate source and basis of all that is morally good; God is Goodness Itself, Justice Itself, Love Itself, etc. In grasping moral goodness we grasp, in our limited way, an aspect of God. Many forms of atheism are associated with moral subjectivism and relativism, the denial of a real, objective, absolute moral standard (a topic discussed in the last part of Professor Geisler's essay). An atheism of this sort cannot rationally press the "argument from evil" against God. For if there is no real, objective moral good and evil, then it cannot be held that suffering *ought* to be defeated, failing to do so is morally evil, or wrong.

After showing that various alleged "disproofs" of God all fail (and in some cases even contain elements that point to God), Professor Geisler "takes up the offensive" against the atheist's position, by pointing to some recent scientific developments that clearly point to God, provide rational grounds for believing in God. They are the three arguments discussed above, for the creation of the universe (because it is "running down"), for the creation of life (because the "prebiotic soup" could not have given rise to life spontaneously), and for the creation of man (on the basis of the results of information theory). Finally, Professor Geisler shows that the denial of a real objective morality, an absolute moral standard of good and evil, in addition to destroying the basis for the "argument from evil," also destroys the basis of human life, that while such a denial may be professed in theory, it cannot be practiced in actual life. For example, all protests that something is unjust appeal to a real standard of justice, and stand in marked contrast to mere expressions of subjective dislike. In being treated unjustly we clearly grasp the objective reality of moral good and evil, though our theorizing may have led us to think that all good and evil are merely subjective, as Professor Geisler's story about the blue folder so vividly brings out.

Turning now to another chapter, Professor Alston points out that Logical Positivism, far from providing a model for all human knowledge, failed to provide an adequate model even for that branch of human knowledge, natural science, where it seemed most to apply, and where adherents of this school of thought devoted their most intense efforts. In his "analogy of the very small child," he adds an important dimension to our understanding of the problem of "God and evil," from which the "argument from evil" against God is derived. The point may, I think, be explained as follows: We are to God as a small child is to his parents, only infinitely more removed from Him in our understanding than the child is from his parents. Suppose the child needs a painful operation to save his life. He is taken to the doctor by his parents. The doctor performs painful surgery, as the parents stand by. "Why do they not prevent the doctor from hurting me? Why do they not defeat this evil?" The child's vision is too small to see why his parents allow his suffering: our vision, as children of God, is also too small to see why God allows our sufferings, and other evils. Just as the child is in no position to judge his parents, so too we are in no position to judge God. And if we cannot be ultimate judges, we cannot press the "argument from evil" as showing that God does not exist.

Diffusing the argument from evil removes an obstacle to believing in God. Are there positive grounds for belief in God? We have already noted several scientifically based grounds for belief in God. We have noted that an absolute standard of moral good and evil, presupposed in the argument from evil against God, actually points to God. There is another important, philosophical argument for God that Professor Alston discusses, the Cosmological Argument. The core idea of this argument is that the universe cannot just be: it requires an explanation, a reason for being, a source of its being. It cannot have that source in itself, for it is a vast collection of individual beings who are essentially dependent beings: they depend on one another for their coming into existence, and often for their continued existence. Thus, works of art depend on artists, rivers depend on rain and geologically formed river beds, the motion of cars and boats on energy, living beings on seeds and parents, and so on. These individual dependent beings when viewed as a whole (the universe) do not cease to be dependent beings. The universe — as the sum total of these beings, all of which are essentially dependent, lacking the ground of their being in themselves — must itself be an essentially dependent being. Why then does it exist, rather than not exist? Where does it come from? What is the ground of its being? That can only be an absolutely independent Being, Who is the Ground of His Own Existence, Who exists necessarily. For if it were another dependent being we would simply be back to our problem (what is the ground of that dependent being, the universe), rather than having reached a solution. Thus the ground of being of the universe must be an absolutely independent Being, Who is the Ground of His Own Being, and exists necessarily.

Such a Being, the Creator of the universe, must be a Personal Being, the Absolute Person, the Absolute Consciousness, the Absolute Knowledge, Will, and Love. For if He is the Ground of our being He cannot be less than what we are, personal beings. If God were an impersonal force, we would be higher than God, as conscious persons, which is absurd. And the act of intending the universe to be, of creating it into actual being, essentially requires a Conscious Person.

We touch here the ultimate meaning of the four scientifically based arguments considered earlier. The first, based on the doctrine that the universe is "running down," points to a beginning in time for the universe, a first moment at which it began to be. But why did it begin to be? It could not have created itself. It could not just pop into existence. It must have come from the Hand of a Creator. The underlying reasoning here is that the universe is ultimately a dependent being, hence dependent for its coming into existence on a Creator. Pointing to that first moment, the moment of the Big Bang, makes vivid for us what the Cosmological Argument brings out: that the universe is not self-sufficient, and must therefore depend on another, a Creator, God.

If it is claimed that the scientific data we have does not rule out the possibility that the Big Bang was not the first moment of existence of the universe, that some physical reality may have already existed, which was given a new form through the Big Bang, nothing changes in regard to the force of the Cosmological Argument. Where did that material come from? Why did it exist rather than not exist?

The other three arguments are related more to the Design Argument than to the Cosmological Argument. The Design Argument says essentially that the wonders of the world, especially life and what stems from it, particularly from human life, could not have come about by mere chance, by the random motion of elementary particles and physical forces. There had to be some design, some plan, some intention, and that of course points to a Grand Designer, God. In its purely philosophic form, the Design Argument is quite general. The scientific data makes it very specific. Thus *life* could not have arisen by chance, because the probability against that is 1 in $10^{40,000}$. *Intelligent life*, human beings, could not have arisen by chance, as the data from information theory shows. And the whole universe was specifically designed for life, as the Anthropic Principle indicates. Thus the findings of modern science corroborate and amplify an ancient philosophical argument, that the universe is too marvelous to be the result of mere chance. It must be the handiwork of a Great Designer, a Grand Artist, God.

The core idea underlying the Cosmological and Design Arguments is the "principle that there has to be an ultimate explanation for everything," as Professor Alston puts it. This brings us back to our starting point, the great fundamental question: Is existence ultimately meaningful, or is it ultimately absurd? If God is, He represents the ultimate meaning of existence, the sufficient reason why it came into existence and the final end towards which it moves as its destiny. If God is not, existence is an accident, a momentary flicker of light between an infinite darkness and void before, and after. Whatever meaning there is — for example, beauty, knowledge, justice — will be destroyed, and rendered void. It will have had only a temporary, fleeting "meaningfulness," but will not be ultimately meaningful, because it will have been destroyed. Bertrand Russell vividly describes this state of affairs of ultimate meaninglessness (something he holds to be virtually certain) as being

> That man is the product of causes which had no prevision of the end they were achieving; that his origin, his growth, his hopes and fears, his loves and his beliefs, are but the outcome of accidental collocations of atoms; that no fire, no heroism, no intensity of thought and feeling, can preserve an individual life beyond the grave; that all the labors of the ages, all the devotion, all the inspiration, all the noonday brightness of human genius, are destined to extinction in the vast death of the solar system, and that the whole temple of man's achievement must inevitably be buried beneath the debris of a universe in ruins.[4]

When I speak of "existence as ultimately meaningful or absurd," I mean not only the physical universe; I mean everything that can be meaningful, that aspires to meaning. I mean above all human existence, each person individually and mankind as a whole. I mean the totality of human experience, including what that experience is of, and refers to, such as love, knowledge, truth, goodness, beauty, happiness, and much more.

Is all this ultimately meaningful? Or is it ultimately absurd? More specifically: do we have reason to believe that existence is ultimately meaningful? Are we rationally justified in holding that the thesis, "existence is ultimately meaningful," is *true*? Truth, that is the all important matter. Whatever we may believe: if it is not true, our belief is vain. Now I want to suggest that the central theme underlying Part II — in fact the whole book — is that we do have good reason to believe that existence is ultimately meaningful, because God is.

There are strong arguments for God's existence, especially the Cosmological and Design Arguments; arguments that are fundamentally philosophical in nature, but amplified and supported by scientific findings, such as those from Information theory and the Anthropic Principle. As Professor McInerny points out, it is not that these arguments represent "strict proofs" as we find them in geometry and formal logic; that is, proofs where it is impossible to assert the premises and deny the conclusion without logical contradiction. It is rather that the arguments for God present us with rational grounds for belief, of the general sort that we have for virtually all our rational convictions. They also function, as Professor McInerny suggests, to "remove impediments to the faith."

If our basis for holding that God is, is not a "strict proof," as in formal logic or mathematics, it is something much deeper, much more appropriate to our existential longings and questionings; and, much more appropriate to God Himself. It is, I think, a fundamental insight into reality. To bring this out let me present what I take to be the major thesis of Professor Lonergan's chapter. He starts with a fundamental assumption: that the human mind can know truth; not all of it, not perfectly, but it can grasp certain essential features of reality. These features include what is fundamental to science, to philosophy, to all other branches of human knowledge, and to common sense awareness of the world. Now if we can grasp certain fundamental features of reality, it follows that reality, or being, is intelligible. But reality is not completely intelligible: there are unanswered questions in science, and mysteries that will always remain beyond our grasp. If reality is not completely intelligible it must be grounded in something else, or in a Someone, a Person, Who has this ultimate intelligibility, or Who is this Ultimate Intelligibility: God.

But is the fundamental assumption true? Can the human mind know truth? Yes; for if we say no we contradict ourselves. If the mind can know no truth it cannot know that it knows no truth. It cannot even understand these questions as meaningful. If all knowledge is denied, the whole existential enterprise cannot get started, the wondering, the questions, the arguments, the conclusions, including of course atheistic conclusions. And science becomes an illusion.

If reality is not completely intelligible, why must it be grounded in something else which is intelligible, which completes the intelligibility? Why can't it remain unintelligible? We must be careful what this means. If it means "unintelligible for us now," there is no reason why this cannot "remain" for us now, while our present existence on this earth continues; no theist would deny this. But if "remain unintelligible" means that it is somehow in itself unintelligible, impossible to understand in its very nature, by any mind, then I think we have the equivalent of ultimate absurdity, or an aspect of it.

Why should we not believe that? We can, of course. There is no "strict proof" against it. But it seems to me such a belief involves an inner contradiction and absurdity. Consider the two fundamental possibilities. Suppose existence is ultimately meaningful. Then my belief that it is ultimately absurd contradicts this; and my belief is absurd.

Suppose existence is ultimately absurd. Then my belief seems at first to be meaningful because it corresponds correctly to reality, to reality as ultimately absurd — except that my belief is part of this reality and thus part of its ultimate absurdity, hence ultimately absurd itself. In other words, if existence is ultimately absurd, we should believe this, because in general we should believe what is true. But then the "meaningfulness" of the correct correspondence between true belief and reality (if we truly believe that reality is ultimately absurd) stands in utter contradiction to the ultimate absurdity of all reality.

Lonergan's starting point is that the real is intelligible (and because of this, that the human mind can know truth). Any plausibility that atheism and agnosticism may have rests ultimately on this basis. For even to say "we know too little to say that God is," is to make an appeal, implicitly, to the intelligibility of reality.

If existence is ultimately meaningful atheism cannot be true. For God *is* the ultimate meaning of reality, its Source and its Destiny.

The thrust of all that has been said here, the central theme of this book, is that we have good reason to believe in God and ultimate meaningfulness. One might say we have rational evidence for God; the kind of evidence, were it lacking, that would make our belief unsubstantiated, and irrational. Yet, in one of the chapters below, "Reason and Belief in God," we find its author, Professor Plantinga, denying that a theist must have rational evidence for his belief in God in order not to be irrational. Is this a denial of the rationality of belief in God? Is it a failure to take the truth question seriously? I think not. For what gives belief in God its "rationality" is something much deeper than what (I think) Professor Plantinga means by "evidence": the evidence of proofs, empirical evidence in science, etc. Belief in God is rational because it is "basic": basic in the sense in which our awareness of ourselves and others is basic, as well as our awareness of the physical world around us, and certain realities like truth and goodness and beauty. All evidence starts from them; it does not "get underneath them" to support them, precisely because they are "basic." They are starting points, in daily life, in science, in philosophy. What is basic constitutes the ultimate ground of our beliefs, of our entire lives. And so, a belief that is basic is not groundless; on the contrary, it is itself a ground for other beliefs.

When Professor Plantinga says that belief in God is basic, he means that it is not (or is not properly) one belief among many, but a fundamental conviction about reality.

> To the believer the entire world speaks of God. Great mountains, surging oceans, verdant forests, blue sky and bright sunshine, friends and family, love in its many forms and various manifestations — the believer sees these things and many more as gifts from God. The universe thus takes on a personal cast for him; the fundamental truth about reality is truth about a *Person*.

That the fundamental truth about reality is truth about a *Person* is, of course, a way (a marvelous way, I think) of saying that God is and that existence is ultimately meaningful; it is a way of saying the two together as one, for they are in themselves one.

This relates directly to Professor Smith's chapter. He refers to Whitehead's concept of "Nature alive," meaning that the lifeless, mechanical processes of nature are not the whole story; that "underneath," at a deeper level, there is more, there is a presence of God in the world, His creation. A further dimension of this is his reference to the "hope that order overcomes and includes the disorder" we find in the universe. For it is *ultimate* meaningfulness that is at stake existentially: there is both meaning and absurdity, good and evil, truth and error, order and disorder. Which one has the last word? Which will triumph in the end? Only if the meaning and good and truth and order we see around us have their roots in God; only if they are manifestations of God, can they triumph in the end. For in themselves they lack power, the power to resist the blind forces of physical nature, especially destructive forces.

Only from God do they have the power to really be. Part of the essence of God that is crucial here, in the question of ultimate meaningfulness or absurdity, is God as Power: not so much the power to move galaxies, or even to create them, but the power to make meaning triumph over absurdity, good over evil, order over disorder, life over death.

We have been speaking of two great alternatives: theism and atheism. But perhaps there is a third, agnosticism; and perhaps it is the reasonable option for a person who is uncertain whether theism or atheism is the truth. Agnosticism represents an attempt at a neutral middle position: "I assert neither that God is, nor that He is not; I simply don't know, and so I leave the question open." That is certainly a position, but is it really neutral? What does this position entail for one's life? Does it not entail the same thing as atheism: that one does not live before God, that one does not reckon with God, that one does not pray to God, does not thank Him? Whether one does not reckon with God because one says, "God is not," or because one says, "I don't know that He is," makes no practical difference. Either way God is not present to the person's consciousness. While there is a logical difference between asserting God is not (atheism) and not asserting that He is (agnosticism), there is no existential difference, no difference for the conscious life of the person. One is as opposed as the other to a commitment to God, to seeing the world as manifesting God, to viewing existence as ultimately meaningful because it comes from God and leads to Him as its destiny. For this reason, as William James explains in his essay, "The Will to Believe,"[5] agnosticism is not a neutral middle position. *"Do not decide, but leave the question* (of God) *open, is itself a passional decision — just like deciding yes or no — and is attended with the same risk of losing the truth."*[6]

Agnosticism is adopted to avoid risk in believing.

But does it succeed in this? From the point of view of someone who is uncertain about God's existence we can say the following. The atheist position is a risk: what if God does exist? The theist position is a risk: what if God does not exist? And the agnostic position? Is that not, existentially, the same risk as that of the atheist? If God does exist, the atheist and agnostic are equally wrong in failing to believe in Him; and to respond to Him, to lead their lives before Him. And if God does not exist, both the atheist and agnostic were correct in their nonbelief.

To say, "do not decide but leave the question open," is itself a decision, and implies risk. There are countless examples of this in daily life. If I hesitate to say yes to marrying a person I love, I do not marry, just as if I had said no. I thereby risk the loss of happiness of marriage just as if I had actually said no. The "do not decide" position is not an escape from the risks of "decide yes" and "decide no"; it is itself a risk, the same risk as "decide no," for *in practice* it is a "decide no." As James puts it in another essay, "our only way ... of doubting, or refusing to believe, that a certain thing *is*, is continuing to act as if it were *not*." Thus, for example, "if I doubt that you are worthy of my confidence, I keep you uninformed of all my secrets just as if (I thought) you were *un*worthy of the same."[7]

Agnosticism is, then, not a third position, but existentially equivalent to atheism; and it is no more reasonable than atheism. Both the atheist and the agnostic lead their lives without God, and run the terrible risk that God is. Is this not something everyone should take with the utmost seriousness? No one has proof that God is not. At most we have difficulties about God (e.g., how can He be all-powerful and all-loving, and still allow such evil in the world?), and what is viewed as insufficient evidence for God. But there *is* evidence for God, as we have seen. And so, at the very least, we must reckon with the tremendous possibility that He does exist. The agnostic and atheist should take seriously that inner voice, "but perhaps God does exist."

If atheism-agnosticism is a risk, is not theism also a risk? "Perhaps God is not." Yes; but which risk is worse? Which "way of going wrong" is worse? To believe, and God is not? Or, not to believe, and God is? Let us weigh them. They are equal on the intellectual level, they are equally errors, failures of belief to correspond to reality. But beyond that? Nothing with regard to the first: belief in God while He is not. But the second: not to believe while God is? This represents a terrible failure on my part to give the response due to God, to acknowledge Him as my Creator, to thank Him for the gift of my existence, to love Him in response to His love for me. The other "way of going wrong," believing God is while He is not, represents no corresponding failure to give a response due. If the atheist is right there is simply the state of affairs that there is no God; no adequate response is due to that.

The failure to give the response due to God if He is, is also the greatest evil, and loss, for the individual person. It is the loss of all that we ultimately long for: love, truth, beauty, liberation from guilt, fulfillment, hope, meaning. For all these are to be found only in God; or not at all.

We cannot of course give ourselves belief. But if we grasp the logic of the non-parallelism just discussed, that the atheist's risk (maybe God does exist) is infinitely worse than the theist's risk (maybe God is not), we can seek God. We can follow Pascal who experienced uncertainty about God, in the clear realization that the question of God, together with that of immortality after death, was the all-important question, on which the ultimate meaningfulness or absurdity of existence depended. Pascal, finding himself in darkness about God, recognized this as a great evil. "Surely then it is a great evil to be thus in doubt, but it is at least an indispensible duty to seek when we are in such doubt."[8] If we are uncertain about God, we should seek Him. We can pray, perhaps in words like this: "Oh God, if you exist, come to me, show me your light, give me faith to believe in You. I want to believe, help my unbelief."

This is of course a risk. If God is not, no one hears my voice, and I have prayed in vain. But not to seek God? Is this not an infinitely worse risk: to fail to seek God when He does exist? We have the same non-parallelism discussed earlier on the level of belief, this time on the level of seeking. If I am lost in the wilderness, is it not better to cry out, at the risk of not being heard, than not to cry out, if someone was there? If we are uncertain of God's existence as Pascal was ("seeing too much to deny (God) and too little to be sure")[9], we are in such a wilderness, our existential situation: where we came from, where we are going, whether existence is ultimately meaningful. Should we not seek, seek God? Is it not better to seek and not find, than not to seek when we could have found?[10]

It should be stressed that uncertainty about God is not the same as agnosticism. Pascal, at one stage of his life, was uncertain about God. But he was never an agnostic. Agnosticism is a specific response to uncertainty, a definite position: "Do not decide, but leave the question open." Pascal's response to uncertainty is exactly the opposite of this: I want to decide, I want the question settled, I want to know; and so I seek God. The contrast to the agnostic "do not decide" is most vividly brought out by Pascal's beautiful phrase: "My heart inclines wholly to know, where is the true good, in order to follow it; nothing would be too dear to me for eternity."[11]

Can an agnostic seek God? Certainly. So can an atheist. But then they are abandoning their original positions, which represent not reckoning with God. If the uncertainty of an agnostic (or atheist) leads him to say, in the spirit of Pascal, "my heart inclines wholly to know God if He is, the truth about God," then he has abandoned the attempt at "safe neutrality" that was supposed to be found in agnosticism. He has then ventured out toward God; toward a faith that represents the opposite commitment to agnosticism, namely leading one's life before God.

Despite sufferings, frustrations and lack of fulfillment, we want to *be*. We shudder at the idea of our non-being, our annihilation. We fear death, in part, because we fear it may represent non-being, annihilation. And the suicide, I suggest, wants to escape from his present mode of being, not his being as such. We want to *be*; we feel, deep down, that existence is good.

We did not give ourselves existence. We received it, and continue to receive it, for we do not, ultimately, hold ourselves in existence. Our existence: what a gift! If we realize this, we will want to give the adequate response to any gift: gratitude. I am happy to be. But not only happy: grateful. Without gratitude for my existence, something that should be will be missing. It cannot be right to simply take my existence for granted, or even to rejoice in it. I should be grateful that I am.

Grateful to whom? Not merely my parents, for they did not know me before I was, and did not "intend" me to be. They may have wanted a child, but they could not have intended *me*. I can and should be grateful to them for all that they gave me afterwards. But to whom can I be grateful that I a*m*, that *I* am?

Only to God, to a God of Love, Who gave me my existence in love, and to Whom I owe love; and gratitude. If God, a God of love, is, I can and should be grateful to Him. If God is not, gratitude for my existence

becomes absurd: part of the general absurdity of existence. I want to be grateful, I feel I should be grateful, I
realize that being grateful is also the best attitude for me
psychologically; yet I cannot be grateful if God is not.

It is useful to ponder the thought that the worst
moment for an atheist, or agnostic, is when he is really
thankful — for his being, for the good things of life,
such as love, truth, beauty — but has no one to thank.[12]

Should I be grateful to God that I am? Should I be
grateful to Him for all His gifts? Is it meaningful to be
grateful to God? Yes, if existence is ultimately meaningful; no, if it is ultimately absurd. The meaningfulness or
absurdity of gratitude for my existence, and for all the
good things of life, represents, in a very specific and
concrete way, the fundamental question that has been
our basic theme here, the question whether existence is
ultimately meaningful.

If we are not sure; if we wonder whether Good will
triumph over Evil (and so provide the answer to the
"argument from evil against God"); if we are not sure,
what will we do? We can make a commitment to "existence is ultimately meaningful," and risk that perhaps it
is ultimately absurd. Or we can make a commitment to
"existence is ultimately absurd," and it may turn out that
it is ultimately meaningful. Which "way of going
wrong" is worse? In the first (existence is ultimately absurd), our error is just one more absurdity; does that
really matter? Can anything *ultimately* matter in a reality
that is ultimately absurd? But in the second (existence is
ultimately meaningful), our error stands in drastic contrast to the meaningfulness of existence. Our commitment puts us outside the mainstream of existence. God
is, but we are not part of His Plan; that cannot be other
than a terrible consequence for us. Is it not better to
believe in, or seek, or hope for ultimate meaningfulness, with the risk that we may lose; than to despair of
ultimate meaningfulness, of the triumph of Good over

Evil, with the terrible risk that existence is, after all, ultimately good?

That, I think, is the ultimate decision each person has to make: *Either*, a commitment to ultimate absurdity, that all will be lost in the end, that the powers of Darkness and the Impersonal will triumph over us and everything that we cherish: love, beauty, truth, meaning, goodness, being, hope. *Or*, a commitment to ultimate meaning, the triumph of Love, Beauty, Truth, Meaning, Goodness, Being, Hope.

The great value of the developments in modern thought brought out here, is that they give a clear rational support to the commitment to Ultimate Meaningfulness, to God Who is that Ultimate Meaningfulness.

During his lifetime, Jean Paul Sartre, the famous French Existentialist, was a passionate atheist. His writings depict an absurd world, absurd because God is absent, because there is no immortality after death. But at the end of his life, he seems to have changed and moved towards God and ultimate meaning. The two themes, "the turn to theism" and the inner connection between God and ultimate meaningfulness, are dramatically expressed in the words of Sartre not long before his death:

> I do not feel that I am the product of chance, a speck of dust in the universe, but someone who was expected, prepared, prefigured. In short, a being whom only a Creator could put here; and this idea of a creating hand refers to God.[13]

Notes

1 *Pensees*, No. 229.

2 *Ibid.*

3 See George Gamow, *One, Two, Three, Infinity* (New York: Mentor Books, 1947), p.16.

4 Bertrand Russell, "A Free Man's Worship," First pub. 1903. Reprinted in *Why I am Not a Christian*, ed., Paul Edwards. (New York: Simon and Schuster, 1957), p.107.

5 First pub. 1896. Reprinted in *The Will to Believe and Other Essays in Popular Philosophy* (New York: Dover, 1956), pp.1-31.

6 Part IV, p.11.

7 "Is Life Worth Living?" First pub. 1895. Dover ed., pp. 32-62. Quotations are from pp.54-55.

8 Pascal, *Pensees*, No. 194.

9 *Ibid.*, No. 229

10 The core idea, that it is better to believe when God is not, than not to believe when God is, is that of Pascal's famous Wager (*Pensees*, No. 233). For a further development of this, a defense of the core idea of the Wager and an attempt to bring out its true meaning, see my paper, "Faith, Doubt and Pascal's Wager," forthcoming in *The Center Journal*. Also in *Modern Thought and the Turn to Theism*, to be published by Eerdman's.

11 *Pensees*, No. 229.

12 See Balduin Schwarz, "Gratitude: The Worst Moment in the Life of an Atheist," presented as a paper at the international conference, "The Reality of God and the Dignity of Man," Dallas, March 7-12, 1983. See also his essay, "Some Reflections on Gratitude," in Balduin Schwarz (ed.), *The Human Person and the World of Values* (New York: Fordham University Press, 1960), pp. 168-91.

13 Quoted by Professor Geisler, below.

SUMMARY STATEMENT
Stephen D. Schwarz

Is my existence as a person ultimately meaningful? Or ultimately absurd? Is the universe, and all that it contains, especially the contents of human experience (love, truth, goodness, etc.), ultimately meaningful? Or absurd? There is both meaning and absurdity, good and evil, order and disorder. Which will triumph in the end? Which "speaks the last word"? We long to be happy, and to *be*; but each of us moves closer and closer to the one great certainty of life: death. Death takes away our present being and present meaningfulness. Is death the absolute end of our being, our annihilation? Or is there something beyond death, something stronger than death? A new life?

The great question of life is whether it is ultimately meaningful or ultimately absurd. Taken in themselves, the elements of our world that are meaningful are subject to powerful physical powers that can, and ultimately will, destroy them. A beloved person dies, the victim of drowning. A beautiful painting is destroyed, the victim of an earthquake. And, in due time, the whole earth will freeze over, or be consumed in a great cosmic explosion. Then all that was meaningful — our experiences of love, beauty, truth, goodness and much more — will be destroyed. Is this the final verdict?

Or is there Something More? An Ultimate Power in Whom meaningful things now rest; Who will preserve them in the end; from Whom they originally came?

Why are there meaningful things at all? Why do we exist? Is it a matter of chance, of blind physical forces? Or were we, and these things, intended?

Was my existence as an individual person intended, meant to be? Or merely a matter of chance?

Why is there anything at all, and not simply nothing? Where did it all come from?

All these questions point to God. Or rather, they point to the Great Alternative: *Either* God is, He is the source and basis of all that is meaningful, He is the Ultimate Power that preserves meaning. And existence is ultimately meaningful. *Or*, God is not, it all happened by chance, the result of blind forces. And existence is ultimately meaningless.

Which of these alternatives is the one that is *true*. Truth, that is the all important question. Better to believe a painful truth than a comforting illusion. Belief in ultimate meaningfulness is useless if it is not true.

More concretely, which of these two alternatives should we accept as true? There is a tradition in Western thought that says that belief in God and ultimate meaningfulness is an illusion; that the world in its immediate physical aspect is all there is; that death — our own individual death and the final destruction of our planet — is the end, the absolute end. It is the view that holds that science alone can give us truth; and since science reveals no ultimate meaningfulness, there isn't any. Further, it is even thought that science somehow destroys the credibility of belief in God and ultimate meaningfulness.

The book, *The Intellectuals Speak Out About God*, presents a very different picture. First, it shows that science, far from indicating a universe devoid of meaning and Divine Presence, actually points to God and ultimate meaningfulness. That is, scientists, without presupposing God's existence or trying to prove it, have come up with findings that point unmistakably to God. An example of this is the Anthropic Principle, a discovery of modern astronomy, that indicates that the universe was made to support life, including human life;

for if certain initial conditions had been only slightly different, life could not have originated.

Second, the book discusses developments in modern thought that open the way to a turn to God and ultimate meaningfulness. An important aspect of this is the collapse of Positivism, a view that limited rationality to science and mathematics, and methods of inquiry modeled on them.

This view would destroy all philosophy — including itself of course! It is now seen, once again, that the scope of rationality is far broader than what Positivism would allow. It includes many modes of rational inquiry, above all philosophic insight into reality, and arguments based on it.

For example, why is there something, and not nothing? Where did the universe, and especially man, come from? Did it all just pop into existence? Even if it is supposed that the universe always existed (though the scientific evidence discussed here indicates otherwise), that still does not answer the question *why* it exists, rather than Nothingness. The only rational answer is that it exists because it was brought into existence by a Power beyond itself, God. And with God comes ultimate meaningfulness. The universe makes sense because it is a Divine Creation, a Divine Design, and has a Divine Purpose.

Belief in God and ultimate meaningfulness is not one belief among others; it is basic, fundamental to the way one lives one's life. It is a way of looking at our own being, and all of reality, namely as having a value and significance beyond what will be destroyed by death, or by cosmic forces. A concrete example of this is gratitude. If I am happy to *be*, can I be grateful for this? Yes, if my existence was intended by a Person; if it was intended in love, by a God of Love. To be grateful to be is a response to God, and an aspect of the fundamental belief, and participation, in the ultimate meaningfulness of existence. Another is hope, the hope of ultimate fulfillment and happiness because death is not annihilation, but a new beginning; the full participation in goodness, truth and beauty that we now experience only partially and imperfectly. The message of this book is that this view, the basic belief in God and ultimate meaningfulness, is rationally justified, is worthy of acceptance.

Two dominant themes in the book, the turn to theism and the inner connection between God and ultimate meaningfulness, are dramatically expressed in the words of Sartre not long before his death:

> I do not feel that I am the product of chance, a speck of dust in the universe, but someone who was expected, prepared, prefigured. In short, a being whom only a Creator could put here; and this idea of a creating hand refers to God.

9
THE COLLAPSE OF MODERN ATHEISM
Norman L. Geisler

Many contemporary trends point to the intellectual demise of atheism. I would like to briefly address three areas in which this has become increasingly evident: philosophy, science, and ethics.

I. The Philosophical Demise of Atheism

When we speak of the demise of atheism, we do not necessarily mean there are less atheists in the world but simply that there are less *reasons* for being one. That is, there is a *collapse* of the *intellectual grounds* for *holding* an *atheist* position.

Atheists have offered various kinds of arguments in support of their view that no God exists. We will examine some of the more important examples and then point to the conditions leading to their collapse.

A. *Cosmological Argument Against God*

Some atheists, like Jean Paul Sartre, offered a kind of cosmological argument against God. It can be summarized as follows:[1]

1) God by definition is *causa sui*, a self-caused being.
2) A self-caused being is impossible.
3) Therefore, it is impossible for God to exist.

Most theists would grant the second premise but would deny the first one. For a theist, God is not self-caused; He is uncaused. And an uncaused being is not a contradiction. Or, if an uncaused being is a contradiction, then so is the atheist's uncaused universe. Conversely, if it is meaningful and non-contradictory to speak of an *uncaused universe*, then it is also meaningful and non-contradictory to speak of an *uncaused God*. And if it is meaningful to speak of an uncaused God, then the argument against a self-caused God turns out to be an argument against a straw God, not the real one.

B. *Ontological Disproof of God*

One atheist boldly suggested an ontological disproof of God that went like this:[2]

1) God is by definition a Necessary Being.

2) Now a Necessary Being must exist necessarily (if it exists at all).

3) But statements about existence cannot be necessary.

4) Therefore, it is impossible for God to exist.

Most theists would grant the first two premises but would challenge the third one. For the very statement ("Statements about existence cannot be necessary") is either a necessary statement or else it is not. If it is not, then its opposite may be true, namely, statements about existence (such as the one about God) can be necessary. In order to be a real disproof of God, the statement must be necessarily true. But if it is necessarily true, then it is self-destructive. For in this case the statement is itself a statement about existence which purports to be necessarily true. But the statement affirms that no such statements (including itself) are possible. So this alleged disproof of God disproves itself. So decisively has this argument met its demise that even its original proponent has subsequently discarded it.

C. *Moral Disproof of God*

Few sophisticated atheists offer an absolute disproof of God on moral grounds, but most atheists find the moral arguments most persuasive. The most famous form of the argument goes like this:[3]

1) If God is all good He would defeat evil.
2) If God is all powerful He could defeat evil.
3) But evil is not defeated.
4) Therefore, no such God exists.

Granting that "defeat" does not entail destroying free choice,[4] most traditional theists would agree with the first two premises but would challenge the third one. One need only point to a crucial missing word in this premise to show its fallacy. Premise 3 should actually read: "But evil is not *yet* defeated." But once the time factor is placed in the premise the conclusion no longer follows. For simply because God has not yet defeated evil does not mean that He *never will* defeat evil in the future.

In fact, with this new factor in the premise the argument can be reworded to show that evil *will* be defeated by a theistic God.

1) If God is all good He would defeat evil
2) If God is all powerful, He can defeat evil.
3) But evil is *not yet* defeated.
4) Therefore, evil *will yet* be defeated.

How do we know? Because an all loving God would do it if He could, and He *can* do it. How do we know He can? Because He is powerful enough to do it. So the theist can say: just wait: God *will* defeat evil. His all good and all powerful nature guarantees that He will defeat it. The existence of a theistic God is the guarantee that the "Lord's Prayer" will be answered — "Thy Kingdom come, Thy will be done on earth as it is in heaven."

Of course the atheist might shore up his third premise and restate the argument thus:

1) If God is all good He would defeat evil.
2) If God is all powerful He could defeat evil.
3b) But evil is not yet defeated, *and it never will be.*
4) Therefore, no such God exists.

This form of the argument is indeed much stronger,

and it would seem to be a disproof of classical theism. However, there is a serious problem with premise 3b. It is this: how does the atheist know for sure that evil never will be defeated? Is the atheist assuming omniscience in order to deny the Omniscient? One thing seems certain: no finite mind is in a position to pontificate about the future. Hence, anyone lacking in omniscience about the future is in no position to press the argument as a disproof of God. Thus here again the rational grounds for atheism collapse.

There is a fundamental fallacy in all attempted moral disproofs of God: where does one get his moral ground to stand on? Certainly not from any absolutely perfect moral standard, for that is what the theist means by God. On the other hand, how can there be absolute moral prescriptions without an absolute moral Prescriber? One former Oxford atheist concluded that atheism was really circular.[5] For it argued that God does not exist because of the injustice in the world. But how can there be injustice unless we assume a standard of justice. Further, how can there be an *ultimate* injustice unless we have an ultimate standard of justice? But an ultimate standard of justice is precisely what the theist believes God to be. Hence, in order for the atheist's argument against God to succeed he must assume the theistic equivalent of God, which is self-defeating. Here again, the grounds for atheism collapse.

The dilemma of the atheist can be put this way. Either he stands inside a theistic position to criticize it as inconsistent or else he moves outside of it and finds his own grounds to stand on. But if he stands inside there is always an answer to his choice. For example, the atheist may argue:

1) An all-wise, all-good, all-powerful God must have a good reason for permitting *all* evil.
2) But there is no good reason for *some* evil.
3) Therefore, no such God exists.

But here again this argument collapses if one is standing *inside* a theistic view. For it can be successfully countered as follows.

1) An all-wise, all-good, all-powerful God has a good reason for everything that happens.
   a) It must be a *good* reason because he is *all*-good.
   b) It must be a *wise* reason because he is *all*-wise.
   c) He must have permitted it because he is all-powerful.
2) Evil does occur.
3) Therefore, such a God has a good reason for all evil that does occur.

The reason the atheist failed to see this point is that he confuses two premises:

1) We do not know of any good reason for some evil.
2) God knows of no good reason for some evil.

It is obvious that these two premises are not equivalent, unless the atheist is equal to God in knowledge and benevolence. Here again the atheist would have to be God in order to refute God. Thus from the *inside* of theism there is no inconsistency nor refutation of theism, since it is logically *possible* that God has a good reason we know nothing about. Indeed, if he is all-wise and all-good it is *necessary* that he has such a reason, even if he has not revealed it to us.

But suppose the atheist seeks some ground outside of theism on which to stand? The lack of such grounds to stand on was brought home forcefully to me a few years ago when I confronted an atheist philosophy professor with this dilemma:

1) Either your grounds for rejecting God because of injustice are based on an ultimate standard of justice or else they are not.

2) If your grounds are ultimate then you are using an ultimate moral standard to eliminate God whom theists hold is the ultimate moral standard.

3) If your grounds are not ultimate, then your argument fails because the injustice you perceive may only be immediate and not ultimate at all.

I was surprised by his reply. It went something like this: "My argument that there is no God is not based on any ultimate moral standard. It is based on *my own benign moral feelings*."[6] Not all atheists are this frank, but all who take their stand outside an ultimate or absolute find that ultimately they have no basis on which to criticize God except their own relative and subjective feelings.

In the final analysis there is no rational *disproof* of God; there is only a moral *distaste* of God. This reminds one of Nietzsche's similar reaction in the *Anti Christ* when he exclaimed: "If one were to *prove* this God of the Christians to us, we should be even less able to believe in him."[7] With this kind of unreasonableness the intellectual bankruptcy of atheism becomes apparent. Lacking rational justification it manifests itself in existential reactions.

D.   *Existential "Arguments" Against God*

As strange as it may seem in view of the foregoing discussion, some have attempted to eliminate God from the very nature of their existential experience. Jean Paul Sartre is an example. His argument can be summarized this way:[8]

1) If God exists then I am not free (since God has determined everything).

2) But I *am* free.

3) Therefore, God does not exist.

In support of his second premise Sartre insisted that he was absolutely free. Man, he said, cannot be free. We are condemned to freedom. In Sartre's own words, "I *am* my freedom. No sooner had you (Zeus) created me than I ceased to be yours."[9] But if I am free to choose my own way, then there can be no God to determine my course. But I *am* free. Therefore, no such God exists.

Let us grant Sartre that man is free. Does it necessarily follow, therefore, that God does not exist? The problem here is in the first premise: If God exists, then I am not free. Why? The reason seems to be the fallacy of either/or. It assumes that *both* God's determination *and* man's freedom are impossible. On closer analysis this does not necessarily follow, at least not for a theistic God who knows the future. Take for example any free act you performed yesterday. Let us consider the clothes you chose to wear yesterday. That choice is now a once-for-all *determined* event that cannot be changed. Yet we have agreed that it was a *free* act. Hence, freedom *and* determination are not contradictory when we speak about the past. But if God is omniscient and knows the future, then future free acts are determined with the same certainty that past ones are. For God cannot be wrong about what He omnisciently knows will occur. Thus, all acts are determined, even the free ones.

There is no contradiction between saying God has *determined* all events and man *freely* chooses some events. All we need to add is that God has determined that we *freely* choose these events.[10] In this way both freedom and determination are compatible, and the existential argument against God collapses.

There are other existential ways to argue against God. One of the more popular ones goes like this:
1) If there were a God, then life would be meaningful.
2) But life is empty and futile.
3) Therefore, there is no God.

The problem with all these arguments is their radical subjectivity. No doubt life is meaningless to many.

But does that necessarily imply there is no meaning? Or does it imply only that they have not found that meaning? Simply because one dies of thirst in search of an oasis does not necessarily mean there is no water anywhere. And would we not consider anyone cruelly unjust who discourages someone else from looking for water (or God) simply because he has not found it (or Him)?[11]

Apparently even Jean Paul Sartre who declared "man is a useless passion" and believed that life is an empty bubble on the sea of nothingness did not give up himself. Not long before Sartre's death the *Nouvel Observateur* recorded a dialogue with Sartre and a Marxist in which Sartre reportedly said, "I do not feel that I am the product of chance, a speck of dust in the universe, but someone who was expected, prepared, prefigured. In short, a being whom only a Creator could put here; and this idea of a creating hand refers to God." Sartre's former companion, Simone de Beauvoir, was shocked. She said, "all my friends, all the Sartrians, and the editorial team ... supported me in my consternation."[12] Indeed, if Sartre rejected the absurdity of life in a chance universe for a belief in a purposeful Creator, one can understand the consternation of his atheist colleagues. For if this confession of the father of modern atheistic existentialism is so, then with it we witness the existential collapse of existential atheism. Apparently even Sartre who had early admitted that "atheism is a cruel and long range affair" could not himself live it to the end.

II.   The Scientific Collapse of Atheism

In the realm of science the kingpin of traditional atheism is materialism. This takes on two major forms: physical reductionism and the eternality of the material universe.

> a) The first affirms how long matter has existed (namely, forever).

b) The second aspect of materialism declares the *nature* of all that exists is material.

c) From this emerges a third aspect of materialism, spontaneous biogenesis or self-organization of life from non-living chemicals. An examination of each of these areas reveals the collapse of modern atheistic explanations.

A.   *Is the Universe Eternal?*

Professor Jastrow has done more than perhaps any other astronomer to announce the implausibility of the eternality of the material universe. Dr. Jastrow pinpointed the evidence for a beginning of the universe succinctly in these words: "Now three lines of evidence — the motions of the galaxies, the laws of thermodynamics, and the life story of the stars — pointed to one conclusion; all indicated that the Universe had a beginning."[13]

Let's examine just one of these lines of evidence briefly — the second law of thermodynamics. According to this law, in a closed system (such as the materialist conceives the whole universe to be) the amount of usable energy is decreasing. That is, there is a heat loss. This process is going on throughout the whole universe as nuclear fission occurs. But if the universe is "running down" then it must have had a beginning. In Dr. Jastrows words, "Now we see how the astronomical evidence leads to a biblical view of the origin of the world. The details differ, but the essential elements in the astronomical and biblical accounts of Genesis are the same: the chain of events leading to man commenced suddenly and sharply at a definite moment in time, in a flash of light and energy."[14]

Some had hoped to find a source for *fresh hydrogen atoms* coming into the universe which would maintain it in a steady state. But no observational evidence for the coming into existence of such atoms has been found. And even if it were discovered that hydrogen atoms were somewhere being *created* this would naturally lead to the idea of a Creator — an idea which the materialist wishes to avoid.

Despite the speculations about a steady-state universe, all evidence indicates it is running down and headed for an ultimate demise. Some have suggested the universe may *rebound* from this exhaustion. This is, however, purely speculative. The scientific evidence indicates that only the creation of fresh hydrogen atoms could enable the universe to rebound. But this again would seem to necessitate *some creative Force* beyond the universe. Further, even if the universe could rebound on its own, according to the second law of thermodynamics it would rebound less and less each time until it is finally exhausted — even though it would take longer to do so.

But if the universe will *eventually collapse* then the cornerstone of atheism will also collapse with it. For if the *universe is not eternal*, then traditional atheism faces *an utter lack of rational explanation*. This dilemma was put well by the British atheist, Anthony Kenny, when he wrote: "According to the big bang theory, the whole matter of the universe began to exist at a particular time in the remote past. A proponent of such a theory, at least if he is an atheist, must believe that the matter of the universe *came from nothing and by nothing*."[15]

It must be extremely painful for an atheistic philosopher to fall back on such irrational speculation as to suggest that the universe was created "by nothing." Even the skeptic, David Hume, declared, "I never asserted so absurd a Proposition as *that anything might arise without a cause*: I only maintained, that our certainty of the falsehood of that proposition proceeded neither from intuition nor demonstration; but from another source."[16]

Again Professor Jastrow has stated the embarrassment well: "For the scientist who has lived by his faith in the power of reason, the story ends like a bad dream. He has scaled the mountain of ignorance; he is about to conquer the highest peak; as he pulls himself over the final rock, he is greeted by a band of theologians who have been sitting there for centuries."[17]

Atheists have often chided theists for believing in *ex nihilo* creation, that God made something out of nothing. Despite their protest there is no absurdity in declaring that Someone made something out of nothing. But to declare that "*nothing* made something out of nothing" is something else. When a position has reached this point of irrational desperation it has collapsed beyond the possibility of rationally rebounding.

B.   *Is Man Reducible to Matter?*

Another foundational stone of atheism is physical reductionism. This is the belief that man is either matter or reducible to it. Certainly there is no logically necessary connection between the denial of God and the denial of the reality of the mind (or soul).[18] However, reducing man to his material components is a logical extension of materialism which in turn is the cornerstone of traditional atheism.

The extreme form of materialism believes that mind *is* material. More moderate forms hold that mind *is reducible* to matter or is *dependent on* matter.

The problem with the strong form of materialism has been put this way: "If my mental processes are determined wholly by the motions of atoms in my brain, I have no reason to suppose that my beliefs are true ... and hence I have no reason for supposing my brain to be composed of atoms."[19] In short, if materialism is *true*, then I have no reason to believe there is any such thing as truth — even the truth of the theory of materialism. For truth is not material, at least not the truth about *all* material.

Another way to show the fallacy of materialism is to note that it is a form of reductionism. The materialist says in effect "I am nothing but my body." But "nothing but" statements imply "more than" knowledge. If there were nothing but matter, how could pure matter know it?

A personal encounter with a materialist who taught science at an Ivy League school dramatically illustrates just how completely materialistic reductionism has collapsed. The professor declared to me that he did not believe in mind, soul or anything immaterial. He believed that only molecules and atoms existed. When I asked him what a scientific *theory* was, he replied, "It is magic." When I recovered from my shock, I asked again to make sure he was serious. He reaffirmed his contention that science theories were only magic. He reminded me that the origin of science was magic; chemistry coming from alchemy, and so on. I then asked him for the rational basis for his conclusion that scientific theories were not real immaterial states of an immaterial mind. His reply was even more revealing. "The basis for my belief that magic is the source of my theory of materialism is *faith*!" With that I was left speechless. Faith in magic is the basis of materialism! Herein is the demise of materialism. It collapses into magic.[20]

The soft form of materialism is not quite so blatant but it too has collapsed under the scrutiny of modern science and philosophy. However, reducing man to his material components is a logical extension of a materialistic view of the universe which is a kingpin of modern atheism.

The extreme form of materialism believes that mind (or soul) *is* matter. More moderate forms believe mind is *reducible to* matter or *dependent on* it. However, from a scientific perspective much has happened in our generation to lay bare the clay feet of materialism. Most noteworthy among this is the Nobel prize winning work of Sir John Eccles.[21] His work on the brain demonstrated that the mind or intention is more than physical. He has shown that the supplementary motor area of the brain is fired by mere *intention* to do something, without the motor cortex of the brain (which controls muscle movements) operating. So, in effect, the mind is to the brain what an archivist is to a library. The former is not reducible to the latter.

From a philosophical point it should come as no surprise that the mind cannot be reduced to matter. For a theory which reduces everything to matter is saying that the irrational is the basis of the rational. In other words, ultimately there is no *rational* basis for their materialistic philosophy. For if materialism is true then all reason — even the reason one is a materialist — is based in non-reason.[22] The dilemma is this: either there is a rational ground for materialism or there is not. If there is, then they must admit that reason (or mind) is the basis of their materialism, which destroys their view. If there is not a rational basis for materialism then it is left without rational justification. In this event we have again evidence of the rational collapse of the materialistic pillar of atheism.

It will not suffice for a materialist to claim that there is a rational ground for his views while at the same time claiming that mind is reducible to or dependent on matter. For if mind is dependent on matter, then matter cannot be dependent on mind. Each cannot be the grounds for the other. The materialist cannot have it both ways.

C. *Did Life Arise from Non-Life?*

Despite the fact that Pasteur long ago disproved spontaneous generation, materialistic scientists continue to believe in the chemical evolution of life. The reason for their accepting this unscientific conclusion was stated very well by J.W.N. Sullivan in *The Limitation of Science*: "It became an accepted doctrine that life never arises except from life. So far as actual evidence goes, this is still the only possible conclusion. But since it is a conclusion that seems to lead back to some supernatural creative act, it is a conclusion that scientific men find very difficult of acceptance."[23] But a reluctance to accept a Creator of life is not scientific grounds for rejecting the evidence for creation.

Recently two brave scientists launched an assault on the materialistic view of chemical evolution in their landmark book, *Evolution from Space*. In it, the astronomers, Sir Fred Hoyle and N.C. Wickramasinghe concluded to their own surprise that even if the whole universe were a kind of prebiotic soup the chances against life arising spontaneously would still be only 1 in $10^{40,000}$. This, they vividly say, would be about like the chances of a Boeing 747 resulting from a tornado raging through a junk yard. Indeed, the chances of a spontaneous origin of life are about that of finding one atom in the whole universe![24]

Other scientists have admitted the odds are "beyond all probability." And one Nobel Prize winning biologist, George Wald, even declared that spontaneous generation is "impossible." In spite of this he insists that it *did* happen! This kind of faith rivals that of Abraham, Job, and Daniel. It too points to the scientific collapse of the materialistic explanations.

The implications of the latest discovery in the realm of biogenesis have not yet been fully exposed or digested by the intellectual community. In an article in *The Theoretical Journal of Biology* (1981),[25] Herbert P. Yockey revealed his discovery about the connection between linguistic information theory and the information code in living systems. Information theory was first described by Claude E. Shannon of Bell Laboratory in 1948.[26] Information theory provides a mathematical basis for specifying the theoretical information carrying capacity of any communication channel. Its ability to show the information patterns of a written language is mathematically expressible. It is also a fact of genetics that there is a certain mathematically expressible pattern in the chemical structure of living things. Yockey's unique contribution resulted from comparing the information in a language and in a living organism.

First, Yockey noted that "The statistical structure of any printed language ranges through letter frequencies, diagrams, trigrams, word frequencies, etc., spelling rules, grammar and so forth and, therefore, can be represented by a *Markov process* given the states of the system, the p and the *p(j/b) probabilities.*"[27] When he compared this mathematical pattern represented by the letter frequency, etc., of a *written language*, as known through the information theory to that known to exist in *living systems*, he discovered that it was *exactly the same*. Yockey adds this comment: "It is important to understand that we are not reasoning by analogy. The sequence hypothesis applies directly to the protein and the genetic text as well as to written language and therefore the treatment is mathematically identical."[28]

But if the *mathematic relation* between *information in a DNA* and *information in a written language* are *identical*, then we can conclude that what we observe to be the *cause* for *information* in a *language* will have to be *posited* for the *source* of *information* in the DNA as well. But what we always observe to be the cause of information is *intelligence*. Thus it is scientifically necessary to posit *intelligence* as the *cause* of the *first living cell*. For observation of repeated and uniform experience teaches us that the information in science research papers result only from intelligent beings, not from *dropping marbles randomly* on an electronic typewriter. Also, repeated experience of similar situations teaches us that the information conveyed in a volume of the encyclopedia never occurs by random forces or non-intelligent laws. Yet the *information* in even the *simplest form of life* is equal to that in a *volume* of the *encyclopedia*, and the genetic information in a human brain is more than the information in *all the major libraries of the world!*[29] Now it goes without saying that if it takes intelligence to produce the information in a single sentence, then it also takes intelligence to create the first simple form of life, to say nothing of the human brain. With this new discovery of the relation between information theory and the DNA we are witnessing another aspect of the scientific collapse of atheistic explanations of origin.

III. The Ethical Demise of Atheism

Atheism has always had difficulty in the realm of ethics. On the one hand, atheists would like to maintain some *objective* ethical ground from which to *attack* God via the *problem of evil*. On the other hand, they want to proclaim the *subjectivity* of ethical norms in *terms of the society or the individual*. On the one hand, atheist would like to join with theist in condemning the Nazi atrocities of the holocaust. On the other hand, they would like to maintain that all is relative to the situation. But can they have it both ways?

A. *Atheists Claim that all is Relative*

Humanist Manifestos I and II are a representative source for atheists' ethical principles. The First Manifesto (1933) had such notable signators as philosophers Edwin A. Burtt and Roy W. Sellars, along with the father of American education, John Dewey. In it, they declared that there are no divinely given values: "Humanism asserts that the nature of the universe depicted by modern science makes unacceptable any supernatural or cosmic guarantees of human values."[30]

In *Humanist Manifesto II* (1973) an impressive array of names including Isaac Asimov, B.F. Skinner, Sir Julian Huxley and Jacques Monod placed their signatures on these statements about ethics: "We affirm that moral values derive their source from human experience. Ethics is autonomous and situational, needing no theological or ideological sanction. Ethics stems from human need and interest. To deny this distorts the whole basis of life. Human life has meaning because we create and develop our futures."[31]

Some atheists have been even more frank about their disbelief in objective or absolute moral principles. Friedrich Neitzsche wrote in a famous passage in *Joyful Wisdom*, "'Where is God gone?' he called out. I mean to tell you! *We have killed him,* — you and I! We are all his murderers! ... do we not hear the noise of the grave-diggers who are burying God? Do we not smell the divine putrefaction? — for even Gods putrefy! God is dead! God remains dead! And we have killed him!" In his famous, *Thus Spoke Zarathustra*, Nietzsche declared, "I beseech you, my brothers, *remain faithful to the earth,* and do not believe those who speak to you of other worldly hopes! ... Once the sin against God was the greatest sin; but God died, and these sinners died with Him. To sin against the earth is now the most dreadful thing ... "[32]

In view of God's death, Nietzsche called himself an "immoralist" who desired to pass beyond all traditional morality the way chemistry passed beyond alchemy, and astronomy beyond astrology.[33] Even general ethical principles, such as: "Injure no man, rather help all men so far as you are able," are questioned by Nietzsche. "In short, moralities too are but a *symbolic language of the passions* ... "[34] The Christian morality of love is singled out for special attack by Nietzsche. "What? An act of love is supposed to be 'unegoistic'? Why, you idiots ... 'How about praising the one who sacrifices himself?'" For "every unselfish morality which takes itself as an absolute and seeks to apply itself to Everyman sins not only against taste, but does worse: it is an incentive to sins of omission."[35]

Nietzsche reserves his strongest words for Christian ethics. In *Ecce Homo* he wrote, "Christian morality is the most malignant form of all falsehood ... It is really poisonous, decadent, weakening. It produces nincompoops not men." He adds elsewhere, "I condemn Christianity and confront it with the most terrible accusation that an accuser has ever had in his mouth. To my mind it is the greatest of all conceivable corruptions ... I call it the one immortal blemish of mankind."[36]

Along with God, Nietzsche rejected all moral absolutes. Not only did he attempt to reject all *traditional* value, but he also rejected all *absolute* values altogether. "I shall repeat a hundred times," he wrote, "that 'immediate certainty' as well as 'absolute knowledge' and 'thing in itself' are all contradictions in terms."[37] For Nietzsche both truth and value are on a sliding scale with no absolute standard. "Whatever forces us," Nietzsche asks, "to assume at all that there is an essential difference between 'true' and 'false'? Is it not sufficient to assume levels of semblance, lighter and darker shadows and tones of semblance as it were, different 'values' in the painter's sense of the term?"[38] Nietzsche asks, "what if nothing any longer proves itself divine, except it be error, blindness, and falsehood; what if God Himself turns out to be our most persistent lie?"[39] Indeed, the whole of Nietzsche's *Anti Christ* is devoted to the destruction of absolute truth.

B. *Atheists' Lives Betray their Belief in Moral Absolutes*

Although not all atheists have been as militant as Nietzsche in rejecting moral absolutes, nevertheless most have been just as emphatic. However, there is a serious problem with this view which is evident in the *lives* of atheists. Few atheists, for example, really live a life totally devoid of all absolutes. For instance, few really hate, murder, torture or rape anyone they wish. Indeed, few really even *believe* that these things should ever be done. In fact, most atheists live their lives guided by what amounts to a moral absolute. For example, for many humanists the *absolute* is *mankind*. For John Dewey it was human *progress*, and so on. Dr. Paul Tillich believed everyone has some ultimate to which he is committed.[40] Without *this center* he would lack any *integrating point for his life*. Certainly most atheists have something to which they are unconditionally committed.

Furthermore, few, if any, atheists really believe Hitler was right. Few atheists actually believe there is any ethically good sense in which the Nazis *ought* to have attempted the genocide of Jews.

The inability of atheists to really believe and live a totally relative ethic was brought home forcefully to me by a true story about a Midwestern philosophy student. He wrote a research paper arguing that there are no objective or absolute moral principles. Judged by its research, scholarship, documentation, and argumentation most would have agreed it was easily an A paper. The professor, however, placed these words on the paper: "F — *I do not like blue folders*." When the student received his paper, he stormed into the professor's office waving his paper and protesting: "This is not *fair*! This is not *just*! Why should I be graded on the basis of the color of my paper? It should have been graded on its contents, not on its color!" When the student had settled down, the professor asked quietly, "Was this the paper which argued that there are no objective moral principles such as fairness and justice, and which argued that everything is a matter of one's subjective likes or dislikes?" "Yes, yes!" the student replied. "Well, then," said the professor, "I do not *like* blue folders. The grade will remain an F!" Immediately the face of the young man changed. Suddenly he understood that he really did believe in objective moral principles such as fairness and justice. The lesson having been learned, the professor changed the grade to an A and the young man left with a new understanding of the objective nature of morality. It is easy to *say* there are no moral laws, but it is much more difficult to really *live* as if there are none.

C. *Atheists' Talk Betrays their Belief in Moral Absolutes*

Despite their explicit disclaimers about absolutes, moral relativists do not avoid absolutes of their own. For example, while Joseph Fletcher said, "the situationist avoids words like 'never' and 'perfect' and 'always' and 'complete' as he avoids the plague, as he avoids 'absolutely.'"[41] Yet in the same book Fletcher declares "Love is the *only* norm," and "*no* unwanted babies should *ever* be born."[42] But "only" and "no" are just as absolutistic as "never" and "always."

The same kind of inconsistency is apparent in the *Humanist Manifestos*. We read strong imperatives like "This world *must* renounce the resort to violence and force ..." Again, "it is a *planetary imperative* to reduce the level of military expenditures and turn these savings to peaceful and people-oriented uses."[43] Other humanists speak of moral duties as "absolutely essential."[44] The Second Manifesto calls for a moral commitment which "transcends ... church, state, party, class, or race."[45] What are these but humanist ways of stating their belief in moral absolutes?

That secular humanist moral principles should be understood in a universal sense can be seen from the exceptionless way they believe in principles such as *tolerance* and *freedom*. One can search their writings in vain for any real exceptions to these moral principles. Where do they ever give the impression that they believe there are any exceptions to the basic humanistic command to treat humans with respect? In point of fact this norm functions like an absolute in this system. The most recent "Secular Humanist Declaration" (1981) says explicitly, "we oppose *any* tyranny over the mind of man, *any* effort ... to shackle free thought."[45] This surely is absolutistic in tone and wording.

D. *The Undeniability of Absolutes*

There is an important reason why atheists *live* and even *talk* as though there really are moral absolutes. It is because absolutes are absolutely undeniable. Take for example, Joseph Fletcher's claim that all is relative. Reduced to simple English, it is *self-destructive*. It says in effect, *"we should never use the word never. Never!* Or, we should always avoid using the word always. Always!"* How do they know there are no absolutes? Are they absolutely sure? If so, then there is an absolute — their absolute certainty. If it is not absolutely certain there are no absolutes then there may be some. In either case, it is impossible to absolutely deny all absolutes. But if there is (or even can be) a moral absolute, then the atheist's relativistic ethic collapses.

One thing seems clear: the atheist has no firm moral ground on which to stand and from which to proclaim his position. He cannot stand on the pinnacle of his own absolute and relativize everything. For if all is relative then so is the basis of his ethics. One can only move the earth if he has a firm place for his fulcrum.

Will Durant summed up the groundlessness of modern man well when he said, "You and I are living on a shadow ... because we are operating on the Christian ethical code which was given us, unfused with the Christian faith ... But what will happen to our children ...? We are not giving them an ethics warmed up with a religious faith. They are living on the shadow of a shadow."[46]

Indeed, it is difficult to live on the shadow of a shadow. But that is precisely where modern man is living, since he has denied the reality of God. But alas this is no longer necessary for contemporary man. Both science and philosophy have opened up new doors through which we may walk and discover the reality of God and thereby a firm basis for the dignity of man.

Notes

1 Jean Paul Sartre, *Being and Nothingness* (New York: Washington Square Press, 1966), trans. Hazel E. Barnes, p. 758 f.

2 J.N. Findlay, "Can God's Existence Be Disproved?" in *The Ontological Argument*, ed. Alvin Plantinga (Garden City, New York: Doubleday, 1965), p. 111 f.

3 See Pierre Bayle, *Selections from Bayle's Dictionary*, trans. R.H. Popkin (Indianapolis: Bobbs-Merrill, 1965), p. 157 f.

4 If "defeat" evil necessitates destroying free will then one can object that 1) this is too high a price to pay, and 2) once free moral choices are destroyed there is no longer a moral problem of evil.

5 C.S. Lewis, *Mere Christianity* (New York: Macmillan, 1960), pp. 45, 46.

6 Summarized from a recording of a debate with a philosophy professor at Lake County Junior College, north of Chicago, Illinois.

7 Friedrich Nietzsche, *The Anti Christ* in *The Portable Nietzsche*, trans. Walter Kaufmann (New York: The Viking Press, 1968), p. 627.

8 Jean Paul Sartre, *ibid.*, pt. four, ch. 1.

9 Jean Paul Sartre, *The Flies* in *No Exit and Three Other Plays* (New York: Vintage Books, 1946), pp. 121-123.

10 Aquinas put it this way: "Things known by God are contingent because of their proximate causes, while the knowledge of God, which is the first cause, is necessary." *Summa Theologica* I, 14, 13, ad. 1, trans. Anton C. Pegis (New York: Random House, 1944), Vol. One, p. 155.

11 For an elaboration of this point see my *Is Man the Measure: An Evaluation of Contemporary Humanism* (Grand Rapids: Baker Book House, 1983), pp. 169-171.

12 From a dialogue with a marxist recorded in the *Nouvel Observateur* as reported by Thomas Molnar, *National Review*, 11 June 1982, p. 677.

13 Robert Jastrow, *God and the Astronomers* (New York: W. W. Norton, 1978), p. 111.

14 *Ibid.*, p. 14.

15 Anthony Kenny, *The Five Ways: St. Thomas Aquinas' Proofs of God's Existence* (New York: Schocken Books, 1969), p. 66.

16 David Hume, *The Letters of David Hume*, 2 volumes, ed. J.Y.T. Greig (Oxford: Clarendon Press, 1932), I: 187.

17 Robert Jastrow, *ibid.*, p. 15.

18 There are in fact some philosophers such as J.M.E. McTaggart and C.J. Ducasse who believe in the immortality of the soul but not in God.

19 J.B.S. Haldane, *Possible Worlds* (p. 209), quoted by C.S. Lewis in *Miracles* (New York: Macmillan, 1947), p. 22.

20 Perhaps this should not be so surprising since, as C.S. Lewis notes, both science and magic arise from a similar desire — the desire to have power over nature. *The Abolition of Man* (New York: Macmillan, 1947), pp. 87-88.

21 Karl Popper and John Eccles, *The Self and Its Brain* (New York: Springer-Verlag, 1981) revised edition.

22 See C.S. Lewis, *Miracles*, pp. 19-24.

23 J.W.N. Sullivan, *The Limitations of Science* (New York: A Mentor Book, 1963), p. 94.

24 Sir Fred Hoyle and N.C. Wickramasinghe, *Evolution from Space* (London: Dent. 1981), pp. 24-26.

25 H.P. Yockey, "Self Organization Origin of Life Scenarios and Information Theory" in *The Journal of Theoretical Biology* (1981) 91, 13-31.

26 See Claude Shannon, "Mathematical Theory of Communication" (July and October, 1948), *Bell Systems Technical Journal*.

27 Yockey, *ibid.*, p. 16.
28 *Ibid.*
29 See Carl Sagan, *Cosmos* (New York: Random House, 1980), p. 278.
30 See Paul Kurtz, *Humanist Manifestos I and II* (Buffalo: Prometheus, 1973), p. 8.
31 *Ibid.*, p. 17.
32 Friedrich Nietzsche, *Joyful Wisdom* (Sect. 125) trans. Thomas Common (Frederick Ungar Publishing Co., 1960), pp. 167, 168; and *Thus Spoke Zarathustra* (Prologue 3) trans. Walter Kaufmann (New York: Viking Press, 1966), p. 125.
33 Nietzsche, *Beyond Good and Evil* (32) trans. Marianne Cowan (Chicago: Henry Regnery Co., 1966), p. 39.
34 *Ibid.*, (186, 187), pp. 93-94.
35 *Ibid.*, (220), pp. 144-145.
36 Nietzsche, *The Anti Christ*, p. 230.
37 Nietzsche, *Beyond Good and Evil* (16), p. 17.
38 *Ibid.*, (34), p. 41.
39 Nietzsche, *Joyful Wisdom* (344), pp. 279-280.
40 See Paul Tillich, *Ultimate Concern* (London: SCM Press, Ltd., 1965), pp. 7,8,11, 30.
41 Joseph Fletcher, *Situation Ethics: The New Morality* (Philadelphia: Westminster Press, 1966), p. 44.
42 *Ibid.*, p. 39.
43 Paul Kurtz, *Humanist Manifestos I and II*, p. 21.
44 See Corliss Lamont, *The Philosophy of Humanism* (New York: Philosophical Library, 1949), p. 273 f.
45 See "A Secular Humanist Declaration" in *Free Inquiry* (Winter 1980-81), ed. Paul Kurtz, p. 4.
46 As quoted in *Chicago Sun-Times*, 24 August 1975, Section 1 B, p. 8.

10
FROM POSITIVISM TO BELIEF
IN GOD
Professor William Alston

What is the best way to talk about the basis or the ground that a person can have for believing in the existence of God?

Well, the thing that I'm most interested in is trying to understand the way in which our experience of God operating in our lives constitutes a basis for belief. I don't like to use the term "religious experience." "Religious experience" is a very sprawling, cover-all term. I'm thinking specifically of experiences of encounter with God, awareness of God. I'm also thinking of quite common, ordinary, run-of-the-mill encounters. I'm not thinking of super-spectacular mystical experiences that you read about in St. Teresa and St. John of the Cross. Those are very interesting; I'm not pooh-poohing them. That's just not what I'm talking about. I'm looking for some way of seeing how the ordinary religious life of ordinary, devoted, committed Christians provides them with a basis for beliefs about God. I don't think I can extract the whole of Christian theology out of this. But I think that the assurance that many people have that God is real, and that God is at work in their lives, is much more similar to the kind of assurance they have about the physical environment than most people think. The work that I'm doing on this involves a major effort to work out the epistemology of sense-perception. And there are a lot of things to be done here on the phenomenology of awareness of God, just to clear a lot of junk out of the way and get rid of a lot of unwarranted prejudices against the kind of position I'm taking. When somebody says they experience the presence of God, people say that's just their interpretation, that's not what they really experience. You have to show that, in the same way, when somebody says they see a telephone over there, you can say that is just their interpretation.

Do you see, in the last decade or so, a shift away from Positivism?

Oh, definitely. Yes.

How widespread and how deep is this change?

Well, I think it's very significant, and, as far as lip service goes, it's almost whole. But I think there are still Positivist assumptions under the surface in a lot of places. For example, a lot of the people who had recently been attacking Realism — Hilary Putnam, Richard Rorty and so forth — they are quite explicitly using Verificationist arguments. But yes, I think, as far as the period is concerned when everybody was afraid to violate Positivist restrictions, we're pretty much past that.

What was responsible for the demise of Positivism?

I think it was really the failure of Positivist philosophers to produce any significant results along their lines. The thing sounded very impressive as a program. They were going to develop this criterion of meaningfulness that would show what distinguishes genuinely cognitive empirical statements from others but they never succeeded in working out this criterion in such a way that it wouldn't exclude most of science. Of course, they did not want to do that. So, it's just generally been abandoned. It just never worked out.

There were always people who were not seduced by Positivism. But, as far as the large group of people who embraced it [is concerned], I think what happened was that it just didn't pan out. So far, I've just been talking about the Positivist criterion of meaningfulness, the verifiability criterion of meaningfulness. That was only one thing that didn't pan out. There was also — these are connected, of course — the program of exhibiting the logical structure of scientific theories in a certain way and, of course, this way changed as the program developed. The original idea was that we were going to show how all of your apparently theoretical, non-observable statements about postulated entities, [which] couldn't be observed, could be defined or explicated in terms of observables. That didn't work, so the program was changed to partial definitions of these things, and we would show that they had some empirical content by showing that they had some implications for observables. But then the people trying to work that out came to realize that the only way you can get any consequences in observable terms of theoretical statements was to add a lot of additional premises and how do you keep that from being arbitrary? If you put in the right subsidiary premises you can derive anything. Nobody ever solved that problem. So, the Positivist program for exhibiting the logical structure of theories in their terms never worked. And then, of course, there was the Kuhnian revolution which I think definitely succeeded in revealing that the considerations that lead to the establishment or abandonment of a theory can't be logically codified in the way the Positivists thought. They are much more elusive and much more complex, and they can't be reduced to any logical rules. There's no effective way of taking a theory or a body of data and telling whether the theory is acceptable given that body of data. It's always a question of what the competitors of this theory are; what might you be accepting instead of that? And then there's a question of which of these competitors does a better job; and there's no cut and dry answer to what makes one better than the other. It turns out to be more like a matter of deciding whether Schumann's symphonies are better than Berlioz'.

How should the Christian theist respond to traditional objections to belief in the existence of God, such as the problem of evil?

I am strongly tempted to take a "we can't expect to understand the details" line. I'm rather impressed by, let's say, the analogy of the very small child not being able to grasp or appreciate the standards of conduct followed or inculcated by his parents. Let's endow this child with very unusually righteous and morally praiseworthy parents for the sake of this illustration. Very often the child (you can make the child as young as you like) won't be able to understand why the parents are behaving the way they are. The child, at that stage of development is not in a position to grasp the content of the moral principles of the parents. And, since we are much further from God than such a child is from his parents, I don't know if we have any right to expect to do any better. A lot of discussion on the problem of evil presupposes that we have morality all figured out and we're in possession of the last word on the subject of how a perfectly good God would act; and if anybody suggests that, maybe, God doesn't follow the same standards that we do, you get a lot of righteous indignation. John Stuart Mill is a case in point. It just seems to me unreasonable to think that we are in a position to grasp the standards that God would employ. That's the main resource we have in dealing with the problem of evil.

How can Christian thinkers be most effective in presenting Christianity to non-believers?

I guess the answer to this is going to depend on what you think about natural theology. You've got to decide about that. I find myself in something of a transition in my attitude toward this. I guess I've never taken natural theology terribly seriously. Forget what philosophers can do specifically, for the moment. I still think that by far the best way to convert atheists is to preach the Gospel, administer the sacraments, and live a Christian life in a way that is visible to people. I certainly don't think many people are going to be converted by arguments. But, I guess I take the traditional theistic arguments more seriously now than I would have before. I still don't think they come up to the most exaggerated claims that could conceivably be made for them. I don't think that they succeed in proving anything in any strong sense of that term. But I'm beginning to think that they do help to display the rationality of the position. With respect to the cosmological argument, I now rather think of it in this way: the cosmological argument shows you what you are committed to if you are prepared to accept the principle that there has to be an ultimate explanation for everything. Now, it's a little stronger than that: it's not what you are committed to, if that happens to be your taste. I think it can be effectively argued that it is by no means an unreasonable stance to take to suppose that there is an ultimate explanation for everything. And, since that is not an unreasonable position, and since there can only be an ultimate explanation for everything if there exists a Necessary Being that has certain characteristics, being a theist is not an unreasonable position to take. So, I think you can go that far. But to have a living faith, I think people have to be receptive to experiencing the presence of God. There may be exceptional cases.

Are there any skeptical arguments you find substantial? And what do you think of Antony Flew's "presumption of atheism"?

I can't see that the latter amounts to anything. I can't see any rational basis for any presumption of anything. I think that's a sleight of hand that he's trying to pull there. I think that the Naturalist who is convinced that there isn't anything beyond what we can discover through sense-perception, and what science tells us about, is simply shutting himself off from some of the ways we have to find out what there is. So what do you do with a person like that to shake him out of this? You might remove objections he has to the theistic orientation and you might be able to show him it's not unreasonable. And you might be able to show him that there is some sort of presumptive case, by appropriate use of traditional theistic arguments. But probably, in the end, he's going to have to open himself up to God if he's going to move beyond his position. And that's not the philosopher's special province; it's the province of any Christian.

11
THE RATIONALITY OF BELIEF IN GOD

Professor John E. Smith

Do you see any definite or clearly articulated turn towards theism in modern thought?

There is a concern for religious questions which is becoming quite urgent and this is accompanied by a sense that long standing moral and religious commitments have eroded, partly as a result of the authority of science and its accomplishments. But I see a turning point in the form of a quest for purpose, orientation and a source of meaning that gives point to what we are doing. A number of scientists are showing a concern for philosophical questions these days and in other areas of inquiry there is a renewed interest in the ethical dimension of human activities, including that of research itself. It is not easy to say whether we are witnessing a return to theism as a doctrine or not, but there is no question that at present there is a greater uneasiness about our capacity to live without God than was the case a decade ago.

Do you see this development as being a result also of such advancements in modern science as have done away with the mechanistic world view?

Certainly. You cannot begin to turn in the direction of religion if you are constantly being told, either from the side of scientists, or, what is more likely, from the proponents of scientistic philosophy, that the move is futile and without meaning. But I think that new lines of communication have opened up and one of the main reasons is to be found in the contribution made by the history of science. For a long time philosophers accepted oversimplified views of the progressive character of science and as a result came to regard their own enterprise as hopelessly outmoded. The history of science has presented a new picture; the gap between science and philosophy has been narrowed because the old contrast between the two can no longer be maintained. Kant claimed that the hallmark of a science is that it has no room for differing "schools" of thought and that, on this account, philosophy is no science because of the existence of such schools. But, as recent studies show there are in the sciences themselves different opinions about basic matters — the species problem, for example — and this fact is regarded not as a defect but as a goad to further inquiry. Also, among scientists there has arisen a new interest in the human significance of what science discloses about the world. There are those like Lewis Thomas, for example, who are making most successful efforts to relate scientific knowledge to other aspects of life. This sort of thing has not always happened and, in fact, there are scientists at present who are raising basically philosophical question when many philosophers have abandoned these questions in their efforts to emulate the methods of the sciences. That's very interesting!

And yet popular scientific writers like Carl Sagan and Isaac Asimov present emphatically mechanistic views. How do you view this?

Well, I think they are being dogmatic and that the tide is against them. You can go back to Whitehead for a clue here; in considering what he called "Nature lifeless" —

the mechanical view — Whitehead maintained that the mechanical view succeeds in eliminating meaning and purpose not because they are not there but because the position does not allow them to be there. There will always be those who will try to reduce the world to materialist proportions. But then, to appeal to Whitehead again, it is, as he said, a phenomenon worthy of study to find people animated by the purpose of showing that purpose is an illusion! No mechnical determinism can be correct if, as Peirce, Whitehead and Hartshorne argued, there are real possibilities in the world which is to say that, with regard to any outcome of any process, there was more than one alternative possible. Without real possibility there can be neither freedom nor creativity.

How best can the theistic point of view be presented to modern man? How useful do you think the traditional arguments are in this context?

What we have to show is that these arguments are not geometrical proofs, but rather what I call attempts to show patterns of rationality in the world and our experience of it and of ourselves. What, for example, the ontological argument basically says is that if you understand what is to be meant by "God" and at the same time fail to see the necessity of the reality of that Being, then you are not talking about God but about something else. The cosmological arguments are different; they start with the fact of finite existence and propose to show that if anything exists then something exists of necessity. These seem more obvious in their intent because it is difficult to deny the existence of the world as a starting point; there is, however, the problem that, if one takes causality in a narrow efficient sense, one cannot arrive at a mode of existence other than *finite* existence. Tillich used to take these arguments apart for the purpose of showing their roots in experience and how patterns of rationality arise in the attempt to see how they lead the mind to God. Without, however, experience and engagement, the proofs do not have coercive force. Many have argued that, if the proofs are coercive in themselves, it is difficult to account for the fact that they often are rejected by those who can understand them best. On the other hand, there are genuine logical transitions in the proofs, but they cannot be understood without some form of experiential engagement. The rational development alone is like a flower that has no roots.

I have had some success in presenting the arguments as the discovery of rational patterns in our experience, an experience that all can have. Everyone can confront the order in the world and can experience the finitude and transciency of things; everyone can observe the purposeful movement of things and events towards ends and goals; everyone can meditate on the meaning of what is meant by "God" and all can be led to consider what is implied in all these experiences, namely, that they point away from themselves to a Ground that makes them intelligible or reasonable. If, however, reason is reduced to purely formal proportions, as it has indeed been, and the reality it is to know is reduced to merely brute fact, then there can be no rational thought about matters of supreme importance. This explains why those who accept the narrow view of reason are forced either to declare religion meaningless or to attempt to salvage it by making it a matter of sheer faith — *fideism* — totally lacking in any sort of rationality. The truth is, as Whitehead claimed, brute fact can give no reasons.

What would you say are the main features and the underlying fallacies of the approaches adopted by prominent contemporary atheists?

Well, I think that many of those who reject God are really disappointed rationalists. They would like to have a coercive demonstration but they do not find any without flaws. There is a story about Russell's having been asked what he would say if, after his death, he found himself in the presence of God. His answer was, "you should have given me more evidence." Now that is an answer that is intelligible; someone is saying that there is insufficient evidence. I want, however, to distinguish that response from a view that is more difficult to cope with. I mean the view, largely represented by Sartre, according to which God *ought* not to be. The thesis is that if God is, man is not and only if God is not can man be. That is something new and it is based on the assumption that if man has to accept his existence from Another, he cannot truly be. In this regard, Sartre's account of man's project to be God is far more instructive than has been noticed. Sartre chooses as his conception of God the character of being *Causa sui* — cause of Himself — and it is this feature that is to be assumed by man in his project of being self-caused or creating himself. In short, the idea of God envisaged is tailored for the occasion. It is interesting to speculate about what would happen to man's project to be God were God to be thought of in terms of the "Suffering Servant." Such a conception would not work at all since it contains no hint of a being creating itself. The idea that man cannot be himself if God is real represents a different and more sophisticated denial of God than that to be found in discussion of proofs and disproofs for the existence of God. The Sartrean approach draws heavily on the absurdity of existence and the belief that whatever value there may be can be only as the result of its being created by human beings. This view may have had its place at a time when heroic resistance was called for and could be sustained only by the belief that human beings possessed the power that is reserved for God.

At present the most urgent problem is that of nihilism, the belief that nothing matters and that life is a kind of game in which the prize goes to the most clever. And to make matters worse, there are those who do not believe sufficiently in the truth of their own nihilism to live as if their outlook were true!

Is Positivism still present in contemporary philosophy?

Positivism as an official position seems to be dead, but whether this is true or not it seems clear that the outlook of classical British empiricism is still very much alive. A good indication of this survival is found in Ayer's attempt to solidify the theory that Pragmatism was no more than an American version of the empiricism. This view is totally erroneous. Peirce, Royce, James, Dewey all made a full-scale attack on the conception of *experience* bequeathed to us by Locke and Hume; as Dewey put it, that conception is itself decidedly unempirical!

Do you see a direct line from David Hume to contemporary British empiricism?

There can be no question. The major difference in the present situation is that while Hume had at his disposal only the traditional psychological logic known as the association of ideas, contemporary "empiricists" have the far more powerful tool of mathematical logic. The basic assumptions, however, remain and they are not likely to be questioned by those whose main concern is to preserve them intact.

12
MODERN PHILOSOPHY AND THE TURN TO BELIEF IN GOD
I
Professor Alvin Plantinga

Do you see a definite shift towards theism in modern thought?

I think there is a definite shift towards theism, but I don't think that nearly all philosophers are theists now. But theism is a lot more respectable and there's less hostility towards it and more receptiveness towards it.

And what could be the main reasons for this shift?

I don't know if anybody knows. I think people make guesses but nobody's got any real knowledge. It's correlated with other changes: there's more interest in religion generally now than there was say 20 to 30 years ago in the Western world and there is a sort of loosening up with respect to science, in ways of thinking about science. Those things all fit together though I certainly wouldn't know which caused which. Probably they're all due to some other cause.

Do you think the shift away from Mechanism in science had some effect?

Yes. That's not, at any rate, nearly so monolithically endorsed as it was 20 to 30 years ago. One can respectably dissent from it as one couldn't then. So I think there have been significant shifts.

What approach do you think would be most effective for a Christian thinker dealing with skeptics?

I think that the Christian community has to do a lot of different things; there is not just one thing to do. Certainly, the Christian community ought to engage in dialogue with skeptics, respond to skeptical objections and questions, respond to atheological arguments and objections to Christianity; and ought to produce arguments for God's existence. Arguments that will appeal to specific kinds of people and specific circumstances.

How can theism be presented most effectively in modern thought?

Well, it should be done in a thousand different ways. It should be done by way of arguments, by way of working out a Christian view of looking at things. It should be done in literature, it should be done in science. A Christian should produce alternatives to mechanistic biology for example. If indeed mechanistic biology is incompatible with Christian theism, then mechanistic biology needs revision, needs to be changed; there needs to be an alternative developed to it and the like. So there is no single thing that should be done: there's a whole host of things which people should work at.

(In response to questions on a previous occasion, Professor Plantinga had this to say.)

Could you comment on the rationality of belief in God?

As you can see from "Reason and Belief in God," I don't think argument for the existence of God is necessary any more than argument for the existence of other persons, the past, and material objects. Belief in God, like belief in these other things, is properly basic.

Is it conceivable that the universe always existed and that it had no Creator?

It is conceivable that matter is eternal and the universe is a product of chance — just as it is conceivable that the world popped into existence just 5 minutes ago, complete with all its apparent memories and traces of the past. But nothing follows from this conceivability, with respect to the propriety or impropriety of either theism or atheism, except that atheism isn't inconceivable.

What is your response to the problem of evil, to the dilemma posed by the existence of evil in a universe which, Christians believe, was created by an infinitely good God?

What I have to say on the argument from evil can be found in *God, Freedom and Evil* (Eerdmans); there's no way, I think, in which I can usefully summarize it, except to say, with Augustine, Aquinas and the Christian tradition that there is no contradiction in the joint assertion of (1) God is omnipotent, omniscient and wholly good and (2) there is evil; this can be shown by the free will defense. That, of course, leaves the question, "why *does* God permit all this evil?" We don't know. All we know is that it's perfectly possible that He could achieve a better overall total state of affairs by creating free beings and permitting evil than by not doing so; and perhaps that's why He permits it. What we do know is that He (God) has promised that all things work together for good, for those who love and follow Him.

13
MODERN PHILOSOPHY AND THE TURN TO BELIEF IN GOD
II
Professor Ralph McInerny

Do you see any definite turn towards theism in philosophy?

Oh yes. In the sense that it's a far different thing now than it was when I first came into philosophy, when the main drift in philosophical analysis seemed to be calling into question any kind of theism, of philosophical theism, let alone religion. Now that's no longer the case. There are very many, and generally well-received, philosophical attempts to show the reasonableness of theism and more than that, of religious beliefs. It's a very different picture. There are signs like the Society of Christian Philosophers. The idea behind that was that you didn't always want to be talking just about preliminary subjects, "does God exist?" and so forth, but could get into some of the more traditional and profound theological questions. Most meetings are well-attended; there are about three every year. So these are good signs. Sometimes you're not as happy as you'd like to be with some philosophical attitudes to theism even though they are favorable. For example, fideism is just unacceptable to the Roman Catholic tradition.

(In Professor Norman Malcolm) there was a case where Wittgenstein's development made taking religion and ethics seriously possible. And philosophers are as much influenced by that as they are by arguments. It's a perfectly human thing that, if a very powerful figure starts taking things seriously that had not been taken seriously for a while, this has a great deal of influence, independently of what he might be saying. It's that extra dimension of one's role as a teacher. It's best never to forget that people are not just hearing your lecture and your arguments. You're conveying a whole sense of what the use of the mind is like, what's possible and what isn't. And that disposes people. We're always being disposed one way or the other. For a long time exposure to higher education exposed people to the notion that there was something suspicious about religious behavior. They didn't know why but it was just in the atmosphere. And that has a very bad effect over a long period of time. It may be that no one ever heard a serious argument on behalf of that emphasis. But it begins to take moral courage to oppose that. Things are a little bit easier for Christian philosophers now and it's not as unrespectable as it used to be. But that has its dangers. You start getting too comfortable, doing the right deed for the wrong reason, being too quickly convinced that you have got a good argument and so on.

Do you think any specific events, like developments in science, are responsible for this turn to theism?

Maybe. But none of the philosophers I live with are influenced by that sort of thing. I think some of the developments in modal logic, like "possible worlds" ontologies, have had as much happy effect on philosophical theism as any scientific discovery. One thing, I think, has really changed relevant to your question on developments in science. For centuries both theists and non-theists felt that there were just water-tight arguments for or against something. But it's almost impossible now to find someone who thinks that there are arguments of that kind about substantive things. So what Thomas would call "demonstration" or what was apodictic reasoning for Aristotle, almost nobody has any confidence you can have arguments like that. That makes theism philosophically much easier than it was. Nobody is really saying that he has this air-tight refutation. That argument of Sartre's, that is about the last one I can recall, I mean his claim that the concept of God is totally incoherent. Now, it's as if, if you can't conclusively refute a position, then it's at least possible that that position is true. So nobody can say it is irrational to accept it. It's very rare that someone thinks he can really refute theism. So what you get are arguments against it but no one thinks of them as conclusive. That leaves theism wide open, in the sense that I can say I'm being reasonable.

What would you say are the underlying fallacies of contemporary atheism?

It's hard for me sometimes to regard atheism as an intellectual position. It's not a heavily worked out theory and so forth. It seems to me it's not a matter of winning arguments when it comes to people who are having difficulties about religion. One of the great contributions of Cardinal Newman in *The Grammar of Assent* and *The Apologia* was to draw our attention to how changes take place in peoples' lives. You want something to change their lives — not just change their minds. And the odd thing is that you can be convinced by an argument or stopped by a refutation and that doesn't convince you existentially. This is a longer process from the natural point of view, to change your life. And you don't do it by syllogism. Newman drew attention to this in the religious realm. Error has to be refuted. There's no doubt about that. But the thing is, that doesn't accomplish much. No one enjoys being refuted. It alienates them. Even when you are doing philosophy, you have to retain the realization that Christianity isn't "ours" in some kind of ownership, and you don't want to do anything to create a further obstacle to someone accepting it.

How could a Christian apologist be most effective?

Arguments are important. But more important is the way you argue, because it's the kind of triumphalism of an argument or refutation that again alienates people. The whole purpose of it is to draw people to the truth. Just to put them down is not going to be very helpful. Even in the intellectual life, even in universities, even in talking by way of arguments and that kind of thing, you have to keep in mind the more important form of persuasion; which is *being* something and not just talking in a funny fashion. That's what really moves people and again that's not irrelevant. As I mentioned before, when a very important philosopher will start taking certain questions seriously, it creates a whole new interest in them. Look at the greatly influential philosophers of the 20th century; Wittgenstein, Heidegger, Husserl. And you see the admiration that their students had for them. Clearly this was a more than intellectual kind of thing. [Cult-worship but] sometimes in a good sense. They are seeing something embodied. Wittgenstein when he wrote the *Tractatus* thought there wasn't anything for philosophy to do, so he quit his job. He was a consistent man. After the *Tractatus* he took a job teaching high school in Austria, something where there was a subject matter. But then he lost the conviction that he had put philosophy out of business, and he went back to teaching it.

Which one of the traditional arguments for God's existence do you find most persuasive?

The Third Way. Necessity and contingency.

Do you see the argument as presented in Aquinas as proving God's existence?

Yes, I think it does. I haven't seen any argument against it that obtains. But what stops people is always ... take just causality. If this is caused by that and that by that, why can't you go on forever? And there is a sense in which you can. For Thomas it was perfectly conceivable that the world had always been and that meant that there would always have been causes of that kind. He didn't think of the world as a necessary object. But it's making the transition from this cause and that effect and so on, taken singly, to that *kind* of thing and saying that *not everything* could be of that kind. Explain this one by that one and so on but why should there be *any* of them? I think that's the nerve of the proof. And I think when people see what the change of perspective is, it's pretty hard to resist.

But again you come to what does Thomas claim for a proof for the existence of God. He doesn't think it's going to change anybody's life. It's perfectly possible to accept the proof for the existence of God as sound and continue to lead a horrendous life. What you want is to bring the totality of life into conformity with those convictions and that's a moral task. I think the proofs are sound, but any conversion story I've read where the narrator holds that there are sound proofs for the existence of God will say that they didn't have much to do with his conversion. C.S. Lewis says this, Newman says this. But those arguments are important. They remove impediments to the faith. That is, if there is a sound

argument that God exists, that's an impediment removed to the claim that God became man in Jesus
Christ. Obviously if you don't think there is a God, the
Incarnation isn't going to make much sense. But it's a
big picture, it seems to me, and you don't want to claim
that the proof will do it, and that's why you have to use
the material in a particular way. If you are going to remove an obstacle, you don't want to create another
obstacle.

14
THE COMMON MAN AND GOD:
INTERVIEWS WITH THE "FINEST PHILOSOPHIC THINKER OF THE TWENTIETH CENTURY" (*Time*)
Bernard J. F. Lonergan

(Professor Lonergan preferred that the interviews which the editor had with him be reported not in interview form but in the context of an essay on his views on the issues under discussion.)

Simply in terms of the impact he has had on the world of philosophy, Bernard Lonergan has been one of the most influential philosophers of the twentieth century. What follows is a brief report on one aspect of his thought: the justification of belief in the existence and reality of God, particularly when the belief in question is held by one who has no pretense to philosophical sophistication. This report is based both on a limited study of the libraries of Lonergania available (of these, Lonergan's works and F.E. Crowe's commentaries have been of most help) as well as on interviews which the editor had with Lonergan.

Something must be said by way of introduction about Lonergan's influence in philosophy because he is well known to be a philosopher's philosopher whose thought is not easily accessible to "the common man." *Time* magazine said of him that he "is considered by many intellectuals to be the finest philosophic thinker of the 20th century."[1] One measure of the high regard in which he is held is the fact that there have been over one hundred and fifty doctoral dissertations written on his thought and, more important, he had the distinction of becoming the first philosopher to have witnessed, in his lifetime, an entire conference of fellow-philosophers convened solely in order to study his thought. At this congress, said *Time*, "77 of the best minds in Europe and the Americas gathered to examine Lonergan's profoundly challenging work."[2] *Insight*, his monumental work on human knowledge — which "has become a philosophic classic comparable in scope to Hume's 'Inquiry Concerning Human Understanding'"[3] — has had a phenomenal impact on philosophy in the Continent, in the United States, and in the British Isles. In *Insight*, "he develops an all-embracing theory of knowledge that includes every area of human understanding, not least of them the awareness of God."[4] Lonergan's significance for the Christian thinker has been impressively expressed in *Christianity Today*: "So who is Bernard J.F. Lonergan? Just possibly the most important orthodox philosopher-theologian of the century in the Anglo-American Christian world ... For evangelicals seriously interested in grappling with the critical problem of providing an adequate philosophical underpinning for an orthodox Christian faith in the contemporary world, Bernard Lonergan is a name to remember."[5]

Lonergan's main concern in *Insight* is to explore the structure of human knowledge, to discover how human beings know and the validity of their knowledge. Epistemology, in his work, is prior to metaphysics in the sense that he analyzes the methodology of knowing ("Insight as Activity," the first section of *Insight*) before analyzing the objects or content of knowlege ("Insight as Knowledge," the second section of *Insight*). As E.L. Mascall has said, in his title, Lonergan makes the point that "knowing always consists in penetrating beneath the immediately apprehended surface of an object into its intelligible being. Insight is *in*-sight, seeing *into* the observed object."[6] And in the introduction to *Insight* Lonergan writes, "Thoroughly understand what it is to understand, and not only will you understand the broad lines of all there is to be understood but you will possess a fixed base, an invariant pattern, opening upon all further developments of understanding."[7] In the body of the book he analyzes various types of knowledge and, as he said in one interview, he was "bringing out insight in mathematics, insight in physics, insight in common sense, insight in judgment, insight in the notion of being, insight in the notion of objectivity. All these lead to ... metaphysics."[8] Inquiry into the data of experience yields understanding, insight into it. In order to find out if what is understood is correct, it is subjected to reflection and this results in judgment. In the same interview Lonergan said, "The empiricists and the rationalists had no notion of judgment. By science you know conclusions. By understanding you know principles. But by judgement you know whether your principles are true and whether your conclusions are true. That's where judgement comes in ... The chapter 'Positions and Counter-Positions' in *Insight* describes my approach to philosophy. What you do is start out from the data. Your senses of act, your act of inquiry, your insight into the data, your formulations of your insights, your reflection on your formulation. You assemble the pros and cons for your insight and then it may dawn on you that you may have something. I tie things down by positions and counter-positions."[9] Lonergan argues for the truth of a position by showing that the counter-position leads to contradictions.

Lonergan's famous proof of God's existence is presented in chapter 19 of *Insight* ("General Transcendent Knowledge"). Proof, as Lonergan understands it, "is not some automatic process that results in a judgment ... But grasping it [a relevant virtually unconditioned] and making the consequent judgment is an immanent act of rational consciousness that each has to perform for himself and no one else can perform for him."[10] Unlike some traditional, time-tested approaches — to which his can be considered complementary — Lonergan begins with the subject, with "self-appropriation"; "know oneself" for then one can know all around one. Details of his argument cannot possibly be presented here (it appears in what has been described as "the most difficult chapter of his most difficult book") but some of the general themes can be touched on. "The existence of God," says Lonergan, "is known as the conclusion to an argument and, while such arguments are many, all of them, I believe, are included in the following general form. If the real is completely intelligible, God exists. But the real is completely intelligible. Therefore, God exists."[11] It is assumed that the real and being are one and the same because the former is not merely an "object of thought" but is also an "object of affirmation."[12] The fact that the mind can come to know being through what Lonergan calls "intelligent grasp and reasonable affirmation"[13] — and that the mind can know truth is one of Lonergan's fundamental assumptions, an assumption which cannot be challenged without self-contradiction — makes it clear that being is intelligible. And, if the questioning dynamism of the mind is permitted in its entirety, it becomes clear too that being is completely intelligible. Since "material reality" is not completely intelligible in itself it has to be grounded in something which has "an intelligibility that is at once complete and real."[14] This complete and real intelligibility is identified "with the unrestricted act of understanding that possesses the properties of God and accounts for everything else."[15]

The dynamic and unrestricted nature of man's openness to questioning implies a corresponding complete intelligibility. Lonergan said in an interview, "Anything we learn comes through questions and answers.

And where do the questions come from? The number of questions you can ask is unlimited. And, consequently, there has to be an intelligible world. What makes the world intelligible? What's the one basis on which you can assume that the world is intelligible? It's not just a matter of fact. The atheist can say that it's a matter of fact. That's not being intelligent, reasonable. Merely a matter of fact? It is 'I refuse to think. I refuse to inquire.' That's all it means. That's what comes from being an atheist. Why do you ask the questions? Are your questions intelligent or unintelligent? If they are intelligent you are presupposing something intelligible, to be understood. The only argument that has a sure foundation is based upon your understanding yourself, your own concerns, your own questions. They're your questions. You have to live with them and give the answers. Honest answers or crooked answers. That's up to you to decide."[16] And in an address he gave he said, " ... if human knowing consists in asking and answering questions, if ever further questions arise, if the further questions are given honest answers then, as I have argued elsewhere at some length, we can and do arrive at knowledge of God."[17]

Lonergan's other famous book is *Method in Theology*. At the risk of gross over-simplification it could be said that in *Insight* he concentrates on the knowledge of God attained through man's "upward" intellectual movement while in *Method* he emphasizes the knowledge of God that comes as a gift, from "above downwards," with man being drawn in love to the transcendent mystery that is God. "Religion," he writes in *Method*, "is the ... word God speaks to us by flooding our hearts with his love."[18] The question of God recurs "in a new form. For now it is primarily a question of decision. Will I love him in return or will I refuse? ... Only secondarily does there arise the questions of God's existence and nature, and they are the questions either of the lover seeking to know him or of the unbeliever seeking to escape him."[19] In an interview Lonergan confirmed that *Insight* and *Method* complemented each other and, he said, "even when I was doing the first one I intended *Method in Theology* all along."[20]

The focal point of this report is what Lonergan has to say about the basis of a belief in God which is not intellectually articulated. In *Insight* he writes, " ... because it is difficult to know what our knowing is, it also is difficult to know what our knowledge of God is. But just as our knowing is prior to an analysis of knowledge and far easier than it, so too our knowledge of God is both earlier and easier than any attempt to give it formal expression."[21] And in *Philosophy of God, and Theology*, he writes, "I do not think it difficult to establish God's existence. I do think it a life-long labor to analyze and refute all the objections that philosophers have thought up against the existence of God. But I see no pressing need for every student of religion to penetrate into that labyrinth and then work his way out."[22] Asked further about such objections, in an interview, Lonergan responded, "The difficulty with the question of the existence of God is answering the objections of the philosophers. You have to understand all of the philosophers to be able to answer all of their objections. That's a big job. And, [this humorously] as far as I can see, they're crazy, most of them must be wrong. They never agree with one another."[23] Asked what would justify the ordinary man in believing in God without studying the philosophers, he said, "It depends on if he has difficulties or not. If he has difficulties and not merely difficulties but doubts. Newman said ten thousand difficulties do not make a doubt. A doubt is existential. A difficulty is intellectual, something you don't understand. The thing I do in *Method* is this: we have questions which have answers. But why should our understanding provide a real answer to these questions? What makes us think the world is intelligible? What's the condition of the possibility of the world being intelligible? Does it exist? Is that so? And we have sufficient evidence that it is so. What is the condition of the possibility of our having sufficient evidence that it is so. What is the condition of the possibility of our having sufficient evidence of being wrong in saying that something actually exists? We're not merely looking at it. We say this is right and that is wrong. Man is certain of it. What's the condition of the possibility of my feeling what is right or wrong corresponding with what is really right or wrong? How could that be possible? Well, you need a First Cause Who is Intelligence Itself and Truth Itself and Justice Itself and lives up to that in all He does. And in making us, too, the way we are built, to ask these questions. As Plato and Mr. Voegelin discovered, the reason we search for the Ground of Being is that the Ground of Being is moving us to this search."[24]

About the conditions of a believer being certain in his belief in God he said, "The discernment of spirits. You make an election in a retreat. And you have all sorts of doubts and worries. And you make an office election. And you have great peace of soul. In the one case you are like the two disciples walking to Emmaus, saying 'We were hoping He will restore Israel but now everything's all finished.' Later, after our Lord has spoken to them, they say, 'Our hearts burnt within us when He explained what's on the way.' People say 'I have peace of soul.' That's a good sign. What have the philosophers got? Well, you ask a question. Nature, according to Aristotle, is an immanent principle of movement and rest. In man, raising questions is the principle of movement; answering them satisfactorily, the principle of rest. At first the principle of movement. Do you know the answer? Let's wait till you get rest. Do you give the wrong answer? You're getting further questions all along. You make a judgment. Then all sorts of difficulties start cropping up in your mind. You change your judgment and there are no difficulties at all: you rest. [So peace of soul is a strong indication of one's being right or wrong?] Yes. It's a sign that you can rest. You have rest, you are resting. [By their fruits you shall know them?] Yes. [But it's also possible to find rest in a wrong conclusion?] Yes. But that's because you've deceived yourself. [How can you find out whether or not you have deceived yourself?] You know it. The thing is, there are all sorts of things which could be so. How do I know you're not a neurotic? I don't. How do I know I'm not? I don't. The existence of God is beyond reasonable doubt. You can be certain you're not mistaken ... by judgment you know whether your principles are true and your conclusions are true. Can judgment be certain? Why not? Are you sitting there? Are you talking? Are you certain of that?"[25]

Asked about the theological roots of unbelief, of why philosophers can fail to apprehend fundamental truths, Lonergan said, "Well, there's such a thing as scotosis. In *Insight*, Chapter 6, I talk of scotosis, the darkening of intellect, the effects of original sin, the weakening of will, the propensity to evil. These things have been around for a long time ... the thing is, why did Adam sin? If there were a reason, not merely an excuse, but a reason, it wouldn't have been a sin. So, when you ask me why these people talk and think the way they do, I say: It's the darkening of intellect due to sin."[26]

Bernard Lonergan has also made an important contribution to Christology and to Trinitarian theology. Asked if he considered belief in the divinity of Christ to be essential to Christianity, he said, "Do you think we were saved by a preacher? That was the argument at Nicea. We weren't saved by a preacher. That was a point made by Athanasius. Your eternal destiny is not decided by a preacher."[27] About contemporary discussions in Christology he said, "People think they can give their own meaning to 'person.' That isn't the question. That isn't what the Church defined. That isn't the conclusion derived from Scripture and Tradition. People don't know the Councils. They think all this should be brushed aside. They know better. There's no evidence that they know better. You can't be a human person and be a divine Person. It's one Person Who has a human nature and a divine nature, a human consciousness and a divine consciousness. If you were both a man and a dog, you know yourself as a man by your human consciousness and you know yourself as a dog by your dog consciousness. Except it couldn't happen to you. You need an infinite Subject to have this."[28] When asked to what he attributed the contemporary confusion in Christology he said, "Loose thinking: the modern age, we're different ... this sort of nonsense."[29]

Notes

1 "The Answer is the Question," *Time*, April 20, 1970, p.65.
2 Ibid.
3 "A Great Christian Mind," *Newsweek*, April 20, 1970, p.75.
4 "The Answer is the Question," op. cit., p.65.
5 "Bernard J.F. Lonergan: A Name to Remember," *Christianity Today* April 24, 1970, p.38.
6 E.L. Mascall, *The Openness of Being*, The Westminster Press, Philadelphia, 1971, p.84.
7 Bernard J.F. Lonergan, *Insight*, Harper & Row, San Francisco, 1957, p.xxviii.

8 Personal Interview with Bernard Lonergan (I), August 1981.

9 Ibid.

10 Lonergan, op. cit., p.672.

11 Ibid.

12 Ibid., p.673.

13 Ibid., p.657.

14 Ibid., p.676.

15 Ibid., p.675.

16 Personal Interview with Bernard Lonergan (II), August 21, 1982.

17 Bernard J.F. Lonergan, *Natural Knowledge of God*, 1968.

18 Bernard J.F. Lonergan, *Method in Theology*, Herder & Herder and Seabury, 1972, p.112.

19 Ibid., p.116.

20 Personal Interview with Bernard Lonergan (I).

21 *Insight*, op. cit., p.683.

22 Bernard J.F. Lonergan, *Philosophy of God, and Theology*, 1973, pp.55-56.

23 Personal Interview with Bernard Lonergan (I).

24 Ibid.

25 Ibid.

26 Ibid.

27 Personal Interview with Bernard Lonergan (II).

28 Ibid.

29 Ibid.

15
REASON AND BELIEF IN GOD
Professor Alvin Plantinga

Belief in God is the heart and center of the Christian religion — as it is of Judaism and Islam. Of course Christians may disagree, at least in emphasis, as to how to think of God; for example, some may emphasize His hatred of sin, others, His love of His creatures. Furthermore, one may find, even among professedly Christian theologians, super-sophisticates who proclaim the liberation of Christianity from belief in God, seeking to replace it by trust in "Being Itself" or the "Ground of Being" or some such thing. It remains true, however, that belief in God is the foundation of Christianity.

In this paper I want to discuss a connected constellation of questions: does the believer-in-God accept the existence of God by *faith*? Is belief in God contrary to reason, unreasonable, irrational? Must one have *evidence* to be rational or reasonable in believing in God? Suppose belief in God is *not* rational; does that matter? And what about proofs of God's existence? Many Reformed or Calvinist thinkers and theologians have taken a jaundiced view of natural theology, thought of as the attempt to give proofs or arguments for the existence of God; are they right? What underlies this hostility to an undertaking that, on the surface, at least, looks perfectly harmless and possibly useful? These are some of the questions I propose to discuss. They fall under the general rubric *faith and reason*, if a general rubric is required.

I believe Reformed or Calvinist thinkers have had important things to say on these topics and that their fundamental insights here are correct. What they say, however, has been for the most part unclear, ill-focused and unduly inexplicit. I shall try to remedy these ills; I shall try to state and clearly develop their insight; and I shall try to connect these insights with more general epistemological considerations.

What the Reformers meant to hold is that it is entirely right, rational, reasonable and proper to believe in God without any evidence or argument at all; in this respect belief in God resembles belief in the past, in the existence of other persons, and in the existence of material objects. I shall try to state and clearly articulate this claim, and defend it against objections.

My first topic, then, is the evidentialist objection to theistic belief. Many philosophers — W.K. Clifford,[1] Brand Blanshard,[2] Bertrand Russell,[3] Michael Scriven,[4] and Anthony Flew,[5] to name a few — have argued that belief in God is irrational or unreasonable or not rationally acceptable or intellectually irresponsible or somehow noetically below par because, as they say, there is *insufficient evidence* for it. Bertrand Russell was once asked what he would say if, after dying, he were brought into the presence of God and asked why he hadn't been a believer. Russell's reply: "I'd say, not enough evidence, God! Not enough evidence!"[6]

But how shall we construe 'theistic belief' here? I have been speaking of 'belief in God'; but this isn't entirely accurate. For the subject under discussion is not really the rational acceptability of belief *in* God, but the rationality of belief that God exists — that there *is* such a person as God.

And belief in God is not at all the same thing as belief that there is such a person as God. To believe that God exists is simply to accept as true a certain proposition: perhaps the proposition that there is a personal

being who has created the world, who has no beginning, and who is perfect in wisdom, justice, knowledge
and power. According to the book of James, the devils
do that, and they tremble. The devils do not believe *in*
God, however; and belief in God is quite another matter.
One who repeats the words of the Apostles' Creed — "I
believe in God the Father Almighty, ..." and means
what he says is not simply announcing the fact that he
accepts a certain proposition as true; much more is involved than that. Belief in God means *trusting* God, accepting God, accepting His purposes, committing one's
life to Him and living in His presence. To the believer
the entire world speaks of God. Great mountains, surging oceans, verdant forests, blue sky and bright sunshine, friends and family, love in its many forms and
various manifestations — the believer sees these things
and many more as gifts from God. The universe thus
takes on a personal cast for him; the fundamental truth
about reality is truth about a *Person*. So believing in God
is indeed more than accepting the proposition that God
exists. But if it is more than that, it is also at least that.
One can't sensibly believe in God and thank Him for the
mountains without believing that there *is* such a person
to be thanked, and that He is in some way responsible
for the mountains. Nor can one trust in God and commit oneself to Him without believing that He exists; as
the author of Hebrews says, "He who would come to
God must believe that He is and that He is a rewarder of
those who seek Him" (Hebrews 11:6).

So belief in God must be distinguished from the
belief that God exists. Having made this distinction,
however, I shall ignore it for the most part, using 'belief
in God' as a synonym for 'belief that there is such a
person as God.' The question I want to address, therefore, is the question whether belief in God — belief in
the existence of God — is rationally acceptable. But what
is it to believe or assert that God exists? Just which belief

is it into the rational acceptability of which I propose to inquire? Which God do I mean to speak of? The answer, in brief, is: the God of Abraham, Isaac and Jacob; the God of Jewish and Christian revelation: the God of the *Bible*.

To believe that God exists, therefore, is first of all to hold a *belief* of a certain sort — an existential belief. To assert that God exists is to make an *assertion*. It is to answer at the most basic level, the ontological question 'what is there?' This may seem excessively obvious. I wouldn't so much as mention it, were it not for the fact that some philosophers and theologians seem to disagree. Oddly enough, they seem to use the phrase 'belief in God' and even 'belief that God exists' in such a way that to believe in God is not to hold any such existential beliefs at all.

As *I* use the phrase 'belief in God,' however, that phrase denotes a belief, not a resolve or the adoption of a policy. And the assertion that God exists is an *existential* assertion, not the assertion of an intention to carry out a certain policy, behavioral or otherwise. To believe or assert that God exists is to believe or assert that there exists a being of a certain very special sort.

What sort? Some contemporary theologians, under the baneful influence of Kant, apparently hold that the name 'God,' as used by Christians and others, denotes an *idea*, or a *concept* or a *mental construct* of some kind.

Now these are puzzling suggestions. And when Christians say that God has created the world, for example, are they really claiming that an image or imaginative construct, whatever precisely that may be, has created the world? That seems at best preposterous. In any event, the belief I mean to identify and discuss is not the belief that there exists some sort of imaginative construct or mental construction or anything of the sort. It is instead the belief, first, that there exists a *person* of a certain sort — a being who acts, holds beliefs, and has aims and purposes. This person, secondly, is immaterial, exists *a se*, is perfect in goodness, knowledge and power, and is such that the world depends on him for its existence.

Now many objections have been put forward to belief in God. First, there is the claim that there really *isn't* any such thing as belief in God, because the sentence "God exists" is, strictly speaking, nonsense.[7] This is the positivists' contention that such sentences as "God exists" are unverifiable and hence "cognitively meaningless" (to use their charming phrase), in which case they altogether fail to express propositions. On this view those who claim to believe in God are in the pitiable position of claiming to believe a proposition that as a matter of fact doesn't so much as exist. This objection, fortunately, has retreated into the obscurity it so richly deserves and I shall say no more about it.[8]

Secondly, there is the claim that belief in God is *internally inconsistent* in that it is impossible, in the broadly logical sense, that there be any such person as theists say God is. For example, theists say that God is a person who has no body but nonetheless acts in the world; some philosophers have retorted that the idea of a bodiless person is impossible, and the idea of a bodiless person *acting* is *obviously* impossible. Some versions of some of these objections are of great interest, but I don't propose to discuss them here. Let me just record my opinion that none of them is at all compelling; so far as I can see, the concept of God is perfectly coherent. Thirdly, some critics have urged that the existence of God is incompatible with other beliefs that are plainly true and typically accepted by theists. The most widely urged objection to theistic belief, the deductive argument from evil, falls into this category. According to this objection, the existence of an omnipotent, omniscient, and wholly good God is *logically* incompatible with the presence of evil in the world — a presence, conceded and indeed insisted upon by theists.[9] For their part, theists have argued that there is no inconsistency here;[10] and I think the present consensus, even among those who urge some form of the argument from evil, is that the deductive form of the argument from evil is unsuccessful.

And of course Flew, along with Russell, Clifford and many others, holds that in fact there aren't sufficient grounds or evidence for belief in God. Flew, therefore, seems to endorse the following two principles:

> (A) It is irrational or unreasonable to accept theistic belief in the absence of sufficient evidence or reasons

and

> (B) We have no evidence or at any rate not sufficient evidence of the proposition that God exists.

What about the various arguments that have been proposed for the existence of God — the traditional cosmological and teleological arguments for example? What about the versions of the *moral* argument as developed, for example, by A.E. Taylor and more recently by Robert Adams? What about the broadly inductive or probabilistic arguments developed by F.R. Tennant, C.S. Lewis, E.L. Mascall, Basil Mitchell, Richard Swinburne, and others? What about the ontological argument in its contemporary version? Don't any of these provide evidence? Notice: the question is not whether these arguments, taken singly or in combinations, constitute *proofs* of God's existence; no doubt they don't. The question is only whether someone might be rationally justified in believing in the existence of God on the basis of the alleged evidence offered by them; and that's a radically different question.

Consider the ontological argument for example; in its contemporary formulations.[11]

This argument is just as satisfactory, I think, as any

serious argument philosophers have proposed for any important conclusion, as satisfactory as Wittgenstein's private language argument, or Quine's argument for the radical indeterminacy of translation, or Armstrong's argument that mental events are identical with brain events, or Kripke's argument that they *aren't* identical with brain events. Of course you may think none of these arguments is *successful*; and perhaps you are right. Still, a philosopher who accepts, say, the conclusion that there can't be a private language on the basis of Wittgenstein's argument does not thereby stand convicted of irrationality. And the ontological argument provides as good grounds for the existence of God as does any serious philosophical argument for any important philosophical conclusion. I am therefore inclined to think (B) false.

At present, however, I'm interested in the objector's other premise — the claim that it is irrational or unreasonable to accept theistic belief in the absence of evidence or reasons. Why suppose *that's* true? Why should we think a theist must have evidence, or reason to think there *is* evidence, if he is not to be irrational? Why not suppose, instead, that he is entirely within his epistemic rights in believing in God's existence even if he has no argument or evidence at all? This is what I want to investigate. Suppose we begin by asking what the objector means by describing a belief as *irrational*. What is the force of his claim that theistic belief is irrational, and how is it to be understood? The first thing to see is that this objection is rooted in a *normative* view. It lays down conditions that must be met by anyone whose system of beliefs is *rational*; and here 'rational' is to be taken as a normative or evaluative term.

Thus, lightly armed, suppose we return to the evidentialist objector. Does he mean to hold that the theist without evidence is violating some intellectual obligation? If so, which one? Does he claim, for example, that

the theist is violating his *ultima facie* intellectual obligation in thus believing? Perhaps he thinks anyone who
believes in God without evidence is violating his all-
things-considered intellectual duty. This however,
seems unduly harsh. What about the 14 year old theist
brought up to believe in God in a community where
everyone believes? This 14 year old theist, we may suppose, doesn't believe in God on the basis of evidence.
He has never heard of the cosmological, teleological or
ontological arguments; in fact no one has ever presented him with any evidence at all. And although he
has often been told about God, he doesn't take that
testimony as evidence, he doesn't reason thus: everyone around here says God loves us and cares for us;
most of what everyone around here says is true: so
probably *that's* true. Instead, he simply believes what
he's taught. Is he violating an all-things-considered intellectual duty? Surely not. And what about the mature
theist — Thomas Aquinas, let's say — who thinks he
does have adequate evidence. Shall we suppose he's violating an all-things-considered intellectual duty here? I
should think not. So construed, the objector's contention is totally implausible.

Finally, while we may perhaps agree that what I
believe is not *directly* within my control, some of my
beliefs are indirectly within my control, at least in part.
First, what I accept has a long term influence upon what
I believe. If I refuse to accept belief in God, and if I try to
ignore or suppress my tendency to believe, then perhaps eventually I will no longer believe. And as Pascal
pointed out, there are other ways to influence one's beliefs. Presumably then, the evidentialist objector could
hold that it is my *prima facie* duty not to accept belief in
God without evidence, and to do what I can to bring it
about that I no longer believe. Although it is not within
my power now to cease believing now, there may be a
series of actions, such that I can now take the first, and

after taking the first, will be able to take the second, and so on; and after taking the whole series of actions I will no longer believe in God. Perhaps the objector thinks it is my *prima facie* duty to undertake whatever sort of regimen will at some time in the future result in my not believing without evidence. Perhaps I should attend a Universalist Unitarian Church, for example, and consort with members of the Rationalist Society of America. Perhaps I should read a lot of Voltaire and Bertrand Russell and Thomas Paine, eschewing St. Augustine and C.S. Lewis and of course, the Bible. Even if I can't, now, stop believing without evidence, perhaps there are other actions I can take, such that if I were to take them, then at some time in the future I won't be in this deplorable condition.

But of course the crucial question here is this: *why* does the objector think these things? Why does he think there *is* a *prima facie* obligation to try not to believe in God without evidence? Or why does he think that to do so is to be in a deplorable condition? Why isn't it permissible and quite satisfactory to believe in God without any evidence — proof or argument — at all? Presumably the objector does not mean to suggest that *no* propositions can be believed or accepted without evidence; for if you have evidence for *every* proposition you believe then (granted certain plausible assumptions about the formal properties of the evidence relation) you will believe infinitely many propositions; and no one has time, these busy days, for that. So presumably *some* propositions can properly be believed and accepted without evidence. Well, why not belief in God? Why is it not entirely acceptable, desirable, right, proper, and rational to accept belief in God without any argument or evidence whatever?

I shall give what I take to be the evidentialist objector's answer to these questions; I shall argue that his answer is not in the least compelling and that the prospects for his project are not bright.

In rejecting natural theology, therefore, these Reformed thinkers mean to say first of all that the propriety or rightness of belief in God in no way depends upon the success or availability of the sort of theistic arguments that form the natural theologian's stock in trade. I think this is their central claim here, and their central insight. As these Reformed thinkers see things, one who takes belief in God as basic is not thereby violating any epistemic duties or revealing a defect in his noetic structure; quite the reverse. The correct or proper way to believe in God, they thought, was not on the basis of arguments from natural theology or anywhere else; the correct way is to take belief in God as basic.

Is Belief in God Properly Basic?

According to the Reformed Thinkers discussed the answer is "yes indeed." I enthusiastically concur in this contention; and I shall try to clarify and develop this view and defend it against some objections. I shall argue first, that one who holds that belief in God is properly basic is not thereby committed to the view that just about *anything* is; I shall argue secondly that even if belief in God is accepted as basic, it is not *groundless*; I shall argue thirdly that one who accepts belief in God (or another belief) as basic may nonetheless be open to arguments *against* that belief; and finally I shall argue that the view I'm defending is not plausibly thought of as a species of *fideism*.

The fact is, I think, that ... [no] ... revealing necessary and sufficient condition for proper basicality follows from clearly self-evident premises by clearly acceptable arguments. And hence the proper way to arrive at such a criterion is, broadly speaking, *inductive*. We must assemble examples of beliefs and conditions such that the former are obviously properly basic in the latter, and examples of beliefs and conditions such that the former are obviously *not* properly basic in the latter. We must then frame hypotheses as to the necessary and sufficient conditions of proper basicality and test these hypotheses by reference to those examples. Under the right conditions, for example, it is clearly rational to believe that you see a human person before you: a being who has thoughts and feelings, who knows and believes things, who makes decisions and acts. It is clear, furthermore, that you are under no obligation to reason to this belief from others you hold; under those conditions that belief is properly basic for you. But then ... [the idea that "For any proposition *A* and person *S*, A is properly basic for *S* if and only if *A* is incorrigible for *S* or self-evident to *S*"] ... must be mistaken; the belief in question, under those circumstances, is properly basic, though neither self-evident nor incorrigible for you. Similarly, you may seem to remember that you had breakfast this morning, and perhaps you know of no reason to suppose your memory is playing you tricks. If so, you are entirely justified in taking that belief as basic. Of course it isn't properly basic on the criteria offered by classical foundationalists; but that fact counts not against you but against those criteria.

Accordingly, criteria for proper basicality must be reached from below rather than above; they should not be presented *ex cathedra* but argued to and tested by a relevant set of examples. But there is no reason to assume, in advance, that everyone will agree on the examples. The Christian will of course suppose that belief in God is entirely proper and rational; if he doesn't accept this belief on the basis of other propositions, he will conclude that it is basic for him and quite properly so. Followers of Bertrand Russell and Madelyn Murray O'Hare may disagree; but how is that relevant? Must my criteria, or those of the Christian community, conform to their examples? Surely not. The Christian community is responsible to *its* set of examples and not to theirs.

The *Ground* of Belief in God

My claim is that belief in God is properly basic; it doesn't follow, however, that it is *groundless*. Let me explain. Suppose we consider perceptual beliefs, memory beliefs, and beliefs ascribing mental states to other persons: such beliefs as

(C) I see a tree

(D) I had breakfast this morning

and

(E) That person is in pain.

Although beliefs of this sort are typically taken as basic, it would be a mistake to describe them as *groundless*. Upon having experiences of a certain sort, I believe that I am perceiving a tree. In this typical case I do not hold this belief on the basis of other beliefs; it is nonetheless not groundless. My having that characteristic sort of experience — to use Professor Chisholm's language, my being appeared treely to — plays a crucial role in the formation of that belief. It also plays a crucial role in its *justification*. Let's say that a belief is *justified* for a person at a time if (a) he is violating no epistemic duties and is within his epistemic rights in accepting it then, and (b) his noetic structure is not defective by virtue of his then accepting it.[12] Then my being appeared to in this characteristic way (together with other circumstances) is what confers on me the right to hold the belief in question; this is what justifies me in accepting it. We could say, if we wish, that this experience is what justifies me in holding it; this is the *ground* of my justification, and, by extension, the ground of the belief itself.

So, being appropriately appeared to, in the perceptual case, is not sufficient for justification; some further condition — a condition hard to state in detail — is clearly necessary. The central point, here, however, is that a belief is properly basic only in certain conditions; these conditions are, we might say, the ground of its justification and, by extension, the ground of the belief itself. In this sense, basic beliefs are not, or are not necessarily, *groundless* beliefs.

Now similar things may be said about belief in God. When the Reformers claim that this belief is properly basic, they do not mean to say, of course, that there are no justifying circumstances for it, or that it is in that sense groundless or gratuitous. Quite the contrary. Calvin holds that God "reveals and daily discloses himself in the whole workmanship of the universe," and the divine art "reveals itself in the innumerable and yet distinct and well ordered variety of the heavenly host." God has so created us that we have a tendency or disposition to see His hand in the world about us. More precisely, there is in us a disposition to believe propositions of the sort *this flower was created by God or this vast and intricate universe was created by God* when we contemplate the flower or behold the starry heavens or think about the vast reaches of the universe.

Calvin recognizes, at least implicitly, that other sorts of conditions may trigger this disposition. Upon reading the Bible, one may be impressed with a deep sense that God is speaking to him. Upon having done what I know is cheap, or wrong, or wicked I may feel guilty in God's sight and form the belief *God disapproves of what I've done.* Upon confession and repentance, I may feel forgiven, forming the belief *God forgives me for what I've done.* A person in grave danger may turn to God, asking for His protection and help; and of course he or she then has the belief that God is indeed able to hear and help if He sees fit. When life is sweet and satisfying, a spontaneous sense of gratitude may well up within the soul; someone in this condition may thank and praise the Lord for his goodness, and will of course have the accompanying belief that indeed the Lord is to be thanked and praised.

There are therefore many conditions and circumstances that call forth belief in God: guilt, gratitude, danger, a sense that He speaks, perception of various parts of the universe. A complete job would explore the phenomenology of all these conditions and of more besides. This is a large and important topic; but here I can only point to the existence of these conditions.

Is Argument Irrelevant to Basic Belief in God?

First, suppose someone accepts belief in God as basic. Doesn't it follow that he will hold this belief in such a way that no argument could move him, or cause him to give it up? Won't he hold it come what may, in the teeth of any evidence or argument with which he could be presented? Doesn't he thereby adopt a posture in which argument and other rational methods of settling disagreement are implicitly declared irrelevant? Surely not. Suppose someone accepts

(F) There is such a person as God

as basic; it doesn't for a moment follow that he will regard argument irrelevant to this belief of his, or that he is committed in advance to rejecting every argument against it. It could be, for example, that he accepts (F) as basic, but also accepts as basic some propositions from which, by arguments whose corresponding conditionals he accepts as basic, it follows that (F) is false. What happens if he is apprised of this fact perhaps by being presented with an argument from those propositions to the denial of (F)? Presumably some change is called for. If he accepts these propositions more strongly than (F), presumably he will give the latter up.

Similarly, suppose someone believes there is no God, but also believes some propositions from which belief in God follows by argument forms he accepts. Presented with an argument from these propositions to the proposition that God exists, such a person may give up his atheism and accept belief in God. On the other hand, his atheistic belief may be stronger than his belief in some of the propositions in question, or his belief in their conjunction. It is possible, indeed, that he *knows* these propositions, but believes some of them less firmly than he believes that there is no God; in that case if you present him with a valid argument from these propositions to the proposition that God exists, you may cause him to give up a proposition he knows to be true. It is thus possible to reduce the extent of someone's knowledge by giving him a sound argument from premises he knows to be true.

Many believers in God have been brought up to believe, but then encountered potential defeaters. They have read books by skeptics, been apprised of the atheological argument from evil, heard it said that theistic belief is just a matter of wish fulfillment or only a means whereby one socio-economic class keeps another in bondage. These circumstances constitute potential defeaters for justification in theistic belief. If the believer is to remain justified, something further is called for — something that *prima facie* defeats the defeaters. Various forms of theistic apologetics serve this function (among others). Thus the *Free Will Defense* is a defeater for the Atheological argument from evil, which is a potential defeater for theistic belief. Suppose I am within my epistemic rights in accepting belief in God as basic and am then presented with a plausible argument — by Democritus, let's say — for the conclusion that the existence of God is logically incompatible with the existence of evil. (Let's add that I am strongly convinced that there *is* evil.) This is a potential defeater for my being rational in accepting theistic belief. What is required, if I am to continue to believe rationally, is a defeater for the defeater. Perhaps I discover a flaw in Democritus' argument, or perhaps I have it on reliable authority that Augustine, say, has discovered a flaw in the argument; then I am once more justified in my original belief.

The Reformed epistemologist isn't a fideist at all

with respect to belief in God. He doesn't hold that there is any conflict between faith and reason here; and he doesn't even hold that we can't attain this fundamental truth by reason; he holds, instead, that it is among the deliverances of reason.

As the Reformed thinker sees things, being self-evident, or incorrigible, or evident to the senses is not a necessary condition of proper basicality. He goes on to add that belief in God is properly basic. He is not thereby committed to the idea that just any or nearly any belief is properly basic, even if he lacks a criterion for proper basicality. Nor is he committed to the view that argument is irrelevant to belief in God, if such belief is properly basic. Furthermore belief in God, like other properly basic beliefs, is not groundless or arbitrary; it is grounded in justification conferring conditions. Finally, the Reformed view that belief in God is properly basic is not felicitously thought of as a version of fideism.

NOTES

1 "The Ethics of Belief," in *Lectures and Essays* (London, Macmillan, 1879), pp. 345 f.
2 *Reason and Belief* (London: Allen & Unwin, 1974), pp. 400 f.
3 "Why I am not a Christian," in *Why I am not a Christian* (New York: Simon & Schuster, 1957), pp. 3 ff.
4 *Primary Philosophy* (New York: McGraw-Hill, 1966), pp. 87 ff.
5 Flew, A.G.N., *The Presumption of Atheism* (London: Pemberton Publishing Co. 1976), pp. 22 f.

6 Salmon, Wesley, "Religion & Science: A New Look at Hume's Dialogues," *Philosophical Studies*, 33, 1978, p. 176.

7 Ayer, A. J., *Language, Truth and Logic*.

8 For further discussion of positivism and its dreaded verifiability criterion of meaning, see my book, *God and Other Minds* (Ithaca, New York: Cornell University Press, 1968), pp. 156-168.

9 This claim has been made by Epicurus, perhaps by David Hume, by some of the French Encyclopedists, by F. H. Bradley, J. McTaggart, and many others. For an influential contemporary statement of the claim, see J. Mackie, "Evil and Omnipotence," *Mind*, 1955, pp. 200 ff.

10 C.S. Lewis, *The Problem of Pain*; and see my *God and Other Minds*, pp. 115-155, *The Nature of Necessity* (Oxford: The Clarendon Press, 1974), chapter 9. A more accessible form of the argument can be found in my *God, Freedom and Evil*, (New York: Harper & Co., 1974 republished in 1979 by W. B. Eerdman's), pp. 1-50.

11 See e.g., my book, *The Nature of Necessity* (Oxford, 1974), chapter X.

12 I do not mean to suggest, of course, that if a person believes a true proposition and is justified (in this sense) in believing it, then it follows that he *knows* it; that is a different (and stronger) sense of the term.

PART III

APOLOGETICS

AND

THEOLOGY

INTRODUCTION
Bill Craig

The average layman would no doubt think that while philosophers and scientists stand opposed to the historic Christian faith, theologians are biased in favor of it. If so, then the foregoing sections must have proved something of a surprise to him, for it is evident that the Christian world and life view has resurged as a viable alternative to post-Enlightenment secularism. But he would be probably even more surprised to discover that, far from being biased in favor of the historic Christian faith, twentieth century theology has in the main deserted it, so that it is theologians themselves who have spearheaded the attack on biblical Christianity. Christian in name only, modern theology has plunged blindly this way and that into Heideggerian existentialism, Schelling's pantheism, Whiteheadian panentheism, neo-liberal deism, Wittgensteinian mysticism, as well as universalism, unitarianism, Marxism, even atheism. The layman can only shake his head in bewilderment at the prospect of Ogden's Christ-less Christianity or Braun and Solle's atheistic Christianity! It was theologians who told us in the sixties that "God is dead" and attempted to build a "theology" around this insight. Fortunately, the layman had too much common sense to be fooled by such chicanery, and the movement — the only indigenous theology which the United States can claim, by the way — faded away as quickly as it appeared. The layman sees through the theological mumbo-jumbo and realizes that if the God described in the Bible does not exist, then Christianity is simply false

and we may as well forget about it. The contrast between the thinking of neo-liberal theology and that of
the average man was poignantly brought home to me by
an editorial in a recent *Bulletin of the Council on the Study
of Religion*, a publication for professors of theology and
religion. The author, after observing that most theologians will never have to make a public confession of
faith at an Inquisition, commented,

> The closest most of us ever come to presenting
> a public image of our profession is an occa-
> sional encounter, on an airplane flight, per-
> haps, going to an American Academy of Re-
> ligion/ Society of Biblical Literature annual
> meeting, when someone innocently asks,
> 'What do you do?'
> The narrow approach — 'I'm into comparative
> hermeneutics' or 'I teach Theravada Buddhism'
> — probably terminates any discussion fairly
> quickly. The broad answer 'I teach religion'
> usually leads to a predictable conversation
> about somebody's bad marriage or drinking
> problem, or an argument about evolution. (To
> avoid this type of encounter, a former col-
> league used to say that he was a mercenary
> soldier — until, one day, he sat next to an army
> captain.)[1]

I cannot express how reprehensible I consider this
attitude to be. The religious professional who disdains
to talk about a person's failing marriage or to answer his
intellectual questions about the Bible is a blot on the
name of Christ. The editorial goes on to suggest that
theologians need to improve their public image by writing on a popular level so that others might discover
"new ways of looking at education, life, and work" and
by joining lobbying organizations to affect legislation

impacting the humanities. What has become of the gospel of Christ? Modern theology has nothing to say to the spiritual needs of ordinary people. That is why neo-liberal churches are dying and their denominational seminaries folding up or merging — having abandoned the historic Christian faith they have nothing to say to modern man, and he is not impressed by their theological doubletalk or their pious invocations of love and social justice. What these churches often preach is humanism cloaked in the robes of Christian vocabulary, but they do not tell us how to overcome the sin and corruption in our own hearts that prevent us from living the lifestyle they espouse. As a result we have an institutional church that sponsors programs aimed at social reform, including wars of liberation, while the church itself is populated with members whose own personal lives disgrace the name of Christ. It is no wonder the man in the street looks at the church as full of hypocrites and wants nothing to do with it. He sees through the charade and will not be fooled by the empty gospel of modern theology.

Moreover, what theology has been saying is characterized by a sort of "mushy-mindedness" (for lack of a better word), that is, a lack of logical rigor and clear thinking. As one who has a foot in both the camp of philosophy and the camp of theology, I can testify that the difference between reading the writings of Anglo-American philosophers on some subject (say, God's omniscience) and the writings of theologians on the same subject is often like the difference between day and night. The former is crisp, clean, analytic, and logically developed; the latter is ambiguous, quasi-mystical, emotive, and characterized by sloppy reasoning. In his recent book, *The Coherence of Theism*, on the intelligibility of the Christian concept of God as omnipotent, omniscient, and so forth, Richard Swinburne voices a similar complaint:

It is one of the intellectual tragedies of our age that when philosophy in English-speaking countries has developed high standards of argument and clear thinking, the style of theological writing has been largely influenced by the continental philosophy of Existentialism, which, despite its considerable other merits, has been distinguished by a very loose and sloppy style of argument. If argument has a place in theology, large-scale theology needs clear and rigorous argument. That point was very well grasped by Thomas Aquinas and Duns Scotus, by Berkeley, Butler, and Paley. It is high time for theology to return to their standards.[2]

Swinburne is absolutely correct. The subject with which he is concerned, for example, while extensively discussed in philosophical journals, is handled cavalierly by theologians, if at all. God is the hidden God, they tell us, *deus absconditus* (it always sounds more impressive in Latin), and therefore we do not know what He is really like. Hence, in the standard theological encyclopedia, *Religion in Geschichte and Gegenwart*, the article on "Eigenschaften Gottes" (attributes of God) is all of about one page long, and one will search in vain for articles on subjects such as omnipotence, omnipresence, and so forth. What these theologians do not seem to grasp is that, as Feuerbach explained, a God without attributes becomes an irrelevancy:

A being without qualities is one which cannot become an object to the mind, and such a being is virtually nonexistent. Where man deprives God of all qualities, God is no longer anything more to him than a negative being. To the truly religious man, God is not a being without qualities, because to him he is a positive, real being. The theory that God cannot be defined, and consequently cannot be known by man, is therefore the offspring of recent times, a product of modern unbelief ... On the ground that God is unknowable, man excuses himself to what is yet remaining of his religious conscience for his forgetfulness of God, his absorption in the world: he denies God practically by his conduct — the world has possession of all his thoughts and inclinations — but he does not deny Him theoretically, he does not attack His existence; he lets that rest. But this existence does not affect or incommode him; it is a merely negative existence, an existence without existence, a self-contradictory existence — a state of being which, as to its effects, is not distinguishable from non-being ... The alleged religious horror of limiting God by positive predicates is only the irreligious wish to know nothing more of God, to banish God from the mind. Dread of limitation is dread of existence. All real existence, i.e., all existence which is truly such, is qualitative, determinative existence ... A God who is injured by determinate qualities has not the courage and the strength to exist. Qualities are the fire, the vital breath, the oxygen, the salt of existence. An existence in general, an existence without qualities, is an insipidity, an absurdity. But there can be no more in God than is supplied by religion. Only where man loses his taste for religion, and thus religion itself becomes insipid, does the existence of God become an insipid existence — an existence without qualities.[3]

Of course, to defend God's various attributes will involve engaging in precisely the sort of vigorous analysis that Swinburne proposes — but modern theology seems to have no interest in such a task.

This "mushy-mindedness" also shows up in biblical as well as systematic theology. New Testament criticism has, quite frankly, become in no inconsiderable measure a sort of intellectual game which the critics play. After all, the New Testament is not a large book, and over the years it has been the recipient of the most prodigious and unbelievable expenditure of intellectual energy, unparalleled by any book in history. There is, after all, only so much that one can say. Yet articles in professional journals continue to pour forth from the presses. It is uninteresting to affirm previously established conclusions, and therefore modern critics, if they are to obtain academic post and reputation, simply must come up with creative, new interpretations and methods. These in turn furnish grist for the publishing mill by serving as the objects of refutation or extrapolation. This is not to depreciate the value of approaches to the gospels such as redaction criticism; but it is to say that such tools have been misused by critics to arrive at false, if novel, conclusions. As one of my New Testament colleagues remarked, if critics were really honest, they would admit that despite all the methodological advances in New Testament criticism, the conclusions of J.B. Lightfoot in the last century concerning the fundamental reliability of the gospel records are still correct. But the game must go on, and so it does.

More specifically, New Testament critics have mishandled the personal claims of Jesus recorded in the gospels. Jesus' claims to divinity served as a linch-pin in the traditional apologetic, as explained by Peter Kreeft in his selection in this section, "The Most Important Argument in Christian Apologetics." However, this apologetic was undermined by the challenge of biblical criticism early in this century that these claims reflect the theology of the early Christian church and were written back into the records. Jesus Himself, it is said, never made any such claims. Recent biblical criticism has, however, largely vindicated the traditional apologetic. For one thing, skeptical critics were guilty of a misuse of the so-called dissimilarity criterion, according to which a saying of Jesus is judged to be historical if it is not similar to motifs present in prior Judaism or subsequent Christian theology. The criterion is a positive test for historicity, since any such dissimilar saying could not have been extrapolated from Jewish thought or retrojected by Christian theology. But many critics misused the tool as a negative proof-stone: if a saying was not dissimilar, then it is unhistorical. This negative use is obviously fallacious because it would require that the Jewish milieu have absolutely no effect on Jesus and Jesus no effect on Christian theology! The proper use of the criterion only establishes historicity; it cannot prove unhistoricity. And it is interesting that through the use of various such criteria of authenticity, a remarkable picture of the historical Jesus has emerged. It has been proved that the Jesus of history was not merely a gentle rabbi, a moral teacher, or even an eschatological prophet. Rather He was a man who believed Himself to be the son of God in a unique sense, claimed divine authority and the right to stand in God's place, thought that He could perform miracles and exorcize demons, and claimed to determine men's eternal destiny based on their response to Him. Horst Georg Pohlmann reports, "In summary, one could say that today there is virtually a consensus concerning that wherein the historical in Jesus is to be seen. It consists in the fact that Jesus came on the scene with an *unheard of authority*, namely with the authority of God, with *the claim of the authority to stand in God's place and speak to us and bring us salvation*."[4] But this is where the "mushy-mindedness" begins. Critics acknowledge these facts about the historical Jesus, but insist that such claims have no implications for the divinity of Christ. Royce Gruenler notes, "It is a striking fact of modern New Testament research that the essential clues for correctly reading the implicit Christological self-understanding of Jesus are abundantly clear ... (There) is absolutely convincing evidence that Jesus did intend to stand in the very place of God Himself. If the ... evidence is followed to its natural conclusion, however, moving with the hinge as the Christological door opens, we are introduced to an even wider horizon which visually encompasses not only implicit claims to Messiahship but explicit Christological claims as well. But radical criticism appears incapable of making that very natural and rational swing."[5] Instead the critics hypostasize some abstraction like the Kingdom of God or Jesus' message and locate Jesus' authority in it rather than in Himself. Gruenler argues to the contrary what I take to be the common sense view that what a person says about himself reveals to us something of his self-understanding. And if this is so, then in Jesus we are confronted with a man whose self-understanding was so radical that it involved a claim of divinity. Jesus' personal claims, concludes Pohlmann, thus involve an implicit Christology:

> This unheard of claim to authority, as it comes to expression in the antitheses of the Sermon on the Mount, for example, is *implicit* Christology, since it presupposes a unity of Jesus with God that is deeper than that of all men, namely a unity of essence. This ... claim to authority is explicable only from the side of his deity. This authority only God himself can claim. With regard to Jesus there are only two possible modes of behavior: either to believe that in him God encounters us or to nail him to the cross as a blasphemer.[6]

It is in the context of these personal claims that Jesus' resurrection takes on such significance. For, as Wolfhart Pannenberg explains in the following interview, the resurrection of Jesus serves as God's decisive vindication of Jesus' personal claims to divine authority. Unfortunately, the subject of the resurrection has also been one of the areas of New Testament studies most plagued by mushy thinking. On the one hand, there has been a dramatic reversal of skepticism concerning the historicity of the resurrection narratives in the gospels and of information furnished by the Apostle Paul. On the other hand, there has been a failure of theology to appreciate the implications of criticism's results.

Three areas in which criticism has supported the historicity of the resurrection deserve mention. First, the historical evidence indicates that the tomb of Jesus was found empty on the first day of the week by a group of His women followers. Pannenberg mentions three lines of supporting evidence in his interview:

1. The empty tomb narrative is part of the pre-Markan passion story and therefore represents a very old tradition. This mitigates the possibility of significant legendary accrual.

2. The earliest Jewish polemic presupposes the empty tomb. Thus we have early evidence from the opponents of Christianity themselves that Jesus' tomb was empty.

3. The origin of the Christian movement in Jerusalem would have been impossible without the empty tomb. The fact that the Christian way was founded in the very city where Jesus was publicly crucified and buried necessitates that the tomb no longer held his corpse.

In addition to these considerations, other scholars have adduced the following lines of evidence:

4. The historical credibility of the burial story supports the empty tomb. If the burial account is reliable, then the site of Jesus' grave would have been known to Jew and Christian alike. But then if it were not empty, belief in the resurrection would have been impossible. Since the burial account is widely recognized as historically reliable, Jesus' tomb must have been empty.

5. Paul's testimony implies the empty tomb. When Paul recites in I Corinthians 15 that Christ died, was buried, and was raised, he as a Jew and former Pharisee assumed as a matter of course that the grave left behind was empty. But that means we have early evidence both from Paul and the tradition which he cites that Jesus' tomb was empty.

6. The phraseology of the empty tomb story indicates a primitive tradition. In the early Christian church it was widely proclaimed that Christ rose "on the first day of the week," which appears to be translation — Greek from Aramaic, the native language of the first disciples. Were the empty tomb story a late legend, it would no doubt have used the accepted "third day" motif.

7. The empty tomb narrative is simple and lacks signs of legendary development. Contrast the account in the apocryphal Gospel of Peter, a second century piece, in which a crowd of spectators witness Jesus emerging from the tomb, his head reaching above the clouds, accompanied by two angels whose heads reach to the clouds, and followed by a talking cross!

8. This discovery of the empty tomb by women is highly probable. Given the low status of women in Jewish society and their being disallowed to serve as legal witnesses, it is remarkable that women discover the empty tomb of Jesus. If the story were a late legend, the male disciples would have naturally been made the discoverers of the empty tomb.

9. The fact that Jesus' tomb was not venerated as a shrine indicates that the tomb was empty. It was customary in Judaism to revere the burial place of a prophet or holy man because his remains abode there. The absence of such veneration of Jesus' tomb suggests that his gravesite was not so revered because his remains did not reside there.

These and other considerations provide ample evidence that Jesus' tomb was found empty by a group of his women followers on the first day of the week. Michael Grant, a professional historian, concludes, " ... the historian ... cannot justifiably deny the empty tomb. True, this discovery, as so often, is differently described by the various Gospels — as critical pagans early pointed out. But if we apply the same sort of criteria that we would apply to any other ancient literary sources, then the evidence is firm and plausible enough to necessitate the conclusion that the tomb was indeed found empty."[7] How amazing is it therefore when the late Norman Perrin, a highly esteemed biblical critic of the University of Chicago, can write, "Scholars are coming increasingly to the conclusion that the empty tomb tradition is an interpretation of the event — a way of saying 'Jesus is risen!' — rather than a description of an aspect of the event itself."[8] Here theology has colored historical judgement — as though the disciples were so soft-headed as to narrate straightforwardly the women's discovery of Jesus' empty tomb that early Sunday morning and then turn around and say, "Ah, but this is not a literal historical fact! It is only an interpretive way of saying 'He is risen!' and for all we know or care his body may still lie in the grave." Van Daalen puts his finger on the problem when he points out that it is extremely difficult to object to the fact of the empty tomb on historical grounds; those who object to the empty tomb do so mainly on the basis of theological or philosophical considerations.[9] These, however, cannot change empirical facts. New Testament critics seem to be increasingly recognizing this fact. According to Jacob Kremer, who has specialized in the study of the resurrection, "By far most exegetes hold firmly ... to the reliability of the biblical statements about the empty tomb ..." and he furnishes a list, to which his own name may be added, of 28 prominent scholars in support.[10] I can think of at least 17 more scholars whom he neglected to mention.

Secondly, the historical evidence indicates that the disciples saw appearances of Jesus after his death. Pannenberg appeals primarily to the evidence furnished by Paul in I Corinthians 15. As he notes, most scholars now admit that the disciples did indeed have visionary experiences of Jesus. Even Perrin admits, "The more we study the tradition with regard to the appearances, the firmer the rock begins to appear upon which they are based."[11] But here again theological presuppositions begin to intrude. For many critics hold that these appearances, while not being subjective visions (hallucinations), were nevertheless not physical appearances either, but were so-called "objective visions." This latter notion unfortunately is typically ill-defined and elusive. Critics sometimes speak as though the percipient of such a vision is actually seeing Jesus in his non-physical, glorified, heavenly body. Such a notion is, however, incoherent, since sight apprehends its object by means of light rays reflected from it, and such a non-physical object cannot so reflect light waves. Hence, the seeing involved must be purely mental. In that case, the appearances would be analogous to certain veridical visions studied by parapsychology, in which someone is seen via a purported telepathic communication from that subject which causes the percipient to project a vision of the subject. In this case, however, the appearances of Jesus would have been precisely what was known in the biblical frame of thought as divine visions. Persons were often conceived to have visions which were not hallucinatory because they were God-induced rather than self-induced. Thus, on the model of objective visions, the resurrection appearances would seem to have been divinely induced visions of Jesus. But the problem is that the entire New Testatment, including Paul himself, is widely recognized as having made a firm distinction between *visions* of Jesus and *appearances* of Jesus. Religious visions, such as Stephen's vision of Christ, were known in the early church, and according to the New Testament witness, the appearances of Jesus were emphatically not visions. The distinction between the two seems clear enough in the New Testament: a vision, even if caused by God, is purely mental in nature, whereas an appearance involves the actual, extramental existence of the perceived object in the external world. Why, then, does contemporary theology resist so obvious and clear a distinction? The answer can only be that modern theology still languishes under the bias against the miraculous which was imported into biblical criticism from eighteenth century Deism. The fount of the construal of the resurrection appearances as objective visions has in our day been Hans Grass's *Ostergeschehen und Osterberichte*.[12] Yet, as John Alsup points out, Grass' insistence that objective visions underlie the physical appearances of the gospels "is predicated upon the impossibility of the material realism of that latter form as an acceptable answer to the 'what happened' question ... Grass superimposes this criterion over the gospel appearance accounts and judges them by their conformity or divergence from it."[13] As a result, " ... the contemporary spectrum of research on the gospel resurrection appearances displays a proclivity to the last century (and Celsus of the second century) in large measure under the influence of Grass' approach. In a sense the gospel stories appear to be something of an embarrassment, their 'realism' is offensive."[14] Modern biblical critics, embarrassed and offended by the physical resurrection described in the gospels, have thus been led to embrace a view of the appearances which is either incoherent or incompatible with widely acknowledged New Testament evidence.

When we press further and inquire why it is that the disciples could not have seen Jesus physically raised from the dead, the thinking gets even mushier. It is said that Jesus rose from the dead in a spiritual body, not a physical body, and therefore did not appear physically. But what does it mean to say he rose from the dead if his body remained in the tomb? Are we to seriously believe that the disciples were so cerebral as to proclaim with a straight face and in the teeth of persecution that Jesus had risen from the dead and appeared to them, but that his body still lay in the grave? The critics respond that even if the tomb were empty, Jesus' physical body was transformed to a spiritual body and so physical appearances could not have occurred. But what in the world is a "spiritual body"? All critics recognize that Paul and the New Testament teach the resurrection of the body, not the immortality of the soul as man's final state. But I challenge any critic to explain the difference between an unextended, immaterial, intangible, "spiritual" body and the immortality of the soul. When Paul speaks of the spiritual body in I Corinthians 15 he is talking about orientation, not substance, just as in I Corinthians 2, when he contrasts the natural man and the spiritual man. Some critics acknowledge this, but still insist that when Paul speaks of the spiritual body, the word "body" (σομα) means the self, the person, the "I," so that Paul is saying that a new spiritual self will be raised in abstraction from the body. Thus, these critics believe that they can affirm in good conscience that they believe in the resurrection of the body, when in fact they deny that the physical body will be raised. Again, however, this reduces the resurrection even more clearly to the immortality of the soul. Worse still, such a view is exegetically unjustified. This interpretation of "body" does not represent the first century understanding, but was imported by Rudolf Bultmann from twentieth century existentialism. According to Robert Jewett, "Bultmann has turned σομα into its virtual opposite: a symbol for that structure of individual existence which is essentially non-physical."[15] Hence, Gundry concludes that existentialist treatments of σομα have been a positive impediment to accurate historical critical exegesis of I Corinthians 15 and have sacrificed theology to a philosophical fashion which is already passe.[16] So while we may rejoice that contemporary biblical criticism has come to acknowledge the fact of the resurrection appearances, we need to urge critics to think more deeply about the nature of those appearances.

Finally, the very origin of the Christian movement is inexplicable without the resurrection of Jesus. All New Testament critics acknowledge that the first disciples firmly *believed* in the resurrection of Jesus. But the question at once arises, how does one account for the origin of that belief? As R.H. Fuller states, even the most skeptical critic must posit some mysterious *x* to get the movement going.[17] But the question is, what was that *x*? Again, many theologians have sought to bar that question as somehow illicit. But such a query is perfectly natural and indeed important. How did the disciples come to believe that Jesus had risen from the dead? If there was no resurrection of Jesus, then one has to explain the disciples' belief as an extrapolation of Judaism. This, however, cannot be plausibly accomplished, since Jewish belief in the doctrine of the resurrection differed from the disciples' belief in Jesus' resurrection in at least two fundamental respects: (1) for Judaism the resurrection always concerned all of mankind or all of the righteous, whereas Jesus' resurrection concerned an isolated individual; (2) in Judaism the resurrection always occurred at the end of the world, whereas Jesus' resurrection took place within history. Given their Jewish background and beliefs, the disciples confronted with Jesus' crucifixion and death would have preserved his remains in a tomb and looked forward to the eschatological resurrection in which he would be united with them again in God's kingdom. As James D.G. Dunn argues, apart from the fact of Jesus' resurrection itself, the disciples' conclusion that he had been raised from the dead would have been extravagant, not to say ridiculous and outrageous.[18] The most plausible explanation of the origin of the Christian movement is thus that Jesus really did rise from the dead.

These represent, as I say, the conclusions of current biblical criticism. One would think that contemporary theology would welcome such substantiation of Christian beliefs. Such a thought would be far from the case, however. Ulrich Wilckens, for example, after arguing that no natural explanation can plausibly account for the facts, nevertheless insists that it is *inherently* impossible to prove the resurrection historically because it is an eschatological event.[19] Similarly, Fuller refers to it as a meta-historical event.[20] But it needs to be asked whether such expressions are not in fact nonsensical with regard to Jesus' resurrection. An eschatalogical event is literally an event at the end of history; thus Jesus' resurrection is not eschatalogical in that sense. If one means that Jesus' resurrection was an event of the same character as some end-time event or an event fraught with divine or existential significance, then no *historical* problem seems to arise thereby, since as an event it has already occurred and is with regard to its facticity susceptible to historical inquiry. A meta-historical event, for its part, seems to be a contradiction in terms. For an event is that which happens. Thus, to be an event is to be part of history. To speak of a meta-historical event is therefore to speak of an event which is not part of history, which is self-contradictory. Many contemporary theologians, still I think under the influence of existentialism, which conceived of evidence as inimical to faith, are incredibly and unjustifiably skittish about any suggestion that Christian commitment might be rationally justified. This results in the spectacle of a Jewish theologian like Pinchas Lapide affirming the historicity of the resurrection of Jesus on the basis of the historical evidence and chastising New Testament critics for their unwarranted skepticism![21]

In conclusion, I have spoken in generalizations about the state of contemporary theology and unleashed some broadsides against it. Of course, such generalizations admit of many exceptions; nevertheless I do not believe they are over-generalizations. What I have said is, I think, generally, if not in every case, true.

By and large, modern theology has lost its message to modern man and is characterized by a sort of "mushy-mindedness," which I have sought to illustrate both in systematics and in biblical theology. It is high time for theologians to catch up with the philosophers and the scientists in the re-affirmation of the biblical gospel, in clarity of reasoning and expression, and in the defense of the rationality of the Christian world view.

Notes

1 Leonard J. Biallas, "Editorial," *Bulletin of the Council on the Study of Religion*, 13, (1982), p. 130.

2 Richard Swinburne, *The Coherence of Theism*, (Oxford: Clarendon Press, 1977), p. 7.

3 Lugdwig Feuerbach, *Das Wesen Des Christentums*, trans. G. Eliot, in *The Existence of God*, ed. J. Hick, Problems of Philosophy Series, (New York: Macmillan Co., 1964), pp. 194-5. Feuerbach's contention that the undefinability of God is the product of modern unbelief is certainly wrong, but I think it is true that modern unbelief perpetuates this notion.

4 Horst Georg Pohlmann, *Abriss der Dogmatik*, 3d rev. ed. (Gutersloh: Gerd Mohn, 1980), p. 230.

5 Royce Gordon Gruenler, *New Approaches to Jesus and the Gospels*, (Grand Rapids: Baker Book House, 1982), p. 74.

6 Pohlmann, *Abriss*, p. 230.

7 Michael Grant, *Jesus: an Historian's Review of the Gospels*, (New York: Charles Scribner's Sons, 1977), p. 176.

8 Norman Perrin, *The Resurrection According to Matthew, Mark, and Luke*, (Philadelphia: Fortress Press, 1977), p. 80.

9 D.H. van Daalen, *The Real Resurrection*, (London: Collins, 1972), p. 41.

10 Jacob Kremer, *Die Osterevangelien — Geschichten um Geschichte*, (Stuttgart: Katholisches Bibelwerk, 1977), pp. 49-50.

11 Perrin, *Resurrection*, p. 80.

12 Hans Grass, *Ostergeschehen und Osterberichte*, 4th ed. (Gottingen: Vandenhoeck & Ruprecht, 1970).

13 John E. Alsup, *The Post-Resurrection Appearance Stories of the Gospel Tradition*, (Stuttgart: Calwer Verlag, 1975), p. 34.

14 Ibid., p. 54.

15 Robert Jewett, *Paul's Anthropological Terms*, AGAJY 10 (Leiden: E.J. Brill, 1971), p. 21.

16 Robert H. Gundry, *Sōma in Biblical Theology*, (Cambridge: Cambridge University Press, 1976), p. 167.

17 R.H. Fuller, *The Formation of the Resurrection Narratives*, (London: SPCK, 1972), p. 2.

18 James D.G. Dunn, *Jesus and the Spirit*, (London: SCM, 1975), p. 132.

19 Ulrich Wilchens, *Augerstehung*, TT 4, (Stuttgart and Berlin: Dreuz Verlag, 1970), pp. 152-4.

20 Fuller, *Formation*, p. 23.

21 Pinchas Lapide, *Auferstehung: ein jüdisches Glaubenserlebnis*, 3d ed. (Kösel: Calwer 1980).

16
C.S. LEWIS AND THE CASE FOR CHRISTIANITY
Peter Kreeft

A few years ago the New York C.S. Lewis Society ran a survey of its members, asking (among other questions) "What quality of Lewis' personality and writings most attracted you to him?" The most frequent replies were: (1) joy, (2) clarity, (3) Christian faith, (4) imagination, (5) understanding, especially of the human soul, and (6) humility. These are also the qualities that make him a great apologist, probably the most effective in our century.

Let us take these features one by one in reverse order, for the last really is first in that it is a prerequisite. Socrates taught us the wisdom of unwisdom, of intellectual humility, as the first lesson, the prerequisite for all others. He was declared by the Delphic oracle to be the wisest man in the world and he interpreted this 'riddle' to mean that though he had no wisdom, he at least knew that he had no wisdom, and so was wiser than the rest of the world 'by this one trifle.' Pascal said that all of philosophy was "not worth an hour's trouble." Gilson commented that Pascal had a right to say this because he was one of the world's greatest philosophers, "and a man always has the right to disdain what he surpasses," while we lesser mortals do not. St. Thomas Aquinas called his monumental *Summa* "straw" and would not finish it after he had received the grace of the contemplative vision of God. Lewis, unlike many apolo-

gists, passes this first test. Evidence for that is ubiq-
uitous in his writings, but focused in "The Apologist's
Evening Prayer":

> From all my lame defeats and oh! much more
> From all the victories that I seemed to score;
> From cleverness shot forth on Thy behalf
> At which, while angels weep, the audience
>   laugh;
> From all my proofs of Thy divinity,
> Thou, who wouldst give no sign, deliver me.
> Thoughts are but coins. Let me not trust,
>   instead
> Of Thee, their thin-worn image of Thy head.
> From all my thoughts, even from my thoughts
>   of Thee,
> O thou fair Silence, fall, and set me free.
> Lord of the narrow gate and the needle's eye,
> Take from me all my trumpery lest I die.

(5) Lewis' understanding of the human soul — his
psychology of religion and of morality — as exemplified
in *The Screwtape Letters, The Great Divorce, Letters to Malcolm, The Four Loves,* and most profoundly of all in *Till
We Have Faces,* goes beyond mere intelligence and observation, beyond any scientific psychology, beyond I-It to
I-Thou. Readers are left creatively uncomfortable, exposed to a large mirror and a searching light. The laby-
rinthine ways down which the Hound of Heaven pur-
sues our skittery and self-deceptive psyche are
observed with candor and written about with wit.

(4) And with imagination. The early Lewis found
his poetic and imaginative life sharply divorced from his
rational life, and Christianity was the catalyst that
brought them together. In the service of faith and reason, the imagination was used perhaps more successfully by Lewis than by any other Christian apologist

in history. I refer not only to his fiction, the space trilogy and the Chronicles of Narnia, but also to his use of unforgettable, illuminating and exquisitely apt images in his essays and theological books. It is a gift; he himself admitted that he always began writing stories with pictures just "bubbling up" in his mind.

(3) Often, apologists leave the impression that they are playing a game; that they are giving reasons for *Christianity* but not, as St. Paul commands us, "to give a reason for the faith that is *in you.*" This is never the case with Lewis. If you doubt the depth of his faith, read *Letters to Malcolm*; if you doubt its honesty, read *A Grief Observed*; if you doubt its effect on his life, ask his friends.

(2) Imagination, faith, *and reason* is his blend; and the rational clarity (not just cleverness) of nearly everything he wrote makes lesser writers envious and, often, suspicious (much as the proud young Augustine was suspicious of Scripture's surface clarity and simplicity, as he relates in the *Confessions*). Yet behind the clear and simple statements of *Mere Christianity* lies far more depth than meets the eye at first reading; and more difficult books like *Miracles* and *The Problem of Pain*, which at first seem only profound, are found later to be surprisingly clear and simple. Another rarity: to fulfill both of reason's ideals, clarity and profundity, at once.

(1) But Lewis' supreme achievement, in apologetics and elsewhere, the diamond crowning the ring, is surely his joy. No writer, not even the Romantics, knew it better or evoked it better. There is simply nothing in literature to compare with "The Weight of Glory" or the "Heaven" chapter in *The Problem of Pain*. Not only does the reader of *Surprised by Joy*, a virtual autobiography of joy, find a soul-mate for life, but he also discovers a deeply felt and deeply thought road to God, which culminates in a (relatively) new and tremendously effective apologetic argument.

The argument has two premises. First, that "no natural desire is in vain," that every innate desire (as distinct from artificially conditioned desires, e.g. for the products of advertising) reveals the existence of some reality that corresponds to it, that would satisfy it. Hunger means food exists; sexual desire means the opposite sex exists; loneliness means society exists; curiosity means knowledge exists. The second premise is that there exists in each of us (and we can find it if only we look deeply and honestly) a desire for which earth offers no possible satisfaction; a longing for we know not what. It is not a mere compensation for earthly unhappiness; on the contrary, it springs up in the midst of the greatest earthly happiness: a sunset, a poem, a symphony, a great love. Something seems to be calling to us *through* them; they seem to point beyond themselves the more we enter into them.

These two premises together necessarily yield the conclusion that the object desired in this deepest of all desires exists. This desire is "like the Seige Perilous in Arthur's castle: the chair in which only one can sit." The conclusion is especially effective because it does not give the suspicious appearance of 'sneaking God in undercover.' The reader is *invited* to call this mysterious *x* 'God,' but not compelled. Like Augustine, Lewis explores our "restless heart" and lets *it* point to the One who alone can satisfy it. Neither he nor the argument as such bears 'the weight of glory'; the heart of the reader bears that weight. We are confronted with experiential evidence. All the argument does is interpret it. I find it extraordinarily effective, especially with agnostics and disillusioned ex-believers, if the desire itself is pointed out and described in identifiable and moving terms — something Lewis is a master at.

There are two other arguments that stand out in Lewis' apologetics as distinctively Lewisian. All three have precedents — Lewis was not a pioneer but a "dwarf standing on the shoulders of giants," as the medievals called themselves, seeing farther than his predecessors only because he stands in and on their tradition.

One of these is the *aut deus aut homo malus* argument. Next to the argument from longing, I find it most effective, and most worthy of extended exploration. (Indeed, I wrote an entire book on the first argument — *Heaven: The Heart's Deepest Longing* — and an entire book on the second — *Between Heaven and Hell* — and only scratched the surface of both.) It argues for the key doctrine of Christ's divinity, which like a skeleton key opens all other Christian doctrinal doors, since if the teacher is divine, you will believe all His teachings. The argument, as old as the Fathers of the Church, says simply that Christ must have been "either God or a bad man" because He *claimed* to be God, and a mere man who claims to be God is *not* a good man but a seriously insane idiot. "Lord, liar or lunatic?" is the way Josh McDowell summarizes the argument. And if His human personality, as known by all readers through the Gospels, makes the last two labels ludicrous, we are left with the first.

A third especially Lewisian argument is the one in Chapter 3 of *Miracles*, "The Self-Contradiction of Naturalism" (later modified to "The Cardinal Difficulty of Naturalism"). If nothing, not even human reasoning, is more than a natural process of material objects moving in space; if my thinking is determined wholly by the atoms in my brain and not by reason — by spirit, soul, or God; then no one thought can be said to be more true or valid than any other, any more than one motor running is more 'true' than another. Materialistic naturalism defeats itself; it is a proof that invalidates proof, an ism that reduces isms from thoughts to things. Like the other two arguments, this does not simply and unqualifiedly prove the existence of God, but it does disprove atheism.

Besides *arguments* — and these three are only high-lights; Lewis loves arguments as children love candy — there are numerous other *areas* of excellence (as distinct from our six *qualities* of excellence) in Lewis' apologetics. These include:

(2) his Christian fiction, especially the Chronicles of Narnia, favorites of vast numbers of children who un-consciously thirst for the kind of living Christian para-bles Jesus offered but the 'dead orthodoxy' or live here-sies of most religious education in our century denies them: a baptism of the imagination;

(3) two long, systematic, carefully argued studies of the two great objections to belief in God (cf. Aquinas' *Summa Theologiae* 1,2,3): the problem of pain and the problem of miracles, or the supernatural. If God is good and almighty, why aren't we happy? And if natural sci-ence can explain all observed events, why add a ra-tionally superfluous God? *The Problem of Pain* and *Mira-cles* remain the classic philosophical studies of these two areas;

(4) the best simple, short, clear and honest intro-duction to Christianity available, *Mere Christianity* — a book instrumental in the conversion of hard heads like Eldridge Cleaver and Chuck Colson;

(5) many clear and pointed essays, notably "The Poison of Subjectivism," "Man or Rabbit?" (which be-gins: "Can't you just lead a good life without believing in Christianity?" — necessary and powerful for modern ethically-serious but religiously-relativistic students), "Priestesses in the Church?" (against the ordination of women), "Why I am Not a Pacifist," "The Humanitarian Theory of Punishment" (defending 'retribution'), "Prayer and Work" (why pray if God knows what we need anyway?), and "Modern Theology and Biblical Criticism," a *demolition* of Bultmann and demythologizing;

(6) deep and wise religious and ethical psychology

in *The Four Loves, Surprised by Joy, Screwtape Letters* and *The Great Divorce*, which together with *Letters to Malcolm* amount to spiritual guidance from a master — not a saint, but a good and trustable guide;

(7) one book on Scripture, *Reflections on the Psalms* — unpretentious but wise;

(8) one sermon, which is worth a lifetime: "The Weight of Glory" — quite simply, the most moving extra-Scriptural sermon I have ever read (and most readers of Lewis concur in that judgment);

(9) his own favorite, his tribute to *his* master, *George MacDonald, An Anthology*: utter gems, comparable only to Pascal's *Pensees*.

Finally, perhaps the greatest cause of his greatness as an apologist was his refusal to search for greatness. His greatest originality was his refusal to strive for originality. ("Our Lord never thought of being original"!) Just as we find our very selves by forgetting them, losing them, letting them go, so we find our greatness by doing humble things like manning the center of the battle line, defending 'mere Christianity' while other, 'bold, original thinkers' fight on the wings; reconquering old territories lost rather than new ones; making old truths new rather than looking for new truths. Lewis once replied to a magazine interviewer's question "How do you manage to be so creative, so imaginative, so original?" with his tongue in his cheek: "Oh, I just remember some of the things my old nurse used to tell me, and I dress it up in fancy language and everyone wonders where I ever got such original ideas." Lewis was nursed by the Word of God, never forgot to be a little child (the absolute entrance requirement for the kingdom, according to the King Himself), and thus attained the measure of greatness, in all these ways like his Master.

17
IS CHRISTIANITY CREDIBLE?
Dr. Thomas Howard

What assumptions of the secularist world view do you find most damaging or inimical to the Christian view of reality?

I suppose I wouldn't have any answer that would be different from any orthodox traditionalist Christian. And I suppose that if we try to chase it right to the center of the question, one way of putting it, one of the assumptions would be the notion that we human beings, we mortals, are autonomous, that we may call our own shots, and that we should call our own shots, and we aren't responsible to any higher tribunal.

My mind angles in on these questions from the standpoint of the human imagination. One sees the witness of human imagination down through the centuries. One of the notions that has intrigued me very much with respect to all poetry and all epic myth is that it has been the eras which have supposed, rightly or wrongly, that the gods were there peering over our shoulder — that there was a divine tribunal to which we were responsible and answerable — it has been those eras which have produced not the craving, fawning, obsequious drama and poetry of defeat, but the great heroic poetry, of us mortal men and women as most majestic and noble. It's when you have the gods on their thrones that you have available an Achilles, or an Arthur or a Charlemagne. It's when you dethrone the gods that you get Willy

Loman or the modern, anti-hero, which is all by way of saying with respect to this question ... I think the notion that we are autonomous is one of the most inimical to the Christian view of reality. The question also asks which ones do I find most damaging. In one sense, you can't damage the Christian view of reality because it's there, and it will not be dismantled.

The notion of our autonomy really is just a version, for the ten thousandth time, of the original error or original sin of egocentrism. I am at the center; I call the shots! That's what happened in Eden, and in effect that's what Pandora did in the Greek myth. "I'm going to make my own decision here." This notion would stand at the polar extreme from the Christian notion that not only are we answerable to God, but that that is the very definition of our freedom, that freedom and obedience are synonymous. They don't have to be held in tension. They are not even complementary; they are synonymous. Freedom and obedience, you see it in art and in literature, for instance when you watch a magnificient ballet dancer — Nureyev. His ability to execute those incredible leaps and those incredible figures is not a matter of his shucking off the discipline, or his obedience to the choreography — that is his obedience. That magnificent perfection and freedom and bliss we see there, his power to do it, is synonymous with his obedience to the choreography, his obedience to what his ballet teachers have told him and how you jump. You see it in an athlete. This magnificent pole vault or playing soccer or gymnastics and everything else. You don't have obedience on the one hand, which is a form of slavery and ruins the guy's creativity, and on the other hand a freedom and individualism and a liberty which stands over against it. You're suddenly looking at an icon of freedom and obedience being synonymous.

So, again, ... I think the root assumption of the secularist world view which is inimical to the Christian view is this notion that we are autonomous. We can see it in any bookstore, in any talk show, any glossy magazine, any journal now, a whole vocabulary and mythology of self-assertion, aggressiveness, self-development. All of this stands at a polar extreme from the gospel. The gospel is nonsense and incomprehensible to the point of view which says, in order to fully reach my fullness and maturity and full potential, I must assert myself. As opposed to this vocabulary is the gospel of the crucifixion and renunciation.

The other assumption of the secularist world view, I suppose, is its assumption that there is no final, absolutely fixed, moral order. And as it's been pointed out a thousand times by the Christian apologist, philosophically speaking, you can't jump from "is" to "ought" ... from the observation of data to the phrase, "You ought to do so and so." That is an impossible abyss to bridge logically, and we live in an era which is under the empiricist myth, you might say, that it's just observation of data which we will accept, and you can't make the jump to any kind of "is-ness," or from "is-ness" to "ought-ness" there.

We have no way, given the secularist point of view, of telling one person what he ought to do as opposed to another, so that if I say," I am a cannibal," there's no way, given the secularist world view, that anybody could say that I shouldn't be a cannibal, because there's no scientific data, there's no empirical data, which can show why I shouldn't be so. If you say, "Yes, but people ought to stay alive," I will ask you, "Why ought they stay alive?" You can't show me why life is better than death, why existence is better than non-existence, as though everything is neutral data. There has to be some transcendent point of reference beyond the mere existence.

Is the restriction of all knowledge to the senses another prominent secular assumption?

Yes, certainly, the restriction of knowledge to sense data is an old empiricist idea. That idea doesn't seem to do justice to the whole scope of what we human beings wish and sense and know to be true. We have aspirations and shafts of longing and desire. We need a consolation which can never come from just sense data. I think, you mentioned positivism, it seems to me it's gone a step further in the modern world from merely restricting what we could talk about as sense-data to almost a view of total despair. That is to say, we do not know what is "out there" and we cannot know what is "out there." We're inside a logical trap; we can't bridge from our internal awareness of things to a real external world, therefore we have Logical Positivism, which doesn't talk about external reality. It talks about talking about external reality. In theology, therefore, you don't talk about God; you talk about "God-talk." Or talk about the meaning of statements. You don't talk about whether there is any reality out there which corresponds to those statements.

I think we see the same thing in the behavioral sciences. You no longer speak of guilt, which would presuppose the notion that there is an ultimate tribunal in front of which I am in fact guilty. This is irrelevant now. It just becomes guilt feelings. Our medicine, our witch-doctors, our prophets and seers are the psychiatrists and psychoanalysts. They're never going to say to me, as I'm trying to work my way up, "Well, you better go make a sacrifice to Zeus! You better go make a sacrifice to Yahweh." They're going to say, "Well, now, dear child, you need to come to grips with your guilt feelings." The focus is at this end. The philosophers of ancient Egypt used to rake through the entrails of sheep to try to find the way out; we rake through our own entrails. So the reality is guilt *feelings*.

But what I, as a human being, want to know is, if the gods are there — if Zeus or Yahweh or Baal or somebody is out there and I need to come to terms with him, then I need to find out. I know no counselor can tell me about that.

What other fallacies do you see in the secularist world view?

It would seem to me that if we really pursued them we would see that the assumptions of the secular world view eventually destroy the possibility of *really* human life, and I don't just mean biological life. It would seem to me that what they do is stultify all possibility of keeping alive and affirming the things which set our life apart from the life of brutes. It will be interesting to see whether it is possible to have, for instance, a poetry; what epic poetry, what oratories, what sonnets will be born of secular humanism? What iconography, what imagery of splendor and grace and nobility and beauty will come from that matrix? My hunch, as a teacher of literature, would be that it's going to turn out to be an arid desert. The human imagination will not settle for that.

On what grounds is Christianity intellectually credible?

Well, I would have to come in at an oblique angle on this question. If the question is, "On what grounds do I consider Christianity logically credible," frankly, I would appeal, when the philosophers and the theologians have done their work, to the witness of myth and the human imagination ... if you look at every tribe, every culture, every society, every civilization since the beginning of time, you see the impossible and burgeoning transcendent wish for a consolation which can never come from just the "meat and potatoes" of immediate existence.

I would remind the contemporary man who claims not to be able to believe in the transcendent, least of all in miraculous things as incarnation, virgin birth, ascension (all those things for which there is no category in physics or the empirical world view), that this is one little ventricle or corner or cul-de-sac of history that we live in. I would appeal to what is called the "senate of the dead." I stand under the judgment of Homer and Dante and Shakespeare, not the other way around. I have no footing on which to judge or assess or to least of all, pigeonhole, Homer and Isaiah and Moses and Thomas Aquinas and Augustine. They judge me, and if I find that that view of things, the view that we mortal creatures stand under the scrutiny of the gods, if I find that incredible, then that says more about me than about history and myth, and I would appeal, I would press home, a question: Where do these myths come from? And the contemporary mind would probably come up with its ready answer, namely "the myths are witnesses to what we wish were true. We have human fathers; we wish there were a cosmic father because our human fathers die. We have the experiences of erotic love here; we wish there were some transcendent reality that that corresponded to." But my question would be "How do you know? How do you know that it's only wish-fulfillment, and how do you know that I'm projecting all the time?" What is the vantage point from which the modern world says "This is all there is to it." We have, as it were, screwed down the manhole covers on the dragons and the great deeps, you might say, but they're going to come up around the cracks. The human imagination won't settle for it.

T.S. Eliot, in his poetry, did not so much oblige someone to believe in the Christian vision as show what it was like to believe. So that when you read "The Journey of the Magi" or "Ash Wednesday" you, at that point, are given a dazzling and a luminous vision of what it is like to be a Christian believer in this world, rather than an overriding philosophical case as to why Christianity is true. And, I myself, would tend to incline toward that rather than the inexorable logic of apologetics which can be done and, I believe, Thomas Aquinas and others have done.

Could you tell us how you wrote *Once Upon a Time?*

Well, the book referred to is a short book called *Once Upon a Time God* or *Dialogue With a Skeptic*. What I did there was to set myself the task of asking myself what would I say *if* somebody asked me the following questions. It was a dialogue between an absolute unbeliever and a voice (which was me I suppose) who is a Christian believer, and I put myself the hardest questions I could think of and tried to say what I would say short of being God or the prophet Isaiah or Thomas Aquinas, who knew everything. But, I as a layman ... what would I wish at least to be able to say ... an inquisition or a catechism from a non-believer, and it really ended up being more a question of showing what it's like, or trying to show what it's like, to be a believer rather than shooting down all possible alternatives.

How credible is Christianity on the imaginative plane?

I suppose the one word answer to that would be *absolutely*, absolutely. Christianity has been called the supreme fiction — not meaning it's the biggest lie there is, but meaning it is a story which stands at the top of, or the taproot of, all other stories, or it's the story that we supremely wish were true. I think Tolkien talks about that in his essay on fairy stories. This is the fact that we wish there to be a god to renew our souls, we wish to have some word from Mount Olympus — from wherever. "If only the god would come." He has come, and He has spoken. And not only that, He hasn't just shouted down from the top of Olympus, but He has shown Himself, He has become one of us. The whole drama of Annunciation and Incarnation, the Passion and the Resurrection and Ascension, those are the taproots of our imagination we wish supremely were true. The icon of the Annunciation, for instance, in which we see in the plain, ordinary flesh of this virgin all of humanity. Words have been spoken to our humanity, "Hail, you'll be crowned with glory!" As modern drama, modern painting, modern philosophy see it, no such words have ever been spoken to us. So on the plane of imagination, it certainly, at least it may be said, that this is the thing that we wish were true more than anything else. In the modern theater you don't find that. The trouble, the dismal thing about human life, is that no "Hail!" has ever been spoken to humanity, whereas the Christian gospel says that — yes, it has. There's the Annunciation, the doctrine of the Ascension, for instance, our flesh has been taken up into the mystery of the Trinity. So our flesh, our mortal flesh, has been raised and crowned with glory. You see this in the medieval and late medieval iconography of the Virgin as queen of heaven, raised and crowned with glory as a theological picture.

Our flesh, as St. Paul teaches, is raised and made to reign with Christ, crowned with glory. And you see that in the picture of the Virgin reigning and crowned, whereas the secular imagination says, "Alas, we wish that were true, but it's not." So on the imaginative level,

Christianity is, I would say, more than absolutely satisfying. It is inexpressibly and incredibly satisfying. The way the Jesuits say the Christian faith, rightly understood, is absolutely satisfying to the human intellect.

Would its imaginative power be an argument for its truth?

Well, I suppose the Freudian answer would be, "No, it's not an argument for what we wish were true." Whereas the secularists would say it's only what you wish were true, the Christian would say that it is there because it is true. I think the little drama, the little scene that shows the different points of view would be seen in Lewis' little book *The Silver Chair*. The children and this marshwiggle, Puddleglum, are talking to the Green Witch, and they are trying to say that this isn't the only world there is — down in this hole. For instance, there's the sun and a sky. And, of course, rather than disagreeing with them, she just strums away on her mandolin, and throws this powder on the fire and says, "Ah, yes, the sun, what could be more quaint. What's it look like?" And Puddleglum says, "It looks like that lamp." And she says, "Aha, yes, that lamp" ... or "Oh, yes, there's a Lion? Tell me about this Lion." "Well, it's a little bit like a cat." "Oh, I see." She doesn't disagree with them. She agrees, and I think that the Christian would always need to lodge in the secular mind, "How do you know which way around it is?" That is, the modern world says religious people talk about God the Father because we have human fathers and wish that there were a cosmic Father. How do they know that our human fathers are not themselves human metaphors for, or little cases in point, that give us a way of getting a foothold into the thing that is really true? Namely, the fact that there is the Father who is the fountain of all fatherhood. I don't think there is any way of absolutely proving that.

Isn't a fundamental insight required?

Yes, and I would think that, at least, a Christian could and should keep lodging in the closed, secular mind, keep lodging the seeds of doubt: maybe secularism is a closed system, maybe it's a little box. You might say to moles or bats, "There is such a thing as light. How do you know there's no such thing as light?"

Would you explain the nature of challenges to faith in the 20th century.

There isn't direct opposition. The moderner says, "You like God, be my guest. God's your thing; coke is mine. Three cheers!" It isn't direct opposition, it's just the shrug of the shoulders and "Oh well, fine. That's your scene!" and so on.

But there are questions which can't be answered on a secularist perspective.

The question of ultimate consolation cannot be answered in the closed world by the secularist. Albert Camus was right. The only ultimately serious philosophical question is the question of suicide. Either life is worth living, or it isn't. And if it's not, then why don't we all put a bullet through our heads. So there is no consolation. But it takes courage to *see that*. And a hundred out of a hundred people, or 99 out of a hundred people, manage to sweep it under the rug, and just bumble along without really staring into the abyss. But you have one or two brave, clear-eyed, prophetic souls like Camus, who are able to see that if there is nothing there, then it is an abyss and there is no reason to keep on living. So, I would think that one of the specific questions that can't be answered by secularism would be: Is there any consolation? Is there balm in Gilead? Hamlet's question is "to be or not to be" and the secularist perspective would have to say, "For some strange reason, we want to be, but there isn't one rag of reason why we should."

And then I think the whole question of "ought" versus "is": there's no footing for any moral imperative, really, in the secular point of view. You cannot establish why we ought to do one thing as opposed to another. Why virtue is better than vice. Why truth is better than falsehood. Why heroism is better than cowardice. You can't establish that on a closed system. That has to come from a transcendent source.

And I think one other specific question can be answered. Why has there been the persistence, in all tribes, in all cultures, in all history, of this tale, this narrative, this drama, this wish, "that the gods have come to see us." Well, how do you explain that? Did that come about from nothing? You can't make a silk purse out of a sow's ear, and there is the silk purse of myth.

Would one have reason to live if one adopts a secularist perspective? And how does Christianity make a difference?

It does make all the difference. It's a rare soul that has the courage or clarity of vision to see that life does not make any sense without some transcendent reason for its being. It's only the Albert Camus and the ones or twos who could see that. The Christian would say, just what your question has implied, namely, that there isn't any reason for being short of this, and that the Christian drama does, in fact, gather up and dramatize and fulfill all the potentialities and aspirations of the human frame.

It's the Christian who keeps opening the cans of angels, we might say, and who sees that all these questions in politics, economics, private morality ... all these questions open out onto titanic vistas. It's the Christians who can keep peeling off the veneer or bursting through the rim of the temporal and saying, "Don't you see what this is saying, can't you see that every single thing just waves flags in front of us, flags of ultimacy?" Whereas secular humanism can keep patting down the dust and keep saying, "This is all there is to it. So far so good." But then when the dragons and the great deeps break loose, where are you?

18
THE MOST IMPORTANT ARGUMENT IN CHRISTIAN APOLOGETICS
Peter Kreeft

This essay essays to judge the logical force of the argument which is, I believe, the most important single argument in all of Christian apologetics. It is the traditional argument for the divinity of Christ, used from the time of the early Fathers of the Church right up to contemporary apologists like C.S. Lewis, known as the *aut deus aut homo malus* argument; Christ is "either God or a bad man."

Two reasons why this seems to be the most important argument in Christian apologetics are:

(1) The 'skeleton key' principle: it opens all the other doctrinal doors. For most Christians believe all the doctrines of their faith not on the basis of their own reasoning or experience of each separate doctrine (at least at first) but on the basis of the authority of Christ the Teacher of those doctrines — whatever the respective roles of Church and Scripture in channeling that authority down the centuries. Christ's identity as the Author is the basis of His authority, and His authority is the basis of all Christian doctrines.

(2) The 'you can't give what you don't have' principle; if Christ is not divine, He cannot give us divine life, zoe, and our destiny as well as His is reduced to human

destiny; death. At stake in the theological issue of Christ's divinity is the practical issue of the destiny of Man; therefore no argument is more practically important to us than the argument for Christ's divinity. And the *aut deus aut homo malus* argument is the strongest such argument.

The argument is effective because even unbelievers do not usually think He is ('was,' they would say) a *bad* man. But, the argument insists, 'only a good man' is the one thing He cannot possibly be. For He claimed to be divine, 'Son of God' as well as 'Son of Man.' A mere man who said such things as these — "Before Abraham was, I AM"; "I and the Father are one"; "Which of you convicts Me of sin?"; "Your sins are forgiven you"; "I am the way, the truth, and the life"; "I am the resurrection and the life" — a mere man who said such things would not be a good or wise man but a bad or foolish man; bad if he knew they were not true, foolish if he did not.

The distance between what you are and what you claim to be is a measure of your insanity (if you believe your claim) or of your deceitfulness (if you do not). If I claimed to be the greatest teacher in America, you would think I was only a vain fool. If I claimed to be the greatest living human being, you would think I was incredibly, hopelessly arrogant. But if I claimed to be God, you would put me beyond the pale, utterly 'flipped.' Jesus is either Who He claimed to be or utterly flipped, if He isn't.

Note that the argument has the form of a disjunctive syllogism; Jesus is either God, or a good man, or a bad man; He is not a good man or a bad man; therefore He is God. The unbeliever must make out either that He is a good man or a bad man. As we have already seen, He cannot be a good man because He claimed to be God; but why couldn't He have been a bad man?

The answer to that question, an essential dimension of the argument, lies outside formal logic. It is His human personality, which almost everyone admits was wise and good and trustable. It is our human credibility detector as well as our logical reasoning that is needed to make the argument work. He established His human credibility first, then claimed divinity within that context of credibility. If you or I had claimed what He claimed, no one would believe us. Why did so many believe Him? For that matter, why did so many believe Buddha when he made an almost equally incredible claim, though a very different one; that he as a mere man had attained the supreme enlightenment, the content of which was that all of us are living in perpetual illusion, from which he alone had awakened; that everything we think is real, the ego and the world, the inside and the outside, is really unreal, *sunyata*, emptiness; that the only reality is *nirvana*, 'extinction,' which is *neti ... neti*, 'not this ... not that,' absolutely indescribable — why would anyone believe this if they had not yet experienced it themselves? Only because they believed *him*, the Buddha, a man 'holy to his fingertips.' Similarly, those who came to know Jesus were quite certain that *whatever* He was, He wasn't a bad man.

This psychological dimension of the argument is paralleled by an incident in *The Lion, the Witch and the Wardrobe*, the first of the Chronicles of Narnia by C.S. Lewis. Four English children are playing hide and seek on a rainy day indoors in a large old country house owned by a wise old Professor Kirke. Lucy, the youngest, hides in a free standing wardrobe in an empty room, and soon discovers that it has no back, but is an opening into a whole other world, Narnia. Lucy goes through and has many adventures in Narnia before she finds her way back through the wardrobe. When she tells her brothers and sister about it, they all find only an ordinary wardrobe with a back. Naturally, they do not believe Lucy at first, and she is in tears all day. Finally, at supper, the Professor resolves the issue by asking Peter, Lucy's older brother, how well he knows Lucy. Quite well, is the answer. And how well do you know the universe? Are you sure such things can't happen? Has science or history or common sense *proved* its impossibility? No. Well, then, Lucy is either insane, or lying, or telling the truth. If you know her well enough to know she isn't insane or lying, and you don't know the universe well enough to be certain she can't be telling the truth, you must believe her. Simple logic. "What do they teach them in the schools nowadays, anyway?"

Like Buddha and Lucy, Jesus says incredible things; and like Buddha and Lucy, Jesus is a credible person. We must either believe His unbelievable claim or disbelieve His believable person.

A better way to put the argument is this: let us divide all human beings into four categories by using two criteria; first, whether they claim to be God or not, and second, whether they are unusually wise and good or not. Thus there are four kinds of people:

    (1) Those who neither claim divinity nor are remarkably wise and good; the vast majority of us;

    (2) Those who do not claim divinity and *are* remarkably wise and good: the saints and sages, like Socrates, Buddha, Moses, and Confucius;

    (3) Those who claim divinity and are not wise; the insane (a divinity complex is a fairly common mental illness);

    (4) Those who both claim divinity and are remarkably wise and good: only one man ever existed who fits into this class, Jesus.

Let us examine the terms of this version of the argument more closely. What is a wise man or spiritual master, what is a divinity complex, and why are they incompatible?

Wise men, saints, gurus, spiritual masters, sages all share three prominent psychological characteristics.

First, they have unusual insight into the human heart, into character. Buddhists call this *prajna*. It includes insight both into universal truths about human nature and into the peculiar needs and vagaries of the individual. This insight is not what we all have; it is not expressed in cliches or platitudes. It is challenging, surprising, unpredictable, and often upsetting. Sages make enemies through their wisdom; they are often assassinated. For they tell us things we need but do not want to hear. They are pioneers, and their radical new insights become future generations' well-worn platitudes, as the first roads to the American West became our superhighways.

Secondly, sages have love, compassion, selflessness — what Buddhists call *karuna*. Wisdom and compassion, *prajna* and *karuna*, are the two highest virtues and the marks of a sage. *Karuna* makes you humble. 'Humble' comes from *humus*, earth. Sages are earthy; they feel at home with you, they are *with* you. They are thinking about you all the time, not about themselves. They have space in themselves for you because they have roomy selves, hospitable houses in their spirit.

Thirdly, sages are creative: unprogrammable, unpin-down-able, unclassifiable. For instance, they are neither 'left' nor 'right.' I once tried to figure out whether I favored the 'left' or the 'right' (I seemed to dislike both) by listing my heroes and then asking whether most of them were 'left' or 'right.' Every one was unclassifiable. Socrates and Jesus, just to take two, were each killed by a conspiracy of Left and Right together; Socrates by dogmatic establishmentarians and skeptical Sophists, Jesus by dogmatic Pharisees and skeptical Sadduccees. Because sages are unclassifiable, they are adaptable to changing human needs and situations. You never know what answer they're going to give. They give the answer they see the questioner needs because they see that the real question is always not the question but the questioner. Thus they are always fascinating to listen to in dialog.

Wisdom, compassion, creativity — in all three of these ways Jesus is a typical sage, like a Zen master, like Solomon, like Socrates.

Now let's look at the psychology of an insane person who has a divinity complex. Three features typical of this syndrome are the exact opposite of the three we have seen in the sage. First, his supposed 'wisdom' always turns out to be platitudes that everyone knows and agrees with already. He got them not from his own pioneering spiritual experience but second hand, verbally. He is a parrot.

Second, his ego is small, hard, brittle, and narrow. He clings to his illusion of divinity "as something to be grasped." He does not "empty himself" because there isn't much of a self there to empty. He is incapable of caring about you for the same reason he is incapable of insight into you; he is only into himself and his claims. You get the feeling you are a mere walk-on in his play. He is god, after all; how could he be humble?

Third, he cannot dialog, only monolog. He is unadaptable, as predictable as a machine; he always gives the same answer to the same question no matter who asks it, for he isn't really aware of you as an other, an individual.

In fact, the three main claimants to wisdom in the world today are secular humanism, pantheism, and theism: irreligion, Oriental religion, and Western religion. Distinguishing Christian theism from the other two options was not an essential part of the argument many centuries ago because neither modern humanism nor ancient pantheism were as well known then, or as widely believed in the past, as they are today. But there has always been something like them; a tendency to confuse Christianity with either something like humanism (remember Arianism, Pelagianism, and Arminianism) or with something like pantheism (remember Gnosticism and the many heterodox mysticisms like those of Origen, John Scotus Erigena, and Eckhart).

Let us first briefly examine the "ecumenical" attempt to assimilate Christ to Krishna and Buddha, then the "Modernist" attempt to impugn the texts on which our knowledge of Christ's claim to divinity rests.

Fritjof Schuon's *The Transcendent Unity of Religions* is perhaps the most convincing attempt to Orientalize Christ; it is certainly typical, especially in its distinction between esoteric and exoteric Christianity. Since exoteric Christianity is clearly not pantheism, it is claimed that esoterically the opposite holds true. There, as Chesterton so Orwellianly puts it, "Christianity and Buddhism are very much alike, especially Buddhism." All religions are equal, but some are more equal than others. The claim is that Jesus was the guru to the Jews, as Lao Tzu to the Chinese; Jesus translated the universal mystical truth, "the perennial philosophy," into Jewish terms, but it was the same truth Krishna and Buddha taught: that all is One, a perfect, eternal, spiritual Reality; that all of us and all of existence *is* that One, beyond individuality, beyond personality, beyond distinction.

Now this simply cannot possibly be so; there is a self-contradiction in the view of Jesus as the guru to the Jews. For if He meant to teach esoteric pantheism, He was the most misleading and ineffective teacher in history, *not* a guru. For He fostered at least six illusions in His exoteric teaching, rather than helping to overcome them, as any pantheist guru would do.

First, Jesus clearly taught that God was personal, not impersonal; a person, though of course not a human person. The name God Himself revealed to Moses and His chosen people, His collective prophet, His mouthpiece to the world, was I AM. What pantheistic mysticism sees as the ultimate illusion, I-ness, egohood, is for a Jew or a Christian the nature of ultimate reality!

Second, I AM is a Creator, and thus distinct from His creation. The created world is therefore *not* God, yet it is real, not illusion. Pantheism teaches that all is God, therefore the universe is either *maya*, illusion, or it is God (or part of God). The concept of creation *ex nihilo* simply did not ever occur to any human mind in all the world's history except to the Jews and those who learned it from them.

Third, the pantheist's God is beyond all dualism, therefore beyond the dualism of knower and known, subject and object. He (It) is therefore unknowable. But for Jews and for Jesus, God makes Himself known, speaks in words and deeds, reveals Himself. Other religions are stories of Man's search for God; the Bible is the story of God's search for Man. Instead of mysticism we have revelation.

Fourth, the pantheist's God, beyond all dualism, is beyond the dualism of good and evil, beyond morality. But the God of Jesus and the Jews is definitively good, not evil, righteous, just, holy, and cares infinitely about our goodness, justice, and holiness. He has a *will*, unlike the pantheist's God (and unlike the pantheist mystic).

Fifth (and most important of all), according to pantheism the meaning of human life is the realization that we are all timelessly one with God; we are all divine already. (For time, like matter, is illusory.) But according to Christ we are *not* divine; worse, we are not even truly human, but fallen. Our destiny is to *become* "partakers of the divine nature," to "put on Christ," to be "born again" from God as our Father. Time is real, and a change as real and radical as birth must occur. For this, faith is necessary, for "believing" is "receiving" the divine nature. And this brings us to our sixth difference.

Without faith, no salvation, no eternal life, no *zoe*, no Heaven. Hell is a real possibility in Jesus' teaching, but not in pantheism (an attractive selling feature!). And the concepts of sin and forgiveness of sin are central to Christianity but not present in pantheism. Without sin, Jesus is not Jesus ("savior"); that's what He saves *from*.

Six dualisms: ego-self vs. other, Creator vs. creature, knower vs. known, good vs. evil, human nature vs. divine nature, and belief vs. unbelief, with Heaven and Hell as their respective destinies — Shuon (and anyone else) can deny these are part of Christ's teachings only by inventing another dualism, one that isn't there, the dualism between exoteric Christianity (which is Christianity) and esoteric Christianity (which is pantheism).

It is true that Eastern religions are esoteric, but Western religions are not; they are religions of a Book, a public revelation. An esoteric Christianity is a pure invention of the modern Orientalizer. There is no evidence in Scripture or tradition for it. It is a hypothesis invented to save a dogma; a rationalization. But even if it were true, it would not be true; it is self-contradictory. For it would not make Christ a guru but a fool, because His exoteric teaching led His followers in exactly the opposite direction from the truth (pantheism) in at least six crucial ways. Jesus couldn't do what any twentieth century writer like Schuon could do; say what he meant so that people could understand it! If that's a guru, I'm a goose.

The last attempt to avoid the conclusion that Christ is divine is the Modernist attack on the Biblical texts. This long battle must be fought with two weapons; textual arguments and psychoanalysis. I will concentrate on the second here because it is usually ignored.

From a psychological point of view, the Modernist's battle of the Bible seems very suspiciously like fudging the data to fit the theory, doctoring the tapes, altering the evidence. The textual issue is an enormously complex smoke screen, a red herring. Higher criticism has not proved the texts unreliable. Most modernist Biblical scholarship has not been objective and scientific, as it claims, but has approached the text with *a priori* religious dogmas, notably that miracles cannot happen and that the supernatural is myth, not fact. For a longer and stronger literary sortie into this question, cf. C.S. Lewis' essay "Fern-Seed and Elephants." I would like to investigate the Modernist *motivation*.

Logically, the motive is simple. The thorn in the Modernist's comfortable ecumenical humanism is the fact that one wise man claimed to be God. Only thus does the *aut deus aut homo malus* argument work. If we can only avoid the claim itself, we're home free with humanism. Jesus was just a man who was later misunderstood or misrepresented. The New Testament writers then either were stupid and *thought* He claimed to be God when He didn't or deliberate liars who *said* He claimed to be God when He didn't. But the first confusion is inconceivable, especially for a Jew — the least likely person in all the world to confuse Creator with creature and the most likely person to detect idolatry and blasphemy in such a confusion. And the second possibility (deliberate forgery) involves the psychological absurdity of saints living and martyrs dying for a known lie; the immense impractical joke of some Jewish fishermen hood-winking the world to believe a blasphemous absurdity at the expense of their own skins.

What motive lies behind the Modernist embracing of such absurdities (or behind the Modernist *evasion* of such absurdities by evading such 'black and white' arguments)? It must be a very strong motive to blissfully wade into such nonsense; it must be a religious motive.

The religion of our society is democracy, brotherhood, socialization, conformity, agreement, popularity. Now Christian *ethics* are not as distinctive as Christian *faith*. Everyone admits the claims of love (in principle, if not in practice), but not everyone admits the claims of faith. Everyone agrees (again, in principle) with Jesus' ethical teachings, but not everyone agrees with His claim to divinity. If only we can classify Christ with other ethical teachers and Christianity with other religions, we will have removed the odium of distinctiveness, the scandal of elitism, the terror of being right where others are wrong.

The logical arguments seem so clearly to point against the Modernist that it seems necessary and inevitable to make such a dangerously judgmental psychoanalysis of his motivation. What is behind the often ingenious attempt to justify the logically impossible is something far more serious than logical inaccuracy or scholarly error. It is a spiritual disease we are all prone to, and it comes straight from Hell. It is called dishonesty, the deliberate turning from known or suspected truth, the refusal to face upsetting, uncomfortable questions, the fear of being wrong, the reluctance to repent, the refusal of Reality's invitation to grow, to change one's mind and perhaps one's nature, to be born again.

We have all entertained this visitor from Hell at times, at least in our back rooms. Our judgment must begin at home. The rarest words to hear from most writers are the words "I was wrong." But they are words everyone must speak before God when we meet Him; we'd better get some practice now. More, whenever we meet Him now, whenever new Truth shines on old minds, those minds must break to grow. The new wine bursts the old wineskins and requires new ones. Christ is the new wine, and the old wineskins are the old earth (which was burst at the Incarnation) and our old self (which is burst at baptism and the New Birth). It is for that spiritual incursion into our being, that 'spiritual marriage,' that He came. It was for that that we were created. And it is for that that He continually arranges the events of all lives by His providence — even events as unlikely as apologetic arguments.

19
THE RELIABILITY OF THE NEW TESTAMENT
Professor F. F. Bruce

What are the main arguments in favor of the reliability of the New Testament documents?

The main arguments for the reliability of the New Testament documents are of the same kind as one would apply to other works of the same period. One applies to them the regular tests of historical criticism and the New Testament documents stand up to those tests remarkably well. [Professor F. F. Bruce establishes this position in great detail in his *The New Testament Documents: Are They Reliable*?]

What are the main pre-conceptions of those critics who reject the historical reliability of the New Testament?

There is one quite influential school which thinks that to put one's reliance on historical accuracy is to detract from personal faith in Jesus Christ, which is the sole ground of justification. The late Rudolf Bultmann from Germany used to argue that the justification by history is just another form of justification by works and equally hostile to justification by faith. [As for those with anti-super-naturalistic pre-conceptions], to approach the New Testament writings with the presupposition that nothing supernatural can ever take place, that any miracle is impossible, is to approach the documents with a prejudice that is just as unjustified in its way as a complete suspension of the critical faculty would be in another way.

Do you see any shift in a more hopeful direction among Biblical critics in that many of them seem to be shedding previous prejudices?

Yes. I think so. Of course there is always the possibility that if they shed previous prejudices they may be importing new ones of their own. But yes, I think so, taking the situation as a whole.

Do you think books like *The Myth of God Incarnate* have had a pernicious influence on the public mind?

Not very pernicious because many people refuse to take seriously the picture of men who are pledged to believe in the Incarnation of God in Christ, men who lead their congregations week by week in affirming their belief in the Incarnation of God in Christ who, at the same time, try to deny that Incarnation. It's no use for a man to stand and lead a worshipping congregation in the words of the creed, saying, "I believe in Jesus Christ, His only Son our Lord, who was conceived by the Holy Spirit and born of the Virgin Mary ..." and so on, if at the same time he denies in his writings or otherwise what he affirms in church. People just won't take him seriously one way or the other. Professor C.F.D. Moule's book on Christology is very good.

20
THE HISTORICITY OF THE RESURRECTION. THE IDENTITY OF CHRIST
Professor Wolfhart Pannenberg

(The contribution from Professor Pannenberg, the renowned author of such classic works as *Theology and the Philosophy of Science* and *Jesus — God and Man*, will be preceded by a news report on his life and work.)

"In the current generation, the two acknowledged theological stars are Tubingen's Jurgen Moltmann and Munich's Wolfhart Pannenberg ... he (Pannenberg) 'is fairly widely recognized to have published more substantive work in theology in the past decade' than any other Protestant ...

"Brought up as a Nazi atheist, he fought his way free of Hitlerian nihilism and underwent an intellectual conversion to Christianity. Pannenberg first won renown in the 1960s as a member of the 'revelation as history' school in theology. He accused the pre-eminent Protestant thinkers, Rudolf Bultmann and Karl Barth, of divorcing Christian faith from history, and therefore from rational thought, by ultimately basing their standards on subjective standards ...

"Pannenberg ... thinks that Bultmann's evasion of the resurrection as a historical event is rationally untenable. As circumstantial evidence he cites the early church's unshakeable belief in it. Unless Christ actually rose from the grave, Pannenberg reasons, how can a historian plausibly account for the blazing fervor of the early Christians? ...

"Adds he: 'I am not the most popular theologian in Germany. I am found guilty for referring to reason.'"

Time March 8, 1974, 64-65.

What evidence do you think there is for the historicity of the Resurrection of Jesus Christ and what do you think about what Bultmann and Barth had to say about this evidence?

Well I myself have taken a very strong position on the subject and I think that, usually, and this applies to Barth and Bultmann, I think that most Christian theologians are not aware when they use the notion "historical," what this notion logically implies. If somebody says that a certain event really took place in the past, then, I think, he makes a statement that implies historicity insofar as that he thinks that he will get away with that statement even if it is put to a test, if it is put to critical questioning. And, of course, the historical-critical instrument is nothing else but the ensemble of means of testing statements affirming something about past events. And so our understanding of what belongs to the historical method is constantly changing according to our changing assessments of what can be used in order to find out what really happened in the past by questioning traditions and other kinds of evidence. Basically what is historical is found out by the questioning of tradition and evidence. And therefore I say, any simple statement on past events, involves a claim to historicity as much as it affirms something to be the case in view of the possibility of being checked. And insofar as such a statement really passes the checks of historical questioning, it may be affirmed to be a historical statement. Of course, not every statement about the past is uttered as explicitly a historical statement. A historical statement, then, is a statement of the past on a level of reflection on the problematics of making such statements and on the kind of questioning that is involved in securing whether a statement is really true. But, by implication, every statement about the past is a historical statement. And, thus, as long as Christians affirm that Jesus really rose from the dead, by implication they make a historical statement.

I think that there are good reasons to continue the basic Christian affirmation that Jesus rose from the dead and, so far as they are good reasons based on the historical questioning of the New Testament sources, that this is a historical statement. This does not imply that there would be no quarrel any more about the issue. All historical statements are such that continue to be questioned and many of them are rejected by some historians; and yet other historians claim that the statements they make are historical statements. And so, a historical statement is not, by definition, beyond dispute. And, certainly, the statement that Jesus rose from the dead will be in dispute until the end of time; and there are reasons why this is so. It's simply because the analogies of our ordinary experience do not know of this kind of resurrection from the dead; simply because it's so unusual not because there is less reliability of the sources than other cases. To the contrary, I think if it be an ordinary event that was recorded in such a way nobody would seriously question its factuality. Simply because of the extremely unusual character of that event, again and again people tend to reject it. But, I think, one who affirms the event should not shrink from also taking the implications of such a statement, that is, to affirm that it is a historical event.

Could you elaborate on some of the reasons which justify the affirmation that Jesus rose from the dead?

There are two traditions: The tradition of the empty tomb and the tradition of the appearances. The tradition of the appearances is not only connected with late witnesses where the literary written form of those witnesses comes decades after this event was supposed to happen (as it is true of the Gospels). But there is the Apostle Paul. And, in the case of the Apostle Paul and of the Pauline writings, which are the oldest in the New Testament, we have a person who not only claimed himself to have seen Jesus Christ but, on the basis of all we know about the Jerusalem community, a person who had been acknowledged by the other main apostles in his claim to apostolicity, in his mission that was based on the appearances of the Risen Christ. Hence there is good reason to assume that the basis of such a recognition of Paul by the Jerusalem apostles had been a recognition of the experience which he claimed to be the basis of his mission. Thus, concerning the witness of Paul we do not have the late form of this tradition, as in some of the Gospel texts, but a very early tradition; a very early witness written down by way of a formula, in I Corinthians 15, maybe a few years after those events happened, and transmitted by a person who himself was one of the primary witnesses. And this is a very strong evidence and, therefore, few scholars, even few rather critical scholars, doubt that there had been visionary experiences.

The whole question, however, is what visionary experiences mean: whether they can be explained psychologically in terms of hallucinations or any other way. Then, of course, it comes to the problem of the psychology of visions, of visionary experiences. And I think there are no sufficient reasons for assuming that hallucinatory phenomena had developed analogous to those which we know on the basis of taking drugs or those which come with certain diseases. These presuppositions are not applicable in the New Testament sources.

There is the other tradition, of the empty tomb, and many scholars have rejected this tradition as a late development. In order to judge this, the primary question is whether the tradition of the tomb is an integral part of the Passion tradition, the Passion story, which usually is assumed to have existed as a literary complex before the rest of the Gospels had been written because it appears virtually identical in the three Synoptic Gospels. But then, if the tomb is an authentic, genuine element of the original framework of the Passion tradition, then the question is where the Passion tradition comes from. And most exegetes, to my knowledge, assume that the Passion tradition may have come from the community of Jerusalem because it deals with places in Jerusalem and with events which have been going on in Jerusalem. Thus, there are good reasons for attributing the Passion narration to the Jerusalem community in the first century. And then, of course, we have a rather old tradition. Still the question is how to judge that tradition. Now I think one of the strongest points in favor of a positive judgement here is what we know about the early disputes between Christians and Jews about the Resurrection. The Jews accepted that the tomb was empty. The dispute, however, was about how this was to be explained. The Jews said the disciples had removed the body. But they did not question the fact that the tomb was empty. That, I think, is a very remarkable point. We have no other indication from early or later Jewish polemics against Christianity that would affirm that the tomb was not empty.

And then, of course, my main reason is a general reflection, given the concreteness of the Jewish understanding of a resurrection from the dead. It would be hardly conceivable that the earliest Christian congregation could have assembled in Jerusalem of all places, where Jesus had died and was buried, if His tomb was intact. There are some people who say, perhaps, the tomb wasn't known and that he was just put into an anonymous tomb together with other criminals. Well, then it would be hardly credible that the disciples would not have interested themselves in where the body of Jesus remained. Some critics say, they were not interested in that question. I can't believe that! Even these critics admit that we should have traces of Jewish polemics against the Christians pointing to the supposed facts that the tomb was not known, or that he was put in an anonymous mass grave. Nothing of that kind. But Jewish polemics assume the tomb was empty but it occurred in another way. Thus, I think, in taking all that together, we have good reason for affirming that we have an old tradition that the tomb was empty when the first Christians started proclaiming the Risen Christ. In early times, some people thought the disciples were traitors. Then, of course, it is hard to understand how they could risk their lives for such a conspiracy. So there are more problems, really, with the critics than with the affirmation of the resurrection of Christ.

Except, of course, for the unusual quality of the event that is stated. As Hume said, in his *Essay Concerning Human Understanding*, he would not believe on any amount of evidence, that something so unusual could have happened. That, of course, is a perfectly dogmatic position, saying that there cannot be what shouldn't be, there cannot be what is unusual. And, of course, more or less unusual things happened in history again and again. Of course, not things of such an extremely unusual character as the resurrection from the dead. So it is to be granted that this is extremely unusual, against custom, as Hume would say. But, I think, this in itself is not a sufficient argument to reject the claim. But, in order to reject the claim of the Easter tradition, it has to be shown that the claim was based on legend or on hallucination, or on something that is analogous to deceptive forms of human experience. And this has not been shown so far.

Turning to another theme, what are your reasons for affirming the basic elements of orthodox Christology?

First, I start to give you my reasons why I think that orthodox Christology, as it has been spelt out in dogmatic definitions of the ancient Church, is basically defendable. I think it is basically defendable as a development from the early Christian message, a development of the implications inherent in the early Christian message. And it starts from the Easter faith of early Christianity; the Easter faith of early Christianity meant by implication that by being raised from the dead, Jesus was confirmed by God in His pre-Easter claim to divine authority in His message. That was spelt out in terms of calling Jesus His Son, the One Who, in His ministry, corresponds to the God Whom He calls the Father. The kind of relatedness to the God Whom He calls the Father was aptly expressed by the title of Son at least by His disciples. And so Jesus is the Son of God not only because of the Easter event but because of being confirmed by the Easter event in His pre-Christian ministry even before. It was an implication of the Easter faith. And that He is the Son of God was the basic affirmation of orthodox Christology. The details of this position I develop in my Christology.

To be a Christian, would one, by definition, have to affirm the divinity of Christ?

Yes. I think that's an implication of the Easter faith of Christianity.

And you cannot describe yourself as a Christian if you do not make this affirmation?

That's basically the argument of my book on Christology: that the affirmation of the divinity of Christ, as it was spelt out by the dogma of Nicea and Constantinople and further developed at Chalcedon, is an implication of the original Easter faith of Christianity.

21
EVIDENCE FOR HISTORICAL ACCURACY OF THE NEW TESTAMENT
Josh McDowell

While I was recently lecturing at Arizona State University, a professsor accompanied by students from his graduate seminar on world literature approached me after a "free-speech" outdoors lecture. He said, "Mr. McDowell, you are basing all your claims about Christ on a second-century document that is obsolete. I showed in class today how the New Testament was written so long after Christ that it could not be accurate in what it recorded."

That professor's opinion about the records concerning Jesus had their source in the conclusions of various critics who assumed that most of the New Testament Scriptures were not written until long after the time of Jesus.

I replied to him, "Sir, your opinions or conclusions about the New Testament are 25 years out of date."

Since the New Testament is the primary historical source for our information about Jesus, it is important to determine its accuracy concerning what it reports.

Search for Truth
When you have a religious faith that appeals to truth, as Christianity does, and is based on searching out truth and preserving that knowledge, you have a built-in *plus* factor for preserving its integrity over the years. Biblical Christianity has such a *plus* factor for researching and preserving truth.

For example, the Bible says, "You shall know the

truth." It doesn't say to ignore it. It says, "You shall know the truth, and the truth shall make you free" (John 8:32). The apostle Paul admonishes the believer to "be diligent to present yourself approved to God as a workman who does not need to be ashamed, handling accurately the word of truth" (2 Timothy 2:15). Throughout the New Testament there is an emphasis on truth, and on preserving that truth.

When you compare the Bible to other literature of antiquity, the historical evidence for the Bible's reliability is overwhelming. If other literature had the same historical evidence, no one would question its authenticity and reliability. But with the Bible two objections are raised. First, it's a religious book and therefore "It can't be trusted." Second, it assumes the existence of the supernatural. For many people, the historical evidence is not the key. The issue for many (although not all) individuals involved in New Testament criticism is, "if there's any element of the supernatural, then it's unhistorical."

Because of that assumption, many critics during the 19th and 20th centuries have attacked the reliability of the New Testament documents. There seems to be a constant barrage of accusations that have now been outdated by archaeological discoveries and research.

Many of those opinions about the records concerning Jesus are based on the conclusions of a German critic, F. C. Baur. Baur assumed that most of the New Testament Scriptures were not written until late in the second century A.D. He concluded that these writings came basically from myths or legends that had developed during the lengthy interval between the lifetime of Jesus and the time those accounts were set down in writing.

By the 20th century, however, archaeological discoveries had gone a long way in confirming the historical accuracy of the New Testament manuscripts, and their first-century origin. Discoveries of early papyri manuscripts (the John Rylands manuscript, A.D. 130; the Chester Beatty Papyri, A.D. 155; and the Bodmer Papyri II, A.D. 200) helped bridge the gap between the time of Christ and existing manuscripts from a later date.

Archaeologist Millar Burrows of Yale has said that one result of comparing New Testament Greek with the language of the papyri is an increase of confidence in the accurate transmission of the text of the New Testament (Millar Burrows, *What Mean These Stones*, Meridian Books, 1956, p. 52).

William F. Albright of Johns Hopkins University, who was one of the world's foremost biblical archaeologists, writes: "We can already say emphatically that there is no longer any solid basis for dating any book of the New Testament after about A.D. 80, two full generations before the date between 130 and 150 given by the more radical New Testament critics of today (William F. Albright, *Recent Discoveries in Bible Lands*, Funk and Wagnall, 1955, p. 136).

A Geographer Testifies

Sir William Ramsey was one of the greatest geographers who ever lived. He was a student of the German historical school which taught that the book of Acts was a product of the mid-second century A.D. and not the first century as it purports to be. After reading modern criticism about the Book of Acts, he became convinced that it was not a trustworthy account of the facts of the time just after Christ (A.D. 50) and therefore was unworthy of consideration by a historian or geographer. So in his research on the history of Asia Minor, Ramsey paid little attention to the New Testament. His archaeological investigation, however, eventually compelled him to consider the writings of Luke, in the Book of Acts in particular. He observed the meticulous accuracy of its historical details about the first century, and gradually his attitude began to change. The evidence forced him to conclude that "Luke is a historian of the first rank ... this author should be placed along with the very greatest of historians" (Sir William Ramsey, *The Bearing of Recent Discoveries on the Trustworthiness of the New Testament*, London: Hodder and Stoughton, 1915, p. 222). Because of Luke's accuracy, Ramsey finally conceded that Acts could not be a second-century document but was rather a mid-first century historical account.

Dr. John A. T. Robinson, lecturer at Trinity College, Cambridge, has been for years one of England's more distinguished critics. Robinson at first accepted the consensus typified by German criticism that the New Testament was written years after the time of Christ, at the end of the first century. But, as "little more than a theological joke," he decided to investigate the arguments on the late dating of all the New Testament books, a field largely dormant since the turn of the century.

Scholarly Sloppiness

The results stunned him. He said that owing to scholarly "sloth," the "tyranny of unexamined assumptions," and "almost willful blindness" by previous authors, much of the past reasoning was untenable. He concluded that the New Testament is the work of the apostles themselves or of contemporaries who worked with them, and that all the New Testament books, including the gospel of John, had to have been written before A.D. 64 (John A.T. Robinson, *Time*, March 21, 1977, p. 95) [See also Robinson's — *Redating the New Testament*, London: SCM Press, 1976].

Robinson challenged his colleagues to try to prove him wrong. If scholars reopen the question, he is convinced, the results will force "the rewriting of many introductions to — and ultimately, theologies of — the New Testament" (ibid).

One can also make a strong case for the reliability of the Scriptures from a legal perspective. The "ancient document" principle under the *Federal Rules of Evidence* (published by West Publishing Co., 1979, Rule 901 [b] [8]) permits the authentication of a document to be made by showing that the document (1) is in such condition as to create no suspicion concerning its authenticity; (2) was in a place where, if authentic, it would likely be; and (3) has been in existence 20 years or more at the time it is offered.

A Legal Perspective

Dr. John Warwick Montgomery, a lawyer, theologian, and dean of the Simon Greenleaf School of Law, comments about the application of the "ancient document" rule to the New Testament documents: "Applied to the gospel records, and reinforced by responsible lower (textual) criticism, this rule would establish competency in any court of law" (John Warwick Montgomery, "Legal Reasoning and Christian Apologetics," *The Law Above the Law*, Christian Legal Society, 1975, pp. 88, 89).

Some critics argue that information about Christ was passed by word of mouth until it was written down in the form of the Gospels. Even though the period was much shorter than previously believed, they conclude that the Gospel accounts took on the forms of tales and myths.

But the period of oral tradition (as defined by the critics) is not long enough to have allowed the alterations in the tradition that those critics have alleged. Dr. Simon Kistemaker, professor of Bible at Reformed Seminary, writes: "Normally, the accumulation of folklore among people of primitive culture takes many generations; it is a gradual process spread over centuries of time. But in conformity with the thinking of the form critic, we must conclude that the Gospel stories were produced and collected within little more than one generation. In terms of the form-critical approach, the formation of the individual Gospel units must be understood as a telescoped project with accelerated course of action" (Simon Kistemaker, *The Gospels in Current Study*, Baker Book House, 1972, pp. 48,49).

A.H. McNeile, former Regius Professor of Divinity at the University of Dublin, points out that form critics do not deal with the tradition of Jesus' words as closely as they should. A careful look at I Corinthians 7:10,12,25 shows the careful preservation and the existence of a genuine tradition of recording these words. In the Jewish religion it was customary for a student to memorize a rabbi's teaching. A good pupil was like "a plastered cistern that loses not a drop" (*Mishna*, Aboth, 2:8) (A.H. McNeile, *An Introduction to the Study of the New Testament*, London: Oxford University Press, 1953, p. 54).

Moreover, if we rely on C.F. Birney's theory (in *The Poetry of Our Lord*, 1925), we can assume that much of the Lord's teaching is in Aramaic poetical form, making it easy to be memorized.

There is strong internal testimony that the Gospels were written at an early date. The Book of Acts records the missionary activity of the early church and was written as a sequel by the same person who wrote the Gospel according to Luke. The Book of Acts ends with the apostle Paul being alive in Rome, his death not being recorded. This would lead us to believe that it was written before he died, since the other major events in his life have been recorded. We have some reason to believe that Paul was put to death in the Neronian persecution of A.D. 64, which means that the Book of Acts was composed before then.

If the Book of Acts was written before A.D. 64, then the Gospel of Luke, to which Acts was a sequel, had to have been composed some time before that, probably in the late fifties or early sixties of the first century. The death of Christ took place around A.D. 30, which would make the composition of Luke at the latest within 30 years of the events.

The early church generally taught that the first Gospel composed was that of Matthew, which would place us still closer to the time of Christ. This evidence leads us to believe that the first three Gospels were all composed within 30 years from the time these events occurred, a time when unfriendly eyewitnesses were still living who could contradict their testimony if it was not accurate (Josh McDowell and Don Stewart, *Answers to Tough Questions*, Here's Life Publishers, 1980, pp. 7,8).

Facts involved in the issue led W.F. Albright to comment:

> Every book of the New Testament was written ... between the forties and the eighties of the first century A.D. (very probably sometime between about A.D. 50 and 75) (William F. Albright, *Christianity Today*, Vol. 7, Jan. 18, 1963, p. 3).

The historical reliability of the Scripture should be tested by the same criteria used to test all historical documents. Military historian C. Sanders lists and explains three basic principles of historiography: the bibliographical test, the internal evidence test, and the external evidence test (C. Sanders, *Introduction to Research in English Literary History*, Macmillan Company, 1952, pp. 143 ff).

IS THERE MANUSCRIPT EVIDENCE?

Bibliographical Test

The *bibliographical test* is an examination of the textual transmission by which documents reach us. In other words, not having the original documents, how reliable are the copies we have in regard to the number of manuscripts and the time interval between the original and the extant copies?

A common misconception is that the text of the Bible has not come down to us as it was originally written. Accusations abound of zealous monks changing the biblical text throughout church history.

The problem is not lack of evidence. When research into biblical reliability was completed and my book *Evidence That Demands a Verdict* was released in 1973, I was able to document 14,000 manuscripts and portions of manuscripts in Greek and other early versions of the New Testament. Recently we updated and reissued *Evidence* because of the vast amount of new research material available. Now we are able to document 24,633 manuscripts and portions of the New Testament.

The significance of the number of manuscripts documenting the New Testament is even greater when one realizes that in all of ancient history the second book in terms of manuscript authority is *the Iliad*, by Homer. It has only 643 surviving manuscripts.

The New Testament was originally composed in Greek. There are approximately 5,500 copies in existence that contain all or part of the New Testament. Although we do not possess the originals, copies exist from a very early date. The earliest fragment dates about A.D. 120, with about 50 other fragments dating within 150-200 years from the time of composition.

Two major manuscripts, Codex Vaticanus (A.D. 325) and Codex Sinaiticus (A.D. 350), a complete copy, date within 250 years of the time of composition. That may seem like a long time span, but it is minimal compared to most ancient works. The first complete copy of the *Odyssey* is from 2,200 years after it was written. New Testament Greek scholar J. Harold Greenlee comments:

Since scholars accept as generally trustworthy the writings of the ancient classics even though the earliest MSS were written so long after the original writings and the number of extant MSS is in many instances so small, it is clear that the reliability of the text of the New Testament is likewise assured (J. Harold Greenlee, *Introduction to New Testament Textual Criticism*, William B. Eerdmans Publishing Co. 1964, p. 15).

Many ancient writings have been transmitted to us by only a handful of manuscripts (Catullus — three copies, the earliest one is 1,600 years after he wrote; Herodotus — eight copies, and a 1,300 year gap.)

Many people consider Thucydides one of the most accurate of ancient historians, and only eight manuscripts have survived. Of Aristotle, 49 manuscripts survive.

Not only do the New Testament documents have more manuscript evidence and a shorter time interval between the original (called an *Autograph*) and the earliest copy, but they were also translated into several other languages at an early date. Translation of a document into another language was rare in the ancient world, so this is an added textual verification for the New Testament. The number of copies of these versions is in excess of 18,000, with possibly as many as 25,000. This is further evidence that helps us establish the New Testament text.

Less than 10 years ago, 36,000 quotations of the Scriptures by the early church fathers could be documented. But more recently, as a result of research done at the British Museum, we are now able to document, in early church writings, 89,000 quotations from the New Testament. Without any Bibles or manuscripts — they could all be thrown away or burned — one could reconstruct all but 11 verses of the entire New Testament from material written within 150 and 200 years of the time of Jesus Christ.

F. F. Bruce, New Testament scholar at Malchester University in England, makes the following observation:

> The evidence for our New Testment writings is ever so much greater than the evidence for many writings of classical authors, the authenticity of which no one dreams of questioning.

He also states,

> And if the New Testament were a collection of secular writings, their authenticity would generally be regarded as beyond all doubt (F.F. Bruce, *The New Testament Documents; Are They Reliable?* Rev. ed., William B. Eerdmans Publishing Co., 1977, p. 15).

Manuscript expert Sir Frederic Kenyon, former director and principal librarian of the British Museum, was one of the foremost experts on ancient manuscripts and their authority. Shortly before his death, he wrote concerning the New Testament:

> The interval between the dates of original composition (of the New Testament) and the earliest extant evidence becomes so small as to be in fact negligible, and the last foundation for any doubt that the Scriptures have come down to us substantially as they were written has now been removed. Both the authenticity and the general integrity of the books of the New Testament may be regarded as finally established (Sir Frederic Kenyon, *The Bible and Archaeology*, Harper and Row, Publishers, 1940, pp. 288,289).

Of *the Iliad*, Bruce Metzger, Princeton textual critic, observes:

> In the entire range of ancient Greek and Latin literature, *the Iliad* ranks next to the New Testament in possessing the greatest amount of manuscript testimony (Bruce Metzger, *Chapters in the History of New Testament Textual Criticism*, William B. Eerdmans Publishing Co., 1963, p. 144). Of all the literary compositions by the Greek people, the Homeric poems are the best suited for comparison with the Bible (ibid, p. 145).

Of course, we must apply the same bibliographical test not only to secular literature and the Bible, but also to other religious literature like the Qur'an. There are no original manuscripts available today of the text of the Qur'an dating from the time of Muhammad. Muslims allege that the Qur'an standardized by the third Caliph Uthman still exists, though there are at least 20 early Qur'an manuscripts which claim this coveted origin. One is on display at the Topkapi Museum in Istanbul, another is in the Soviet State Library, and others are preserved elsewhere in the Muslim world. All are written in early kufic script, but if even one could be attributed to Uthman, this still leaves a gap of over a generation between the death of Muhammad and the oldest Qur'an manuscript. In fact there is only one manuscript of the Qur'an surviving in the Medinan al-mail script (Medina being the city where Muhammad spent his last years) and this text is known to date from the eighth century — at least 150 years after the death of Muhammad. It is preserved in the British Museum and is on permanent display. Because neither Christians nor Muslims have *original* copies of their Scriptures, the test of reliability has to be applied in the same way to the transcribed copies that have survived. In both cases the result is the same — the Bible and the Qur'an have been remarkably preserved in its earliest known form.

The bibliographical test that we have briefly applied to the New Testament determines only that the text we have now is what was originally recorded. One still has to determine whether and to what extent that written record is credible.

IS THE NEW TESTAMENT TEXT CREDIBLE?

Internal Evidence Test

Internal criticism, the second test of historicity listed by Sanders, deals with the credibility of the text.

Two factors must guide the application of this test. The first is that in the event of an apparent inaccuracy or discrepancy, the literary critic follows Aristotle's dictum that "The benefit of the doubt is to be given to the document itself, and not arrogated by the critic to himself." In other words, as John Montgomery emphasizes in his lectures: "One must listen to the claims of the document under analysis, and not assume fraud or error unless the author disqualifies himself by contradictions or known factual inaccuracies" (John Warwick Montgomery, *History and Christianity*, Here's Life Publishers, 1983 p. 29). As a person is innocent until proven guilty in a United States court of law, so a document is innocent, until by a proven discrepancy, or inaccuracy or error, it is shown to be not trustworthy.

When alleged discrepancies or a problem or an error are discovered, certain questions should be asked. First, have we correctly understood the passage, the proper use of the numbers or the words? Second, do we possess all the available knowledge in that matter? Third, can any further light be thrown on it through textual research, archaeology, or historical investigation? All three considerations contribute to investigating textual veracity.

Dr. Robert Horn put it this way:

Difficulties are to be grappled with and problems are to drive us to see clear light. But until such time as we have total and final light on any issue, we are in no position to affirm there is a proven error, an unquestionable objection to an infallible Bible. It is common knowledge that countless objections have been fully resolved since this century began (Robert M. Horn, *The Book That Speaks for Itself*, InterVarsity Press, 1970, pp. 86,87).

When faced with an alleged contradiction, one must appeal to the manuscript evidence, the internal biblical evidence, the documented linguistic evidence, and the canons of textual criticism. Space does not permit us to amplify each of these areas here.

The second factor of the internal evidence test is that the nearness of the witness both geographically and chronologically to the events recorded greatly affects the writer's credibility. How does this affect the New Testament? The New Testament accounts of the life and teachings of Jesus were recorded by men who either had been eyewitnesses themselves or who were recounting the descriptions of eyewitnesses.

Dr. Louis Gottschalk, former professor of history at the University of Chicago, outlines his historical method in an excellent guide used by many for historical investigation. Gottschalk points out that the ability of the writer or the witness to tell the truth is helpful to the historian to determine credibility, "even if it is contained in a document obtained by force or fraud, or is otherwise impeachable, or is based on hearsay evidence, or is from an interested witness" (Louis R. Gottschalk, *Understanding History*. Knopf, 1969, 2nd ed., p. 150).

This "ability to tell the truth," Gottschalk points out, is closely related to the witness' nearness both geographically and chronologically to the events recorded. What about the New Testament accounts?

> Inasmuch as many have undertaken to compile an account of the things accomplished among us, just as those who from the beginning were eyewitnesses and servants of the Word have handed them down to us, it seemed fitting for me as well, having investigated everything carefully from the beginning, to write it out for you in consecutive order, most excellent Theophilus (Luke 1:1-3).
>
> For we did not follow cleverly devised tales when we made known to you the power and coming of our Lord Jesus Christ, but we were eyewitnesses of His majesty (2 Peter 1:16).
>
> What we have seen and heard we proclaim to you also, that you also may have fellowship with us; and indeed our fellowship is with the Father, and with His Son Jesus Christ (I John 1:3).
>
> And he who has seen has borne witness, and his witness is true; and he knows that he is telling the truth, so that you also may believe (John 19:35).
>
> Now in the fifteenth year of the reign of Tiberius Caesar, when Pontius Pilate was governor of Judea, and Herod was tetrarch of Galilee, and his brother Philip was tetrarch of the region of Ituraea and Trachonitis, and Lysanias was tetrarch of Abileen ... (Luke 3:1).

This closeness to the recorded accounts is an extremely effective means of certifying the accuracy of what is retained by a witness. The historian, however, also has to deal with the eyewitness who consciously or unconsciously tells falsehoods even though he is near the event and is competent enough to tell the truth.

The New Testament accounts of Christ were being circulated within the lifetimes of His contemporaries. Those people could have confirmed or denied the accuracy of the accounts. In advocating their case for the gospel, the apostles had appealed (even when confronting their most severe opponents) to common knowledge concerning Jesus. They not only said, "Look, we saw this" or "We heard that ..." but they turned the tables around and right in front of adverse critics said, "You know this also," because if he isn't right in the details, he will be exposed immediately.

Speaking to Jewish people the apostle Peter said: "Men of Israel, listen to these words: Jesus the Nazarene, a man attested to you ..." Not just to us. But a man "attested to you by God with miracles and wonders and signs which God performed through Him ..." Notice this: "In your midst, just as you yourselves know" (Acts 2:22). If they hadn't seen those miracles and signs, Peter would never have gotten out of there alive, let alone thousands come to Christ.

Paul did the same thing. He was brought before the king, and he said (in my loose paraphrase), I'm glad I'm brought before you, because you know of my life from childhood up, and you know the customs of the Jews. Then he started to present the evidence for Christianity, but he was interrupted: "And while Paul was saying this in his defense, King Festus said in a loud voice, 'Paul, you are out of your mind! Your great learning is driving you mad.'" They knew he had great learning. He'd studied under Gamaliel, he'd studied in Tarsus. But Paul said, "I am not out of my mind, most excellent Festus, but I utter words of sober truth." The phrase "of sober truth" in the Greek literally says, "of truth and rationale." Then notice what Paul said, "I am persuaded that none of these things escape the King's notice; for this has not been done in a corner" (Acts 26:24-26).

When I study history, and I want to check out the accuracy of the writer, I check out several things. First, does he have a good character — that is, can he be trusted? Second, is there a consistency in his writings, a consistency of accuracy? Third, is there confrontation? In other words, was the material written down or presented at a time when there were those alive who were aware of the facts surrounding the events or statements recorded?

Concerning the primary-source value of the New Testament eyewitness records, F.F. Bruce makes an astute observation not only about the value of friendly, but also *hostile eyewitnesses:*

And it was not only friendly eyewitnesses that the early preachers had to reckon with; there were others less well disposed who were also conversant with the main facts of the ministry and death of Jesus. The disciples could not afford to risk inaccuracies (not to speak of willful manipulation of the facts) which would at once be exposed by those who would be only too glad to do so. On the contrary, one of the strong points in the original apostolic preaching is the confident appeal to the knowledge of the hearers; they not only said, 'we are witnesses of these things,' but also, 'As you yourselves also know' (Acts 2:22). Had there been any tendency to depart from the facts in any material respect, the possible presence of hostile witnesses in the audiences would have served as a further corrective (Bruce, *Documents,* p. 33).

New Testament scholar Robert Grant of the University of Chicago concludes:

At the time they (the synoptic gospels) were written or may be supposed to have been written, there were eyewitnesses and their testimony was not completely disregarded ... This means that the gospels must be regarded as largely reliable witnesses to the life, death and resurrection of Jesus (Robert Grant, *Historical Introduction to the New Testament*, Harper and Row, 1963, p. 302).

While the multiple number of New Testament eyewitnesses are not a 100 percent guarantee of reliabilty, it would be extremely difficult to argue that each one made the same mistake in identification. The eyewitness accounts of having seen Christ alive after his resurrection would be very convincing in a court of law, especially in view of the extensive testimony.

The Hearsay Rule

McCormick's *Handbook of the Law of Evidence*, an excellent treatise on analyzing evidence, observes that the legal system's insistence upon using only the most reliable sources of information is manifested best in the rule requiring that a witness who testifies to a fact which can be perceived by the senses must actually have observed the fact (McCormick's *Handbook of the Law of Evidence*, Edward W. Cleary, ed., West Publishing Co., 1972, pp. 586, 587).

The emphasis of this hearsay rule is that "hearsay" is not admissible as evidence in a court of law. The Federal Rules of Evidence declares that a witness must testify concerning what he has firsthand knowledge of, not what has come to him indirectly from other sources (Federal Rules of Evidence, Rule 801 and 802).

Concerning the value of a person testifying "of his own knowledge," Dr. John Warwick Montgomery, points out that from a legal perspective the New Testament documents meet the demand for "primary-source" evidence. He writes that the New Testament record is:

> ... fully vindicated by the constant assertions of their authors to be setting forth that which we have heard, which we have seen with our eyes, which we have looked upon and our hands have handled (John Warwick Montgomery, "Legal Reasoning and Christian Apologetics," pp. 88, 89).

Most testimony in the New Testament comes from firsthand knowledge. For example, when Mary went to the tomb, the angel appeared to her and said, "He is not here, He has risen." When Mary repeated that, it was hearsay because she hadn't seen Him herself; she just had heard about it. But then later, Jesus personally appeared to Mary. That took it out of hearsay, and made the evidence a primary source.

Psychological Perspective
Along with the eyewitness accounts, we need to see the psychological perspective of personal testimony. In law today, a whole new field is opening up relating the psychological makeup of a witness, and what he can remember and what he can't. Dr. Elizabeth Loftus, professor of psychology at the University of Washington, wrote, "people who witness fearful events, remember the details of them less accurately than they recall ordinary happenings. Stress or fear disrupts perception and therefore memory. Stress can also affect the person's ability to recall something observed or learned during that period of relative tranquility" (Elizabeth S. Loftus, "The Eyewitness on Trial," Trials, Vol. 16, No. 10, Oct. 1980, pp. 30-35).

Her observations strengthen the eyewitness accounts of the New Testament. You do not find in the post-resurrection accounts of Jesus any fleeting glimpse of a stranger in the darkness of an alley, wielding a knife or a gun. After His resurrection the followers of Christ spent time with someone they knew and loved. Several times Jesus said, "Don't be afraid," so there must have been stress there, and fear. But there was also the repetition of appearances — for over 40 days He appeared with them. After being eyewitnesses for 40 days they became certain in their memories.

The multiple number of New Testament eyewitnesses, and all the variety of appearances, 500 at one time for instance, do not give 100 percent assurance that the witnesses were accurate. However, it would be extremely difficult, and just about contrary to everything we know in history, to argue that each one of them made the same mistake in identification. For example, you have 500 witnesses at one time. Let's take them to a court of law. (We'll only give them six minutes each. When was the last time you were in a court, and you only had an eyewitness given six minutes. Take 500 people, multiply by six minutes given each on the witness stand — that's three thousand minutes of eyewitness testimony. Divide that by 60 minutes an hour, and it comes out to 50 hours of eyewitness testimony. Just for the resurrection.

An area of the internal evidence test relating to the apostles that is often overlooked is the resurrection and its effect on their lives. This aspect is documented extensively in *More Than a Carpenter* (Josh McDowell, Tyndale House Publishers, 1977) and *Evidence That Demands a Verdict* (Josh McDowell, Here's Life Publishers, 1979).

IS THIS THE TRUE ORIGINAL MESSAGE?

Two crucial questions relate to the reliability of the

biblical record we have today: (1) Is what we have now what actually was written down 2,000 years ago? In other words, has the original message been changed down through the centuries? (2) Was what was recorded or written down true? Or was it distorted, stretched, embellished, or tailored by His followers to coincide with their own theology or understanding? We have just discussed the first. Now let's go on to the second question.

Die for a Lie?

Good historical tradition shows us 12 Jewish men, 11 of whom died martyrs' deaths as a tribute to one thing: an empty tomb, and the appearances of Jesus of Nazareth alive after His death by crucifixion. For 40 days after His resurrection, these men walked with Him and lived with Him and ate with Him. His resurrection was accompanied by many "convincing proofs" (Acts 1:3). That phrase "convincing proofs," meaning overwhelming and compelling evidence, was used in law courts of that day.

The critic might say that the apostles died for a lie, but if the resurrection were a lie, there were 12 men who knew it was a lie.

André Kole is considered the world's leading illusionist, often called the magician's magician. He has created and sold more than 1,400 illusionary and magical effects.

When André was a student, he studied psychology. And he was trained in illusion and magic. He was challenged to apply his proficiency to the miracles of Jesus Christ, to attempt to explain them away by principles of modern magic and illusion. He accepted that challenge. He was able to explain several of them, but most of them he could not. There was one in particular that he could not come near to explaining away — the resurrection of Jesus Christ. He said that there is no way through modern illusionary effects or magic that Jesus could have deceived His apostles and followers. There are too many built-in safety factors. He was forced to the conclusion that if the resurrection was a lie, they had to know it.

While it's true that thousands of people throughout history have died for a lie, they did so only if they thought it to be the truth. If the resurrection was a lie, then these men not only died for a lie, but they knew it was a lie.

As the early church father Tertullian said, "No man would be willing to die unless he knew he had the truth" (Gaston F. Poote, *The Transformation of the Twelve*, Abington Press, 1958, p. 12). What happened to these people? Dr. Michael Green of England points out that "the resurrection was the belief that turned heart-broken followers of a crucified Rabbi into the courageous witnesses and martyrs of the early church. This is the one belief that separated the followers of Jesus from the Jews, and turned them into the community of the Resurrection. You can imprison them, flog them, but you could not make them deny their conviction that on the third day, He rose again" (Michael Green, "Editor's Preface," *I Believe in the Resurrection of Jesus* by George Eldon Ladd, William B. Eerdmans Publishing Co., 1975, p. 3).

Dr. Kenneth Scott Latourette, who for years was Sterling Professor of Missions and Oriental History at Yale University observed that "from discouraged, disillusioned men and women, who sadly looked back upon the days when they had hoped that Jesus was here, and would redeem Israel, they were made over into a company of enthusiastic witness" (Kenneth Scott Latourette, *A History of Christianity*, Harper and Row, Publishers, 1937, 1:59).

Dr. Simon Greenleaf, Royal Professor of Law at Harvard University, was one of the great legal minds of our country. His expertise was in the area of reducing the credibility of a witness in a court of law, i.e. to show that someone was lying. After examining Christianity and the resurrection, he became a Christian and went on to write a book explaining the evidence that led him to the conclusion that the resurrection is a well-established historical event (Simon Greenleaf, *An Examination of the Testimony of the Four Evangelists by the Rules of Evidence Administered in the Courts of Justice*, Baker Book House, reprinted 1965, p. 29).

Greenleaf made this observation in support of the veracity and integrity of the testimony of the disciples: "The annals of military warfare afford scarcely an example of the like: heroic constancy, patience, and unflinching courage. They had every possible motive to review carefully the ground of their fate, and the evidences of the great facts and truths they asserted" (ibid).

Die for a Great Cause?

Critics also assert that "dying for a great cause" doesn't prove the truth of that cause. Yes, a lot of people have died for great causes. But the apostles' great cause died on the cross.

Let me take you back in history to see why many Jews who were Jesus' contemporaries denied Him as Messiah. The Jews taught that there would be two Messiahs, not one. One would be the suffering Messiah who would die for the sins of Israel. The other would be the reigning political Messiah, who would relieve them from oppression, the son of David. Jesus denied this, asserting that there were not to be two Messiahs coming once each, but that there would be one Messiah coming twice. Jesus said, "I'm coming the first time to die for your sins, and I'm coming back a second time, to reign throughout the world."

Before the time of Christ, the hierarchy of Judaism had become very self-righteous. Christ accused them of being whitewashed sepulchers. They were under the oppression of the Romans, so, to hold the allegiance of the people, they taught them they didn't need the suffering Messiah. When the Messiah came, the leaders said, he'd be the reigning polical Messiah. He would bring the chariots and cavalry down out of the mountains; he would use every weapon possible, and he would throw the Romans out. And that's what the people believed.

That is why it was so hard for the apostles to understand what Jesus was saying. He said, "I have to die. I have to go to Jerusalem. I'm going to suffer. I'm going to be crucified and buried." They couldn't understand it. Why? From childhood it had been ingrained into them that when the Messiah came, he would reign politically. They thought they were in on something big. They were going to rule with Him.

Professor E. F. Scott points this out when he says that "for the people at large, their Messiah remained what He had been to Isaiah and His contemporaries, the Son of David, who would bring victory and prosperity to the Jewish nation. In the light of the Gospel references, it can hardly be doubted that the popular conception of the Messiah was mainly national and political" (Ernest Findlay Scott, *Kingdom and the Messiah*, Edinburgh: T and T Clark, 1911, p. 55).

Dr. Joseph Klausner, a Jewish scholar, observed "that the Messiah became more and more not only a pre-eminent polical ruler, but also a man of pre-eminent moral qualities" (Joseph Klausner, *The Messianic Idea in Israel*, Macmillan Co., 1955, p. 23).

Another Jewish professor, Dr. Jacob Gardenhus, says that the Jews awaited the Messiah as the one who would deliver them from Roman oppression. The Temple with its sacrificial service was intact, because the Romans did not interfere in Jewish religious affairs. The Messianic hope was basically for national liberation, for a redeemer of a country that was being oppressed.

The Jewish Encyclopedia records that the Jews

"yearned for the promised deliverer of the house of David who would free them from the yoke of the hated foreign usurper, who would put an end to the impious world, and rule, and would establish his own reign of peace and justice in its place" (*The Jewish Encyclopedia*, Funk and Wagnalls Co., 1906, Vol. 8, p. 508).

What was the attitude of the disciples, the followers of Jesus? Were they awaiting a suffering Messiah? No! They were expecting a reigning, political Messiah. When Christ died, not having set up a reign of power, they became discouraged. Their great cause was literally crucified. No wonder they went back to their own homes bewildered.

But then something happened. In a matter of a few days their lives were turned upside down. All but one became a martyr for the cause of the Man who appeared to them after His death. The resurrection is the only thing that could have changed these frightened, discouraged men into men who would dedicate their lives to spreading His message. Once they were convinced of it, they never denied it. Harold Mattingly writes: "The apostles, St. Peter and St. Paul, seal their witnesses with their blood" (Harold Mattingly, *Roman Imperial Civilization*, London: Edward Arnold Publishers, Ltd., 1967, p. 226). I would rather trust them than most people I meet today, who are not willing to walk across the street for what they believe, let alone be persecuted and die for it.

The internal evidence points out that the biblical documents were not written long after the events recorded; they were written during the period when many eyewitnesses were alive. The inescapable conclusion of the internal evidence is that the New Testament picture of Christ can be trusted.

The late historian Will Durant, trained in the discipline of historical investigation, who spent his life analyzing records of antiquity, writes:

Despite the prejudices and theological preconceptions of the evangelists, they record many incidents that mere inventors would have concealed — the competition of the apostles for high places in the Kingdom, their flight after Jesus' arrest, Peter's denial, the failure of Christ to work miracles in Galilee, the references of some authors to his possible insanity, his early uncertainty as to his mission, his confessions of ignorance as to the future, his moments of bitterness, his despairing cry on the cross; no one reading these scenes can doubt the reality of the figure behind them. That a few simple men should in one generation have invented so powerful and appealing a personality, so lofty an ethic, and so inspiring a vision of human brotherhood, would be a miracle far more incredible than any recorded in the Gospels. After two centuries of Higher Criticism the outlines of the life, character, and teaching of Christ remain reasonably clear, and constitute the most fascinating feature in the history of Western man (Will Durant, "Caesar and Christ," *The Story of Civilization*, Simon and Schuster, 1944, 3:557).

ARE THERE OTHER SOURCES OF PROOF?

External Evidence Test

The third test in determining the veracity of a document is that of *external evidence*. The issue here is whether other historical material confirms or denies the internal testimony of the documents themselves. In other words, what sources exist, apart from the literature under analysis, that substantiate its accuracy, reliability, and authenticity?

Two friends of the apostle John affirm the internal evidence from John's accounts. The historian Eusebius preserves some writings of one, Papias, bishop of Hierapolis (A.D. 130):

> The Elder (Apostle John) used to say this also: "Mark, having been the interpreter of Peter, wrote down accurately all that he (Peter) mentioned, whether sayings or doings of Christ, not, however, in order. For he was neither a hearer nor a companion of the Lord; but afterwards, as I said, he accompanied Peter, who adapted his teachings as necessity required, not as though he were making a compilation of the sayings of the Lord. So then Mark made no mistake, writing down in this way some things as he mentioned them; for he paid attention to this one thing, *not to omit anything that he had heard, nor to include any false statement among them*" (Eusebius, Ecclesiastical History, 3:39, italics added).

The second, Irenaeus, Bishop of Lyons (A.D. 180), preserves the writings of Polycarp, Bishop of Smyrna, who had been a Christian for 86 years and was a disciple of John the Apostle:

> So firm is the ground upon which these Gospels rest, that the very heretics themselves bear witness to them, and starting from these, each one of them endeavours to establish his own particular doctrine (Irenaeus, *Against Heresies*, 3:1:1).

Polycarp was saying that the four Gospel accounts about what Christ said and did were so accurate (firm) that even the heretics themselves in the first century could not deny their record of events. Instead of attacking the scriptural account, which would have proven fruitless, the heretics started with the teachings of Christ and developed their own heretical interpretations. Since they weren't able to say, "Jesus didn't say that ..." they instead said, "This is what He meant ..." You are on pretty solid ground when you get those who disagree with you to do that.

Archaeology, too, often provides powerful external evidence. It contributes to biblical criticism, not in the area of inspiration and revelation, but by providing evidence of accuracy about events that are recorded. Archaeologist Joseph Free writes: "Archaeology has confirmed countless passages which have been rejected by critics as unhistorical or contradictory to known facts" (Joseph Free, *Archaeology and Bible History*, Scripture Press, 1969, p. 1).

Notice that in the first verse of Luke 3, there are 15 historical references given by Luke that can be checked for accuracy. "Now in the fifteenth year [that's one historical reference] of the reign of Tiberius Caesar [that's two], when Pontius Pilate [three] was governor [four] of Judea [five], and Herod [six] was tetrarch [seven] of Galilee [eight], and his brother Philip [nine] was tetrarch [ten] of the region of Ituraea and Trachonitis [that's eleven and twelve], and Lysanias [thirteen] was tetrarch [fourteen] of Abilene [fifteen] ..."

The Stones Speak Out

Luke at one time was considered incorrect for referring to the Philippian rulers as *praetors*. According to the "scholars," two *duumuirs* would have ruled the town. However, as usual, Luke was right. Findings have shown that the title of *praetor* was employed by the magistrates of a Roman colony.

Luke's choice of the word *proconsul* as the title for Gallio also has been proven correct, as evidenced by the

Delphi inscription which states in part: "As Lucius Junius Gallio, my friend, and the proconsul of Achaia ..." (compare Acts 18:12). The Delphi inscription (A.D. 52) gives us a fixed time period for establishing Paul's ministry of one and one-half years in Corinth. We know this by the fact, from other sources, that Gallio took office on July 1, that his proconsulship lasted only one year, and that that same year overlapped Paul's work in Corinth.

Luke gives to Publius, the chief man in Malta, the title "Leading man of the Island." This had been considered an error by scholars until inscriptions were unearthed which also gave him the title "first man" (Acts 28:7).

Still another case where Luke's reliability was in question was his usage of *politarchs* to denote the civil authorities of Thessalonica. Since *politarch* is not found in classical literature, Luke again was assumed to be wrong. However, some 19 inscriptions have now been found that make use of the title. Interestingly enough, five of these refer to leaders in Thessalonica (Acts 17:6).

Archaeologists at first questioned Luke's implication that Lystra and Derbe were in Lycaonia and that Iconium was not (Acts 14:6). They based their belief on the writings of Romans such as Cicero who indicated that Iconium was in Lycaonia. Thus, archaeologists said that the book of Acts was unreliable. However, Sir William Ramsay found a monument that showed Iconium to be a Phrygian city. Later discoveries also confirmed this.

Another historical reference made by Luke is to Lysanias as tetrarch of Abilene at the beginning of John the Baptist's ministry in 27 A.D. (Luke 3:1). The only Lysanias known to ancient historians was the one who was killed in 36 B.C. However, an inscription found near Damascus speaks of the "Freedman of Lysanias the Tetrarch" and is dated between 14 and 29 A.D.

It is no wonder that E.M. Blaiklock, professor of classics at Auckland University concludes that "Luke is a consummate historian, to be ranked in his own right with the great writers of the Greeks" (E.M. Blaiklock, *The Acts of the Apostles*, William B. Eerdmans Publishing Co., 1959, p. 89)

IS THE WRITER A MAN OF ACCURACY?
A True Picture
F. F. Bruce notes:

> Where Luke has been suspected of inaccuracy, and accuracy has been vindicated by some inscriptional evidence, it may be legitimate to say that archaeology has confirmed the New Testament record.

Commenting on the overall historical accuracy of Luke, Bruce says:

> A man whose accuracy can be demonstrated in matters where we are able to test it is likely to be accurate even where the means for testing him are not available. Accuracy is a habit of mind, and we know from happy (or unhappy) experience that some people are habitually accurate just as others can be depended upon to be inaccurate. Luke's record entitles him to be regarded as a writer of habitual accuracy" (Josh McDowell, *The Resurrection Factor*, Here's Life Publishers, 1981, pp. 34,35).

There was a time in my life when I myself tried to shatter the historicity and validity of the Scriptures. But I have come to the conclusion that they are historically trustworthy. If a person discards the Bible as unreliable in this sense, then he or she must discard almost all the literature of antiquity. One problem I constantly face is the desire on the part of many to apply one standard or test to secular literature and another to the Bible. We need to apply the same test, whether the literature under investigation is secular or religious, without incorporating presuppositions or assumptions that rule out certain content, this is, the supernatural. (To be aware of the various biases, presuppositions, or prejudices that many people approach history with, consult *More Evidence That Demands a Verdict*, Josh McDowell, Here's Life Publishers, 1979).

I now understand why the classical Roman historian, Dr. A.N. Sherwin-White, concluded that "For the New Testament book of Acts, the confirmation of historicity is overwhelming ... Any attempt to reject its basic historicity, even in matters of detail must now appear absurd. Roman historians have long taken it for granted" (A.N. Sherwin-White, *Roman Society and Roman Law in the New Testament*, Oxford: Clarendon Press, 1963, p. 189).

Dr. Clark Pinnock, now professor of systematic theology at McMaster Divinity School in Ontario, concluded after extensive research: "There exists no document from the ancient world, witnessed by so excellent a set of textual and historical testimonies and offering so superb an array of historical data on which an intelligent decision may be made. An honest person cannot dismiss a source of this kind. Scepticism regarding the historical credentials of Christianity is based upon an irrational bias" (Clark Pinnock, *Set Forth Your Case*, Craig Press, 1968, p. 58).

One can conclude that the New Testament gives an accurate portrait of Christ. This historical account of Him cannot be rationalized away by wishful thinking, historical manipulation, or literary maneuvering. (For those who would like also to investigate the historical

accuracy and reliability of the Old Testament documents, read *More Evidence That Demands a Verdict*, Josh
McDowell, Here's Life Publishers, 1979).

Concerning the Christ of the Bible, Kenneth Scott
Latourette observed that "Never has Jesus had so wide
and so profound an effect upon humanity as in the past
three or four generations. Through Him, millions of individuals have been transformed and have begun to live
the kind of life which he exemplified ... Gauged by the
consequences, the events which have followed the
birth, life, death and resurrection of Jesus have been the
most important events in the history of man. Measured
by His influence, Jesus is central in the human story."

The critics can say what they want, but the Christ of
the Bible transforms lives. The evidence is overwhelming, as brought out in the fact that millions from all
backgrounds, nationalities, races, and professions have
seen themselves elevated to new levels of peace and joy
by turning their lives over to Christ. To those who say it
is a delusion, then WOW! what a powerful delusion.

E.Y. Mullins writes: "A redeemed drunkard, with
vivid memory of past hopeless struggles and new sense
of power through Christ, was replying to the charge that
'his religion was a delusion.' He said: 'Thank God for
the delusion; it has put clothes on my children and
shoes on their feet and bread in their mouths. It has
made a man of me and it has put joy and peace in my
home, which had been a hell. If this is a delusion, may
God send it to the slaves of drink everywhere, for their
slavery is an awful reality.'" (Josh McDowell, *Evidence
That Demands a Verdict*, Here's Life Publishers, 1979,
p. 328).

22
MARXISM AND CHRISTIANITY
Professor Nikolaus Lobkowicz

How do you account for the appeal of Marxism in the Western world?

I think that there are different things. One is that Marx sums up what, since several centuries, has been the prevailing mood in the intellectual life of the Western world. If you think of the philosophical traditions; if you think, for example, of Bacon saying that "knowledge is power"; or if you think of the whole tradition of people like Locke and Rousseau and Hobbes who claimed that society is based on a contract, that it is something man-made which can, therefore, also be re-shaped; if you think that all these philosophers and thinkers believed in progress. So there is a certain obvious way in which Marxism is the ideology of our age.

The second appeal is, I think, the following. Modern society does not have any powerful myth to offer and Marxism is a powerful myth. If you took a young man and presented him with two alternatives: either you can have a nice wife, a nice house, a big car and a lot of cash or, on the other hand, you will get nothing, you will go with us to the ice desert of capitalism, you will fight with us, etc. It is, in a way, quite natural that a young intellectual, a young student, who has guts or ideals, will go to the one who has an ideal for him.

Then, I think, there is something which has been often overlooked. There exists in modern times something like a fascination for absolute ruthlessness. And Marxism had this kind of ruthlessness with a certain degree of intellectuality. In the late thirties when Stalin began his mass executions instead of suggesting that this is an argument for the wrongness of the whole thing, this was something which, in a particular way, fascinated a number of, especially American, authors, at that time — and the same repeated itself after the War — perhaps because it indicated or suggested something absolute.

I would also agree with what Dr. Bochenski said, though I would not put it as strongly, that man is not so rational an animal as he believes. Actually there is something which Aquinas says, in the beginning of his *Summa Contra Gentiles* there is a passage where he says: is it appropriate that God would have revealed things which could be known by natural reason? And he says yes: because human life is short, people are busy with other things and, last but not least, they are silly.

What would you say are the fundamental errors in Marxist-Leninist ideology?

One would not know exactly where to begin. But it would begin with its radical materialism. It would be its idea that history and society solely determine what man is, which amounts to a negation of the notion of person. It would be the notion that there exist laws governing historical developments. It would be the notion of the impossibility of solving basic human issues without radically transforming society in revolutionary ways. At the basis of all this there would be atheism, of course, always; one of the big premises which explains much of these. In one way I would argue that Marxism is little else than a sum of fallacies although, as in any wrong philosophy or *weltanschaung*, there are a certain number of concepts, ideas, etc., which are usable. So, for example, the notion of alienation theory could be used as a meaningful category or that insight, which has been terribly exaggerated by Marx, that the developments of ideas are dependent on economic structures. But, I think, on the whole either you have fallacies or you have elements of Marxism which become obvious parts of social science and which nobody even mentions with reference to Marx or Marxism. And anything else are fallacies!

How can the Christian thinker be most effective in confronting Marxism?

First of all, two things. He has to know his Marxism better than he usually does know it. And he has to know his Christian Faith better than he usually does know it. There exists, precisely among conservative Christians, sometimes, very naive ideas about what Marxism is, sort of the feeling that Soviet ideology is Marxism and that it's the only really powerful stream. Hardly anybody in the Western world would be fascinated by this Soviet ideology! It takes a lot of relatively detailed knowledge to know how the thing emerged and how there are many varieties of it.

The second thing: one of the main reasons Christians succumb to Marxism is that they don't know enough about their own Faith. This is most surprising. A complete lack of information, also a complete lack, what very often happens, of the tradition of ideas in Christianity which, if you are familiar with it, you are much more able to handle different issues in terms of different parts of this tradition.

And the third thing is, the Christian must be willing to transform the whole cultural context of the modern world in a Christian way or to imbue it by a Christian spirit and thereby transform it because one of the reasons why people succumb so easily to Marxism is precisely because the whole texture of the modern world is similar to, is related to, is dependent on, so many ideas. Take for example the completely unilateral insistence on the social. The fact, for example, that we are giving millions to underdeveloped countries purportedly in order to help them to develop their economic structures, in reality, in fact, pouring it into a system which disperses money which never arrives to those who need it. But only sort of as if the whole problem would be only an economic one, only a social one. This is a seduction of Marxist ideas. What has, for example, been completely overlooked for a long time [is] that poverty in many countries has its own kind of culture. When you look at poor people in India, you absolutely reduce it in a one-sided way: this is only a problem of having enough to eat. They, nevertheless, have their own convictions, cultural backgrounds, traditions. The Latin Americans even speak today of a culture of poverty. [To succumb to the temptation of believing] that the only real issue is economic development, actually Marxism never claimed anything else, in a way, only that they sort of radicalized this position.

What would you say about Liberation Theology?

In Liberation Theology there is a disappearance of philosophy and a replacement of philosophy in theology by a social science, and a social science which is understood in a Marxist way. This has nothing to do with a desire to help the poor; it has more to do with the idea that it is the task of the Christian, or the prime task of the Christian, to transform the world in a material way. And, if you think this way, then it is rather natural that you will use a sociology, a Marxist sociology.

23
UNISEXISM
Second Thoughts on Women's "Liberation"
Sheldon Vanauken

To challenge the going *certainties* of one's own day — to challenge, that is, the proclamation of the Spirit of the Age or Zeitgeist — is to level one's lance at a fire-breathing dragon. A perilous hazard. Consider a challenge in the Germany of the 1930s to the proclamations of the Nazis. Or in the land of the free in the 1950s — when Senator Joseph McCarthy was focusing the anti-Communist fear and hate — consider a loud challenge to the effect that a man is innocent until *proved* guilty. Whatever the proclamation of the Spirit of whatever Age, it is in its own age the voice of absolute, unquestionable truth. To question whatever brave new world is a-borning is to risk destruction by the dragon.

It is a female dragon today, loosely named Women's Liberation. Her proclamation, at first the plaintive cry for fairness of a damsel in distress, calling forth (for perhaps the last time) men's chivalry, has now become very shrill indeed, even strident.

Although the dragon (of any age) has fangs and claws, its most fearsome weapon is the blast of righteous and indignant flame from its nostrils that often ends the challenge and the challenger together. This blast almost always is the accusation in tones of scornful contempt, delivered by the wave-of-the-future folk, especially the slightly ageing, with-it young, that the challenger is an old-fashioned relic, a diehard, a stick-in-the-mud, blind to the glorious new world being born. This devastating attack obviates the necessity of a reasoned reply or, indeed, even hearing the challenge.

But how if the challenger has been to the brave new world — been a citizen, in fact — and is now coming back? The "Second Thoughts" of my subtitle imply *first* ones. This article is indeed a challenge to that female dragon and may well unleash the Erinyes. But that chief dragon-weapon, the withering accusation of being a stick-in-the-mud, cannot be used. I have *been* there, hailing the brave new world. And now I am coming back.

I shall begin by tracing my approach to Women's Liberation in order to establish, so to speak, my credentials. These, then, are the "first thoughts."

Long ago, long before Women's Liberation was ever heard of, I had a marriage that was very unusual for its day, in being based on complete equality. (It is described in my book *A Severe Mercy*.) Husbandly authority was ruled out from the beginning — at, I may say, my insistence, not hers. We shared the housework and the cooking — shocking our friends — and the sailing and boatwork as well. Moreover, we made a great effort, for the sake of understanding and closeness, to learn from one another what it was to be of the opposite sex in the world. In short, it was a marriage that could not be faulted by a modern feminist, unless she discredited it on the grounds that we did what we did in the name of love instead of the name of female rights. After all, the militant feminists almost have to see men as oppressors and marriage as a loveless battleground to stay in business.

In the years after my wife's death, I did not change my ideas about fair play for women. As a professor of history and poetry, I made every effort (before Women's Lib) to emphasize the relatively few notable women in history and the few poetesses; and I urged that there should be more women on the faculty.

Then in the earliest 1960s I became at once involved in the Civil Rights or Black Freedom Movement and, later, in the Anti-War Movement. There is no doubt that I was hearing the Spirit of the Age loud and clear. Nor do I remember questioning it much until the late 1960s turn towards violence and the rip-off. Always in the Anti-War Movement days, I was glad the girls were marching too, though sad that in the meetings the girls, most of them, sat silently. And I was angry that during the inner councils of the Movement the girls were relegated to making brownies. At all events, it may be noted that now, before Women's Lib, it was precisely male and female roles I was wrathful about.

In 1968, with the first whispers of what would become Women's Lib even clearer in my ears, I wrote a more or less flaming tract entitled "Freedom for Movement Girls — NOW!!" (It was not yet *de rigueur* to call college girls "women.") In this pamphlet I spoke very angrily about unfairness to our sisters and about men who were radical in everything but the freedom of their women. I took it for granted that if the doctrine of separate but equal was demeaning to blacks (as it was), the somewhat similar though far more ancient order of role differences of the sexes was necessarily equally demeaning to women. I was assuming that the (literally) skindeep differences between blacks and whites were paralleled by no less superficial differences between the sexes. But what if *they* are soul-deep?

I knew quite well that there was an immense body of judgements all through the centuries that men and women are deeply and essentially different; but I said away with them; I *knew*. (That is *exactly* how the Spirit of the Age works.) What is so astonishing in retrospect is that I didn't *think* at all — or, rather, I thought but only on the basis of an accepted but unproved, unquestioned fundamental assumption. I did *not* ask whether those past judgements might be true, whether just possibly the whole might be benefited by the men planning the campaign and the women making the brownies, whether there might be value in role differences. The Spirit of the Age speaks in tones of *final* truth.

So I wrote my booklet about Queen Elizabeth I and Sappho and Jane Austen as being great because they weren't oppressed by men (having no husbands), assuming that the only greatness is the sort that makes the history books. And I wrote about the "myth" of separate roles, using "myth" inaccurately to mean a fiction or lie. And, to replace the cumbersome and imprecise "male-chauvinist," on the model of "racist," I invented and defined two new words, "sexist" and "sexism." This pamphlet was published in the [antiwar] Movement in December of 1968: and in February 1969, the second issue of the Boston "No More Fun and Games: A Journal of Female Liberation" thanked me for giving the women's movement these "important new words." At the close of the pamphlet I said:

> This is Female Freedom, the new radical idea blowing in the wind. Blowing down the illusions of the sexist myth ...

The booklet, as I said, was 1968, well before most of today's feminists had even heard of the as yet unnamed Women's Lib, and before the wearisome word "sexist" had yet been heard in the land. I do, therefore, quite certainly qualify as of the vanguard in hearing and supporting the new proclamation of the Spirit of the Age. The dragon was purring (if they do) about me. Later in the first half of the 1970s, when Lib was really rolling, I remained a strong advocate, writing letters to newspapers in behalf of the perennial ERA and writing articles demanding instant "ordination" of women to the sacramental priesthood and instant appointment of women to everything. Fortunately, I wrote many of these under a pseudonym and so shan't have to eat my words in public; for I now think myself to have been wrong, a not unusual state for me. But I do know every feminist argument, having receptively read them all.

But, surely — some thoughtful reader may be thinking — all this about the Spirit of the Age doesn't affect *Christians*, does it? Christians attend to *eternal* things like the *Holy* Spirit and the Church and the Bible. I might reply that *I* was a Christian in the 1960s, but that would only establish, correctly, that I wasn't attending. But, indeed, have we not heard, to the point of wearisomeness, how the *Holy* Spirit is leading us into new truths? New truths about how, after all, women can be priestesses; and how homosex if loving is, after all, quite virtuous (or, at least, not sin); and how divorce (Jesus just didn't understand) is, after all, not really sinful? New truths that just happen to be contradictory to the New Testament or to what the Church has always believed? New truths that — by the most remarkable coincidence — just happen to be identical to what the other Spirit, the Spirit of the Age, is telling the secular folk? Christians, I fear, hear the Spirit of the Age as others do. And, often, their priests and ministers even more so.

Let me offer one specific example. The great advantage of an unchanging prayer book, like the centuries-old Book of Common Prayer, is, according to C.S. Lewis, that the very thing that the people of any period would most like to change is probably the very thing they most need to hear. In our day Episcopalians heartily disliked having to say in the General Confession that we are "miserable offenders [with] no health in us." Surely we weren't *that* bad. A bit thoughtless perhaps but pretty good chaps. The prayer book was revised: out went the uncomfortable words. The joker (the devil is a joker) is that, according to some of the deepest Christian thinkers, the sense of sin has never in the 20 centuries of Christendom been at such a low ebb, partly because of psychiatric 'explaining away.' We simply do not feel ourselves to be sinners and miserable offenders because of a few unfaithfulnesses to our spouse, a few thousand cheated from somebody, or a few divorces: everyone does it. I heard of a married Episcopal rector who ran off with the wife of the senior warden. A bit funny, isn't it? And, anyway, that sort of thing has always happened, towering passion and all. Yes, but in other centuries the guilty couple have at least buried themselves in darkest Africa, and the clergyman has ceased to practice. But this couple simply went off together to another city, where he became rector of a bigger church. Nobody minds.

The Spirit of the Age, then, is heard by Christian and non-Christian alike. And one of the things it is telling Christians is to measure the Bible by secular values; for we today are "Humanity come of age" and we know far more than Jesus and St. Paul, creatures of their time. (But Jesus said He did perfectly the will of the Father in eternity.) Moreover, we have so happily absorbed the truth that God is love that we interpret it to mean that He wants us to have any little thing that will make us happy, including apples.

But — what have I said? *He?* A snarl from the feminist dragon. God is not He: God who created male and female must comprehend both (as of course He does): this suggestion of God's masculinity — words like *He* and *Father* and even *Son* must be eradicated. (Our *Parent* who art in Heaven!) No matter that Jesus thought He had a Father; we know better. No matter that the masculine principle has always been held to be that which *initiates,* so that the soul, whether of man or woman, has always been *she* in her response to the immense masculinity of God. No matter anything, including truth. It must stop. There is now actually a Feminist Bible, dishonestly translated, in which "the only-begotten Son" (can't have that awful male "begotten"!) becomes "the beloved *Child*," who, instead of crying, "Abba, Father!" mumbles improbably, "My loving parent! Source of my being!" — Is there here just a hint as to why Eve was the first to hear her 'Spirit of the Age'?

There is only one wisdom for Christians: to look with a cool and very skeptical eye at all the things their own age is, precisely, *most certain* of. Especially is this true of the certainties that contradict what has been believed by wise Christians down the centuries.

Unfortunately, Christian or no, I did not have that cool and skeptical eye in writing my Lib booklet. But, as a strong feminist in the 1970s, I gradually became aware of a few flaws — oh, very minor — in the vision of the brave new world. It may be useful to show how these developed. Sometimes little, half-admitted uneasinesses may presage the crumbling of a whole position.

I am a writer, a poet, in love with the English language; and I shall be so (in MacLeish's words) "as long as the iron of English rings from a tongue." I objected to the feminist insistence on calling girls "women" from the first (for the language needs words for people of, roughly, courting age — girls and guys, in America). But the feminist assault on language was just beginning. I understood why they did it, but it was still unforgivable (especially from the half of mankind said to be sensitive to the verbal arts). First came that clumsy three-legged mare, "chairperson" and its sisters, false to the natural rhythms of English — and completely unnecessary since "man" as suffix (as in "wo-man") means simply a human; and the more "chairman" was used for both sexes, the more it would have resumed its old meaning. As it is, the over-used "person" both as suffix and alone is becoming obnoxious. Then came the ugly, unpronounceable growl, "Ms" for any woman who didn't specify otherwise. And I must not forget the abominable usage, "he or she," like falling over a hurdle in mid-sentence, the death of style. This tin-eared abuse of English was a flaw in feminism from the beginning, although at first sadly tolerated.

Some years ago there was a TV program, "The Ascent of Man", in which a fleet-footed lad running was a symbol of man's race to civilization. There were bitter feminist complaints. Why not a female runner? they said. Sympathetic to "Lib" as I was, I felt that the absurd had just raised its head. It was a male runner because running is something that narrow-hipped males do far better than broad-hipped females. That is why we have separate races and sports for women. The program might well have chosen a female scientist to represent biology — but a *runner*? A small, insane absurdity, but a flaw. A straw in the wind.

Then one night, reading something about the possible aftermath of nuclear holocaust, it suddenly struck me that the feminist ideal of society is *artificial*. Not the natural order. It could not survive a minute in nature, by which I mean primitive or survival conditions. A hothouse plant. It could not survive the collapse of mechanical society and the protecting law. If our civilization collapsed, as in Rome's fall, leaving a remnant of us, some turned savage, feminism would disappear overnight, gone like an unreal dream. Once again women would seek the protection of men and go back to keeping the hut and — no more pill — the children: Women's Lib not blowing in the wind but gone with the wind. I had wanted feminism to be the true natural order between man and women, the true relationship. I reluctantly saw that it wasn't (and was hardly a relationship at all). This too, though only a hypothetical situation (at the moment), was more than a flaw: it was a fissure.

But this hypothetical situation not unnaturally led my mind back to the one other time in history when feminism flourished among the sophisticated classes of great cities — in the Rome of the Antonines, on the eve, according to Gibbon, of the decline and fall. The greatest of Roman satirists, Juvenal in his sixth satire, gives us a series of portraits of the "modern woman" who has abandoned her traditional duties and pleasures in order to compete with men, not only in literature and law, including giving unasked and unwanted advice to the generals of the legions, but in joining men barebreasted in the hunting field, learning swordplay as if intending to take to the arena, and swaggering about in men's clothes. With the cry, "I am a human being after all! [*Homo sum!*]" they endeavored, not only to out-think and out-fight the men but, according to Juvenal, to out-drink and out-eat them as well. Needless to add perhaps, sexual lib, then as now, was the order of the day. But Rome fell — and feminism can only flourish in a sophisticated society with strong protective laws and weak moral standards. Roman feminism perished with the imperial civilization that protected it.

C.S. Lewis says somewhere that the sound he loves best is the sound of male laughter. I had never particularly thought about it: why not? But then, recently, a man, clearly in the grip of the Spirit of the Age, mentioned Lewis's remark condemningly, adding with the air of one administering the *coup de grâce*, "And what, pray tell, is wrong with *female* laughter?" What Lewis would have replied was instantly so clear in my mind that I simply relayed it to the man: "Female laughter may be an excellent thing. But [with a blow on the table] it is not the *same* thing." It is possible that Lewis then muttered (I couldn't *quite* hear): "Logic — what *do* these schools teach?" Anyhow, absurdity, unreason, had once again touched the feminist cause. Another straw in the wind, flaw in the wind.

Now I began to notice how difficult it was becoming to *find* the laughter of a group of men only. The pubs and clubs invaded. Was there, after all, something to be said for the Long House, at least now and then?

One crisp fall day as I was walking towards the college, the sudden flight of a bird reminded me of boyhood and being with my father and another man, out with the guns on a frosty morning. And for some reason it occurred to me that I should not have liked to have my mother or my girl cousin along, even supposing they could shoot. This was men hunting as men have always hunted back to the dawn ages. I had been given to thinking that women should be in every scene, like the obligatory black in clothing advertisements. Now I found my feeling about men and guns faintly shocking.

In my youth I was for a couple of years a radio announcer, reading among other things the news-on-the-hour. Showing a bit of incipient feminism, I asked why the women, who did certain sorts of female programs in cooing voices, never got to read the news. The program director pointed out that women's voices were different. And higher, tending to make the needles jump. I went along with these undeniable facts. He then pointed out that when hearing loss occurs as one grows older, the high notes are the first to be lost; and therefore men's voices were more comfortable for the population as a whole. Of course that was back in the days when we could not only admit differences like broad shoulders and broad hips, high-pitched voices and low-pitched ones, but could make decisions as to suitability because of them. But now, in the 1970s, as female announcers did begin to read the news, I noticed that in *that* sort of brisk, authoritative reading they were, in fact, usually shrill on their high notes. And then and later I asked a great many people with hearing loss: and to a woman, as well as to a man, they preferred male newscasters.

In *nothing* is the difference between men and women more immediately obvious than voice. The difference in the voices is the glory of choral singing: the light and soaring purity of the women's voices ascending on the powerful shoulders, as it were, of men's voices. But many feminists were demanding an end to separate parts for the voices. The feminist or unisexist need to deny reality was a deep flaw. Another straw in the wind.

I read a book about the sinking, back in 1912, of the *Titanic.* Everyone knows the story of the gallant gentlemen who stepped back from the lifeboats so that the weaker women and children could be saved. Of course the protection of the female is rooted in our nature: the stags and stallions and other mammals do the same. But this particular writer, mainly concerned with the impact of the sinking on America, had unearthed a new fact. When American women, imagining themselves aboard the doomed liner, read the accounts of her final hours and those chivalrous gentlemen, a good many of the ones who were early feminists abruptly left the movement. They had seen a small floating world in survival conditions. That made me thoughtful.

The foregoing insights — as they seem to me in retrospect to have been — were merely scattered straws in the wind, not all put together as here. They were flaws in a position I strongly supported, so I tried to ignore them — somewhat uneasily. Still I had no thought of re-examining the basic feminist position (or maybe, really, examining it for the first time). As I have said, the roots of my feminist ideals stretched back, before my Christianity, into my early life. And I was not, in the 1960s and early 1970s, inclined to ask what God's will was with respect to Movement goals. Like many others in that troubled time, I was not putting Christ first — and He *must* be first or nowhere. But then in the mid-1970s I was recalled to the Obedience: He *was* first. It was not immediately clear that Christ's being first had anything to do with my practically lifelong feminism, although in reading over my "girls'-lib" booklet I saw little indication that it had been written by a Christian. Still, it didn't seem wrong.

But then, later, I reread my pseudonymous article urging the "ordination" of women; and I saw that my arguments on this *totally* Christian matter, though couched in Christian terms, were, in fact, secular and feminist — and wrong. Very wrong. I saw that I hadn't even genuinely considered what God's will might be but had *assumed* (that fatal assumption) that anything that seemed so right to me *must* be God's will. Penitently, leaving apart all *I* thought to be fair and right, I set myself the question: Can God's intention, expressed in Christ, concerning priestesses be discerned? After much thought, I was ready to write a new article: "Women's Ordination Denies the Incarnation" (*New Oxford Review*, March 1978). I cannot here give the argument for that conclusion. The result of writing it on me was, at first, to see the feminist demand for that one unique office as merely another flaw, albeit an important one, in the still-accepted feminist position.

But in the course of the article I had asked — and answered — a question: "How do we know that men and women are, apart from the plumbing, the same, spiritually the same? We do not, in fact, know that." We simply *do not know*. We are to be raised from the dead, after the Second Coming, in the body, incorruptible. The Church has always held that we shall be masculine and feminine through all eternity. Not vague "neuts" drifting about. And if indeed, as I had concluded, God wills that *men* shall form His priesthood, not women — men who would *because of their maleness* represent Christ, *be* Christ, *in persona Christi*, in the sacrament — then, beyond all doubt, there is an *essential* difference, in their very being, between men and women. Without at first realizing it, I had with my spiritual difference question probed to the very heart of the feminist position which is that there is absolutely *no* substantial difference.

In *A Severe Mercy* I described, half-humorously, how my wife, between whom and me there had been such equality and comradeship, began near the end of her life to change. Reading deeply in the Bible, especially her beloved St. Paul, she began to *want* to be wifely and obedient to her husband. As I said in the book, I was afraid she would actually obey me if I were to issue a command. She was very humble. I truly believe that she was finding it *liberation* to be a traditional (Christian) wife. Not a comrade, not a partner, but a *wife*. Years after her death, in writing the book, I wrote (a month too late for the first edition) a paragraph (Chapter VIII) on the implications of her turn to a Christian wifehood that was not feminist but was liberating. In her mind of course were St. Paul's words on the hierarchical order: that the husband is head of the wife *as* Christ is head of the Church. During the grief following her death, I had realized that, although we both should have fiercely denied it, "I *had* exercised a sort of headship — in the sense of the initiatory or leadership role — that was accepted, even *desired*, by [her] without either of us being aware of it." Such headship is of course not being a boss (which is the debasing of headship, as "clinging-vine-ism" is the debasing of wifely response); but it *is* initiating and leading. I wrote in this same paragraph that I had strong reason for being unable to believe that my subtle headship and her acceptance of it could possibly be any sort of conditioning. And I concluded that its existence left me

> wondering without decision whether, despite all feminist denial, such a relationship were not inbuilt in the creation and *effectively* denied — which, after all, we, loving so deeply, had not been able to do — only at heavy cost to love.

If indeed that relationship or order *is* inbuilt in what God has created, then the acceptance of it *would* be liberation. For woman, for man. For Christian and non-Christian alike. Christians, if they are to remain in the Obedience, must accept the New Testament teaching on male and female nature and roles. But that teaching is in harmony with the vision of other, non-Christian peoples on masculine and feminine human nature. The subtle Chinese with their Yang and Yin. Animus and anima. The deep difference. We deny it at our peril. We cannot make a world that is all warp and no woof without disaster. In the quotation from my book I said that I was "wondering without decision." In the years since, I have come to decision on the plain authority of the New Testament, as well as my own careful observation and deep thought, that male initiation (headship) and female response is the natural order and *is* inbuilt in the structure of Creation.

It was at this point in my thinking that I wrote a poem.

PUSSYCAT
Once I saw a wildcat, newly caged,
A-snarl with savage longing to be free,
Small but unappeasably enraged,
The needle teeth all bared at tyranny.

I thought: Could women once have been
    like that?

    Before the building of the cages,
    Before the bars made home a trap,
    Before the breaking of the ages,
    Before the bowl of milk and slap?

It took awhile to make a pussycat.

The haunted hills and open starry sky —
Do they really linger in your dreams?
    Was there once a savage growl,

Before contented purring on a thigh,
Before the catnip mouse and bowl of cream,
      The pitiful miaul?

But now perhaps the genes are pussycat.

These days, indeed, in talk you greatly dare,
      And after all the law is kind,
And even for the fair what's fair is fair —
      Still, questions linger in my mind.

The difference: whether God intended that?

The lion roars his splendour on the hills:
He *will* be free and if he must he kills.
Small pussy — you have fangs and claws in fact,
But dare you with pawsful of daggers *act*?

Renounce the deference due to ladyhood,
As in your wildcat talk you say you would —
Be *sure*, though, in your blood you hear the call,
Dream still a dream of freedom on the hills.
For it, pussy, will you hazard *all*?

Thus only claim the deference due to lords:
      The ancient courtesy of swords.

The case against Women's "Liberation" is not a case against all that feminists, including me, have ever said. Of *course* a woman should get equal pay for equal work (*with* equal commitment). Of *course* a woman should be a doctor or chemist if she wants to — and is willing to pay the price. Feminists, including Christian ones, who stand for little more than this sort of fair play are not the hard-core feminists I am writing about: namely, the unisexists. The neuterists.

Unisexism is a *fundamental assumption*, that is, one of the deep, unexamined, unproved assumptions that people "just know" must be true (though they often are not). An Oxford don once said that Oxford exists to bring out (in the tutorial) the student's fundamental assumptions (HOW DO YOU *KNOW* THAT?), to be proved or abandoned. Unisexism, then, is the unproved fundamental assumption that men and women are (except for a few trifling external differences that don't affect anything, except in bed) the same, psychologically the same; identical; interchangeable. What appear to be deep psychological differences, so deep indeed as to seem to constitute distinct masculine human nature and feminine human nature, are the result of conditioning through the ages by society. (But HOW DO YOU *KNOW* THAT?) Thus there can be no authentic male headship, no authentic masculinity or femininity, no authentic male and female roles in the family or in society. Interchangeable cogs. The androgynous ideal: boys and girls conditioned so that they will become, respectively, unmasculine (womanish, effeminate) men and unfeminine (mannish) women. Apart from graver objections, mightn't a homogenized humanity be a little bit *dull*?

The unisexist assumption is, in fact, not proved. Moreover, it rests on the further unproved fundamental assumption that the masculine human nature and the feminine human nature that we all observe — and experimental psychology confirms — to be different is the result of conditioning. This is not only unproved but it isn't even very plausible. It is just as likely — far *more* likely — that conditioning *follows* nature: that is, instead of conditioning (teaching little boys to be manly, little girls to be womanly) creating the masculinity and femininity, our *innate* masculinity and femininity create or cause the training. Moreover, I believe that body and psyche are a whole, each acting on the other; and no one, even a unisexist feminist, can be a woman in body without her psyche being shaped by that — without, so to speak, thinking like a woman. Apart from these reasoned disagreements with unisexism, the authority of the Bible makes unisexism quite impossible for Christians. As one disgruntled unisexist says, "The Bible is sexist through and through." It is assuredly not *unisexist*.

The unisexist, though, operates on her unproved fundamental assumption, citing only marginal "evidence" — such as boys and girls making equal marks on tests — that, in fact, proves nothing about the central assumption of identity: after all, the marks say nothing about how the learned facts are assimilated into masculine and feminine minds — what they *do* with them. Indeed, the truth is that the unisexist assumption *cannot* be proved — or disastrously disproved — without massive social engineering along counter-conditioning lines. This is already being subtly attempted in day-care centers, schools, textbooks, and social work.

See the recent child-care *Growing up Free* by the would-be 'Spockess,' Letty Pogrebin, who says: "Masculinity and femininity do not exist for me. They are fictions invented to coerce us into sex roles." (How does she *know* that?) She teaches mothers how to do away with every hint of gender including the Fatherhood of God. (Not much femininity in feminists: 'unisexist' is better — or 'neuterist.') Many kindergarten and other teachers will read this book. Some little children will be brought up by it.

A firm grip on reality is said to be the mark of a healthy mind. Starting as they do from an unproved fundamental assumption and treating it as revealed truth, bending everything to fit, the unisexists are in many ways out of touch with the real world. They wave away the plain differences between the masculine and the feminine on the grounds of a hypothetical identity of hypothetical unconditioned men and women: and they deny unmistakably real, demonstrably real physical differences as being of any importance. A female runner is as good as a male runner — except in a *real* race. A female newscaster is as good as a male one — except to *real* listeners. A female cop is as good as a male

cop — except in subduing a *real* ex-marine crook. A
female fireman is as good as a male one — except in
carrying a *real* victim out of the flames or lifting a *real*
beam. The denial of reality is perhaps the chief mark of
the unisexists. But, amusingly, they are not totally divorced from reality. They may scream for a female runner on TV, but their cries are oddly muted when it
comes to *real* sports. Why no demands for an end to
separate female events? Why not *one* race and let the
best man (pardon the expression) win?

But perhaps unisexism is right, after all, and all my
arguments are wrong? Then the Bible, including the
New Testament, is wrong. And there are, I think, some
other standards to measure unisexism against. One of
these is the common judgement of mankind. This is a
phrase used by C.S. Lewis to mean that which throughout the history of the world has been believed at *all*
times and in *all* places. Of course the Spirit of the Age
contemptously dismisses the past, for we are, at last,
"humanity come of age," and what *we* think is right. But
every period thinks that. Antonine Rome thought it. The
19th century *knew* from its Spirit of the Age that *it* was
humanity come of age, and now wars were a thing of
the barbaric past (but just over the horizon the guns of
August and the trenches). The young Nazis *knew* they
had the secret at last — Nordic racial purity and the rest
of it. Had we not, in view of the noticeable wrong-head-
edness of these past Spirits of the Age, best be cautious
about our own? Especially when it flatly contradicts the
common judgement of mankind? There is no doubt
what *that* is: it is that men and women are *deeply* different, that there is a deep and fundamental difference
between masculine human nature and feminine human
nature. Our science has no evidence to the contrary;
and this has been believed in all times and in all places.
All the feminists can do is mutter about a great male
conspiracy and hint at great pre-conspiracy civilizations

where women ruled. Unfortunately for this fond dream, anthropology tells us flatly that no known society anywhere has ever been ruled by females or has not had role differences. (The Amazons are only a myth and, anyhow, had no men to rule.) And the great male conspiracy — well, if one can believe that, she can believe anything. Fairies at the bottom of the garden. But indeed that common judgement of mankind is rooted in all we know of the early history of the race.

Our forerunners back in the dawn age — not screened from nature by a (perhaps temporary) air-conditioned, central-heated, machine-assisted, insulated culture — had to come to terms with reality or not survive. One of the realities was that, although skins might be light or dark and heads long or round, the huge immutable difference in mankind was male and female. Specialization — lawyers, sailors, merchants — lay far in the future; but here specialization was inbuilt. Women had the babies which needed care and women were inclined to give it; and women were smaller and weaker, not fighters, not as good at running after something or away from it. They were valuable, not only because of their ability to make babies, yet they needed protection. (Rome began, we may recall, with the rape of the Sabine women: Romans carrying off armfuls of them, since the Romans had none. It was not felt to be necessary to ask them, only to get them, after which Rome was a going concern.) Men *of course* did the hunting and fighting (for the women and children) and so very naturally ruled. Equally naturally, the stay-at-home women tended the kids and cooked the bear steaks — and, also naturally, "While you're at it, just sweep out the cave, dear." Despite feminist cursing of role difference, we may doubt that their foremothers objected; for, being close to reality, they knew they needed a hunter to kill the bear and bring home the meat — and to protect them. This natural order endured for *millions* of years: the masculine and the feminine, however denied by unisexists, are rooted in the race. If men taught their sons to be warriors and made them toy spears, it was because their survival depended on it. And if some kindly caveman made a doll for his little cavegirl, it was probably because he saw her cuddling a stick or a bit of dry bone. This is our heritage.

Another standard, besides the common judgement of mankind by which to measure the unisexist denial of any inbuilt maculinity and femininity is nature itself. We are, someone said, "half-angel and half-ape": what is certain is our kinship to the warm blooded, child-suckling mammals. Spiders may eat their husbands, like some feminists, and bees have the matriarchy that feminists vainly seek in man's past; but we are mammals and have lived in close association with other mammals that we have domesticated. Our ancestors, whether in the wild or on farms, lived, in fact, close to nature: consequently, to a farmer or farmwife, unisexism would, I think, have seemed ricidulous — and, above all, *unreal*. Unisexism, indeed, could only have sprouted, I think, in the monster cities cut off from nature and mother earth.

At all events, let us look for a moment at our fellow mammals to see what we are. The stallions, the dogs, the bulls, the tomcats, certainly, haven't been "conditioned" by Daddy saying, "Grow up to be a real bull, lad!" — but that's the way they *do* grow up: the fighting bulls. Or the stallions, hard to break and full of fight. The great war horses of the proud knights were stallions, for in battle the fierce stallions would also fight with teeth and hooves. Male dogs are the adventurers; tomcats make the night hideous with their battles and their conquests of females. No, not models — but what the male is. He fights, he is the hunter, he protects his females and the young. The gallant gentlemen on *Titanic*, the Light Brigade charging the guns — they were doing what males, animal and human, have done for millions of years. But the unisexists say that women will be just as good in combat. But *their* heritage — the patient cows, the gentle mares so safe to ride, the often-ladylike bitches: they take care of the young, as they have done for millions of years; they accept the authority (headship) of the males; they do not fight, unless, with no male about, they must fight to protect their calf or puppies. Not adventurous hearts, not fighting hearts, no challenges flung on the winds — but nurturing, protective hearts. All of this man has always known; but perhaps the city-dwellers, growing up in the wilderness of brick, living in an apartment with one "fixed" cat, are forgetting who they are, what they are. At all events, the whole point with respect to our fellow mammals is that, although we may improve on their behavior (some male mammals occasionally dine on their children), we learn from them what is *in our nature* — what is in our genes.

One school of feminists with pleasing realism admit the differences are innate — *but* urge conditioning towards androgeny anyway. And towards a race of neurotics? Or towards a state like that portrayed in H.G. Wells, *The Time Machine*: the horrifying picture of girlish little weaklings of both sexes in the far future? Androgeny might well end that way.

Not surprisingly, in view of the stallions and stags, the psychologists find that men have a built in propensity for risk-taking — which is of course the reason that young men are so lethal behind the wheel. (Despite skill, they have far more wrecks than girls because of taking chances — or showing off to the female of the species.) The psychologists have a good deal more to say about the real differences between the sexes, particularly that men are goal-oriented and women socially-oriented and nurturing.

The common judgement of mankind, the description of primitive man, the genetic heritage of mammals, and the findings of psychology have been proposed as ways of measuring the claims of unisexism. It may also, I think, be shown to be an excess in a historical perspective. I have often observed what might be called a pendulum swing from the extremes of one age to the opposite extremes of the next. For instance, in the 18th century, the age of the drawing room and elegant manners and dress, gentlemen occasionally drew the curtains in their coaches while crossing the Alps so that they might not be offended by all that untamed nature. That age was succeeded by Romanticism — all skylarks and wild torrents and nightingales. The pendulum. Again, sexual attitudes in Tudor England were merry and sane; under Cromwell's Puritans, theatres were shut and merrymaking repressed. With the succeeding Restoration both the court and the theatres became licentious, and things loosened up for a century. But, then Victoria, who was not amused, and excessive prudery became the order of the day. Now, a century or less later, the opposite excess: a virtually sex-saturated age. The pendulum.

But there's more to it: a relationship between sexual repression or sexual license on the one hand, and the position of women on the other. Sexual license cannot flourish when women aren't available except in brothels. In the Victorian Age "nice women" were notably *not* available, unless of course one married them, for keeps. Lots of lasting marriages, therefore, often felt to be a good thing by women. The ideal of virtuous womanhood, though, required that women be put on a pedestal, sequestered from temptation and unseemly tempting, taught to faint (gracefully) at a risqué remark, and chaperoned against male impulsiveness, which was in any case curbed by innumerable petticoats and corsets. All of this, while most effective in preserving virtue, tended to suggest that females were rather brainless, a view contradicted by certain wise and commanding dowagers. It is perhaps worth emphasizing that this treatment of the female is not typical of the past in general but of the Victorian age which was an extreme. As our day is.

As a passing thought, if the pendulum swings from extreme to extreme, does it pass the point of balance (sanity?) somewhere in between? Could that point of balance, assuming that 1880 and 1980 represent the extremes, have been in the 1920s, when women obtained the vote in both England and America and were admitted to women's colleges at Oxford as degree candidates?

Whatever may be the truth as to a point of balance, there seems to me not a doubt in the world that we represent the equal and opposite excess to that of the Victorians. What could be more an excess than that Feminist Bible? Nineteenth-century Oxford didn't admit girls, but then women's colleges were built among the men's colleges in that university, just as in America completely separate women's colleges, like Smith and Vassar, were founded. When I was at Oxford, I thought the system there — women's and men's colleges in the same university (rather like Harvard-Radcliffe), the girls in the life of the university (lectures, clubs, societies) yet separate — was ideal, balanced between all-one-sex and completely coed. But now Oxford, hearing the Spirit of the Age — and for once *not* examining a fundamental assumption — has gone beyond that beautifully balanced system in a panic rush to mix the individual colleges. As Harvard-Radcliffe have done by, in effect, destroying Radcliffe. Balance or excess? Even more excessive, girls at West Point marching about with especially-made *little* rifles looking very absurd indeed. Does it seem precisely balanced, or even sane, for West Point to have rejected frail or short young *men* on the grounds that for an officer of the United States Army a man's strength and stature might be decisive in battle, and then to admit still-frailer, still-shorter *women* who themselves need protection? Or, again, while it seems entirely sensible to welcome women into the ranks of doctors and the other learned professions (as they were, without too hearty a welcome, back in the 1920s), it seems entirely insane to make them policemen.

To make women policemen and firemen and sergeants in the Marines, to send girls to West Point and Annapolis are all related to my earlier remarks about the male runner and the female newscaster in that all of these are a denial of obvious physical differences between the sexes. A denial of reality. The ancient Greeks are justly admired for their fine effort *to see things as they are*. No future age will admire us for that. What would the lucid intelligence of Aristotle — and Aristophanes! — make of our denial of 'the undeniable'? When they'd done laughing, that is? The Victorians, aware of women's frailer bodies and lighter voices, may have decided that their less-visible minds were also frail and light; but *we*, aware now of women's able minds, decide that their *quite* visible bodies and audible voices can do anything men's can. Seeing things as they are?

And yet the feminists, notably Betty Friedan before the Women's Lib Movement even began, have made one valid point. The traditional job of the woman's role is a shrunken one. Fewer children, for one thing. And it is industry that now makes the clothes, churns the butter, preserves the fruit and makes the jam, and bakes what may doubtfully be called the bread. But, however shrunken, the role of homemaker has *not* disappeared and is still *essential*. The differences that psychology discerns between the sexes — men being goal-oriented, women being nurture-oriented — powerfully suggest that homemaking should remain primarily the woman's responsibility. By and large, if there is going to *be* a home — that is, something more than a place to sleep — woman will make it so. Otherwise *home* will become a word found only in history books. It is the house*wife*,

not the housebond (husband) who can make a domicile
into a home.

But what if the woman has to work outside the
home, as millions do, to make ends meet? There's no
single answer to this complex problem.

One partial solution occurs to me: that business
should accept — or be pressured into accepting — for
any job (assembly line, teacher, secretary) *two-woman
teams* at one full salary. The team would share the responsibility, arrange what hours each would work on a
given day (sometimes morning, sometimes afternoon,
one day more, one day less), and the employer could
count on somebody (whether her hair were red or
brown) being there. Very possibly with far less absen-
teeism. One woman would, so to speak, relieve the
watch, as naval officers do, be filled in on what was
happening, pick up typing the letter if a secretary or
take the next class if a teacher. Actually quite like
nurses. The employer would be guaranteed a full-time
employee; the team would have a stable job between
them. I think millions of women would like such an
arrangement very much indeed. A lot better than any
feminist solution I've heard. A realistic solution to the
problem of the shrunken but still vital role of homemaker in relation to the need for supplementary family
income.

I believe that a great many women would feel themselves to be truly liberated to be allowed to be home-
makers without pressure from either the feminists or
the economy. It has been said that in a good marriage
the man is the head and the woman the heart. If there's
truth in this, there's a corollary: in an individual, the
head works for what the heart longs for — not a question of which rules. And thus it is in the mystery of "one
flesh" of Christian wedlock.

I am not, God knows — and as anyone who has
read *A Severe Mercy* knows — hostile to women. I do not
for a moment believe that men are superior to women —

only different. To me, one of the God-given joys of this life is the radiant, forever intriguing, complementary difference of man and woman, not just superficially sexual but deep and awesome. Man and woman are equal, yes, but equal in importance and value; and not, thank God, identical. Equal in importance as a nut and bolt are entirely equal in importance without being identical — and doing a job together that neither two bolts nor two nuts could do, holding something together. Man and woman do what two men or two women cannot do: they hold humanity together. A man and a little pseudo-man won't do it either. A man and a *woman*. I can fall on my knees, figuratively at least, before the mysterious wonder of womanhood, even as a true woman sees a splendour in manhood. Masculinity — that which initiates and leads, as the eternal masculinity of God does — needs femininity, feminine response, to complement and complete it. Help*meet* is the biblical word: a suitable or fit help, a completion. Thus man and woman together in that awesome mystery of one flesh is what Our Lord hath ordained for us.

It is in the Name of God and His will for us that I challenge the dragon of unisexism: and my lady's glove is pinned to my lance.

24
A CALL TO CONSTANT JOY:
Meditations on the Meaning of Life and Death in the Christian Cosmos
Roy Abraham Varghese

"I will see you again, and your hearts shall rejoice, and your joy no man shall take from you."   John 16:22

"Rejoice evermore."   I Thessalonians 5:16

There is nothing as certain as the fact that every man will die. There is nothing as uncertain as the precise timing of the coming of death. Inevitable and unpredictable though it is, "death is swallowed up in victory" in the Christian cosmos and, in its place, the children of God are offered the everlasting ecstasy of the Kingdom prepared for them "before the foundation of the world." This remarkable revelation, however, has not excited as much enthusiasm in the sons of men as might reasonably be expected. Such being the case, it seems appropriate to meditate on the foundations and framework of this revelation: the grounds on which Christians accept this revelation as the revelation of the Creator, the precise questions which are answered by the revelation, and the difference that these answers should make in one's daily life.

On the face of it one can say this: if the Christian revelation is true and if all the children of God are destined for everlasting union with the Creator of the universe, then every one of their thoughts, emotions, attitudes, perspectives, should "run" on this revelation, should be seen in its light. Christianity, from this perspective, is a call to constant joy. Whether or not this initial impression is justified can be determined only after the kind of personal reflection on the data of experience and revelation attempted here ("To thine own self be true"). The children, however, must not be unduly disturbed if they come to see that a lot of the scholarly emperors around wear hardly any clothes to speak of because "He who stands for nothing falls for everything."

The significance of the claims made in the Christian revelation, and of joy in the Christian cosmos, can be fully grasped only by coming to terms with death. Death is the dark intruder which frustrates every earthly hope. Death terrifies the mighty and the meek. Death seems so obviously to be the total "black-out" of one's existence, the end forever of all that one has become and attained. The thought of "death's dateless night" fills the merriest souls with unutterable grief.

"It is not enough to live, man needs a destiny . . . ," said Albert Camus. Clearly the end of earthly existence can make sense only in terms of human destiny and here the question of whether or not the journey of life has a destination becomes incalculably important. The premises and implications of the atheistic answer to the question are intellectually clear-cut (though the atheist rarely digests them psychologically).

On the atheistic view human beings have come from nowhere and from nothing and are likewise destined to return nowhere, become nothing. In a universe with ten billion galaxies, each with over ten thousand million solar systems, human society and human history are merely activities of specks on a speck — and are about as significant. And, as far as time-scale is concerned, the universe has existed for billions of years and will continue to exist for billions of years. Human history, on the other hand, is a few thousand years old, and will cease altogether when the sun burns itself out. In the face of that final moment, all that the humblest and the greatest souls have achieved will be forgotten forever: it will be as if man had never been. Again, on the atheistic view, the existence of each human being is a result of countless chains of chance occurrences, an accidental result of atoms and electrons blindly bumping into each other. The life of every man and of mankind itself is a frenzied farce enacted for no one's benefit, a jigsaw puzzle invented by no one and adding up to nothing. From the atheistic perspective man's life is an absolute accident and his death is the arbitrary annihilation of all that he achieved or became: both are equally terrifying.

Radically opposed to the atheistic answer to the question of the purpose of human existence is the Christian answer: on the atheistic view man lives on the brink of nothingness, on the Christian view he lives on the edge of eternity. The grounds on which Christians believe that there is a Creator and that He revealed Himself in the fullest possible manner in Jesus Christ must first, however briefly, be examined.

To begin with there is the testimony of "the best and the brightest" in the history of human thought and of the overwhelming majority of mankind who have all believed that everything existing — from galaxies to grains of sand — was brought into existence by an infinite Being existing always, without beginning or end; a Being in Whom beauty, goodness and love not only subsist in supreme degree but Who, because He is the infinite source and perfection of these, is Himself Beauty, Goodness, Love. This is a perception rooted as much in common sense as in a fundamental insight that the existence of finite being is "intrinsically unintelligible" without the existence of an infinite Being. Since something cannot just come to be accidentally or causelessly from nothing — if at any time there was nothing which existed then there would be nothing now or ever — and since the universe exists and could not just have popped into existence without "rhyme or reason", the universe owes its existence to the uncreated and eternal Being, to the "mysterium fascinans et tremendum." Said one of the most famous atheists of the twentieth century, Jean-Paul Sartre, just before his death: "I do not feel that I am the product of chance, a speck of dust in the universe, but someone who was expected, prepared, prefigured. In short, a being whom only a Creator could put here, and this idea of a creating hand refers to God."

God's existence does not, of course, depend on the whims and fancies of modern man and anyone who cares to use his mind or his heart or both will be drawn towards the Divine. Moreover, he will discover that goodness, beauty, love and all that most of mankind has acknowledged as truly great and glorious are therefore (as most of mankind has recognized) droplets from an everlasting fountain, sunbeams from a sun that shines forever, breath from the lips of God.

The existence of God does not in itself relieve the anguish of the atheistic abyss of absurdity. If human life does not have any ultimate purpose such that man survives death and attains some goal eternally then it is doomed to futility and absolute insignificance in relation to reality. To realize the reality of God is not to know His design for mankind or man's ultimate destiny. Left to himself, man is more often than not brainwashed by the beliefs prevalent in his intellectual and cultural environments. If he is to know the purpose of life, which he needs to know if he is to lead life intelligently (i.e. with a definite purpose), only God, Who is outside all eras and environments and is Himself all Truth, can tell Him what it is.

In studying the world religions to find out if God has revealed His design for mankind in the course of human history, one principle must be kept in mind: at a fundamental level the only religion that can even be considered as a possible vehicle of definitive divine revelation would be one that can satisfy two conditions: the religion in question must, firstly, at least claim to make sense of human existence (for if it did not it could not be in tune with the Mind Who made it all) and, secondly, it must claim to have as its Founder God Himself (only He would be sufficient guarantee that its message is His message and that it is true). Of all the world religions, Christianity alone claims both to give purpose and significance to man's life on earth (through its teachings about man's eternal destiny) and to be a revelation of God's purpose for man which was unveiled by God Himself in human history (of no other historical figure but Jesus Christ has anyone made the claim that He was infinite God united with a human nature). Moreover no other religion offers the kind of evidence offered by Christians in grounding their claims, and the essence of this evidence must be briefly noted.

The whole story about Jesus Christ is inestimably incredible. Here was a first century Galilean peasant offering men eternal life if they believed in Him! And this same peasant selected a motley band of followers, made the wildly astounding claim that He was God, and preached "words of eternal life" which hypnotized all who heard Him. Predicting His death at the hands of His enemies Jesus promised also to rise from the dead, a promise which would be the most decisive and fundamental test of all as far as His identity was concerned. When He was crucified on Calvary His disciples fled in terror and despair and denied all knowledge of Him. In the forty days after the crucifixion something happened which transformed these eleven terrified peasants and fishermen into fearless knights of faith who ranged themselves against the mightiest empire of the day and went around the world both preaching the message of their Master and making the simply unimaginable claim that He had appeared to them after His officially conducted execution. And this was no mere freakish spurt of defiant courage, a ripple that "straightened out" in a short while. It was a tidal wave which, if anything, became bigger as the years passed, spreading throughout the world and finally engulfing the very empire which sought to hold it back. Only sheer blank-minded credulity and an utterly perverse dogmatism could lead anyone to continue insisting that this dramatic, sustained change in the disciples was founded on hallucination, hysteria or an ingenious hoax. Their transformation can be adequately explained only in terms of the resurrection accounts found in the Gospels: only an event momentous in the highest degree could have transformed these terrified disciples into dynamos surging in every direction. And when one considers the fact that all through the ages millions of people have claimed to have experienced Christ in their lives so that they too were totally transformed, one finds that the whole stupendous affair remains inexplicable until one accepts Christ Jesus as "My Lord and my God."

All theories, modern and ancient, which try to explain away the mystery and the truth that Jesus Christ is the God-man, are merely a rehash of old heresies — Arian, Deist, Nestorian, Unitarian — that keep coming into and going out of fashion. All of them are theological escape-routes designed to evade the all-important question: was Jesus Christ the God-man or a madman? As escape-routes they have all turned out to be dead ends. But the astounding affirmation that Jesus Christ is the God-man, an affirmation that forms the foundation of Christianity, has blazed forth a triumphant path which, though rough and narrow, has been carved out with the vision of glory.

The revelation of the destination of the journey of life, made by Jesus Christ, is of stupendous significance at many different levels. Few people make any definite plan for their lifetimes in this world. Educations, careers, marriages, and so on are usually determined by chance and circumstances not by previously prepared plans. And if death is to be the complete eclipse of all that man has done and become, then any such plan is, in any case, of no enduring value. What Christianity offers man is not merely a definite plan for his life in this world, but a plan for him that extends forever, a plan for the endless and ecstatic existence he will enjoy after death. And this plan is not an arbitrary concoction. It is the purpose and goal for man's life designed by his Creator, the One Who knows what He had in mind as man's goal when He created man. According to this plan every man is offered the choice of proceeding towards a destination. This destination is not a place to be reached but a person to be reached and that Person is an infinite God Who desires eternal union with the beings He created. Thus Christianity is a launching-pad for a life-plan that encompasses eternity. In the Christian framework men are infinities not zeroes.

From the perspective of this eternal-divine life-plan it is clear that the only real priority for man is to be united forever with God, to do all he can in this life to accept that union through Christ. If one's conduct for a day is going to determine how one is going to live for a thousand years one would obviously try to be at one's best on that day. Since man's choices in this fragment of earthly life (which, when compared to even the "life-span" of the universe, is barely a millisecond) will decide his happiness in all eternity, he would do well to try and choose as best he can. From the Christian perspective his every thought and action here and now is of supreme significance because it is so intimately related to the hereafter. Christianity is not only "relevant" to man's life in this world but it is more relevant than anything else could be. Christians are not misty-eyed idealists but the most hard-headed of realists.

God, Who has no past or future, Who is eternally in the present ("I am Who I am"), always knew of all that exists in His never-ending Now. He knew of the existence of every man, the beginnings of his existence and its final fulfillment, planned it, *always*. (Jeremiah 1:4,5: "Then the word of the Lord came unto me, saying, before I formed thee in the belly and knew thee, and before thou camest forth out of the womb I sanctified thee ...."; Psalm 139:16 "Thy eyes beheld my unformed substance; in thy book were written, every one of them, the days that were formed for me, when as yet there was none of them.") Every man has been in God's mind from all eternity. He "wills the salvation of all men" but He will not force anyone into the Kingdom "prepared before the foundation of the world": the choice between Heaven and Hell must be made by man alone.

The fact that man is a union of matter and spirit makes his physical insignificance in relation to the rest of the universe insignificant. Spirit can know, love and worship. Spirit is capable of union with the Supreme Spirit. In all these respects man is immeasurably superior to the mindless universe.

Christianity is too often thought of in negative terms: as a purely self-denying, joyless religion. In actuality, though some of its external features may seem unattractive to fallen man, it is fundamentally a revelation of incredible optimism while atheism offers only darkest despair. Christianity is irreducibly different from other philosophies and religions — it is ultimate and unique — because it relates the City of Man to the City of God and shows that all man's actions are carried out against the backdrop of eternity and with reference to his eternal destiny. Unlike Macbeth the Christian declares that life is a tale told by infinite wisdom, full of sound and fury, signifying everything: of course one can, if one wants, reduce it to a tale told by an idiot — that idiot being oneself. Of Shakespeare, Ben Jonson said, "He was not of an age but for all time." Of Christ, it can be said, "He was not of time but for all eternity."

The "good news" that came from Galilee is then indeed "tidings of great joy." The Heart of Reality, the immediate and the ultimate truth about things, is Love — a Love that saw fit to incarnate Itself and suffer and die at the hands of those It loved into being. Life itself is a love story with the Love "that moves the sun and the other stars." All the fairy tales are true and the children will live happily ever after in the eternal Eden, in the Promised Land beyond space and time.

Hints of the everlasting union with God that is Heaven are strewn all through man's earthly experience. The more intoxicating he finds the "things of time" the more deeply do they draw him toward the Timeless. The intimations of immortality — Browning's line, "All that men ignored in me," is definitely appropriate — manifest themselves through "thoughts too deep for tears" and insights and intuitions too deep for thoughts, through memories which fill him with a yearning not to be satisfied by a return to the experiences they recall or by any earthly experience. The highest degree of happiness in earthly beauties — the beauties of music, art, nature, and so on — cannot be sustained indefinitely, and sooner or later these lose their glamour and glory. Earthly beauties, however, are just formulae hiding the endless secrets of that infinite beauty which man can never cease enjoying.

The exact nature of Heaven is a mystery, not because of darkness, but because of excess of light. So much is suggestive of it that man does not know where to start, where to wind up. By its very nature, it is unimaginable because the immediate knowledge and love of God is something man cannot enjoy in this life and hence cannot describe or grasp. But man does know that Heaven is a union with the Creator of this immense universe, with the Author of all the love, goodness, and joy around him, with the One in Whom all these are found in perfection. He does know that such union cannot but bring him the highest possible satisfaction and happiness. All physical and spiritual pleasures in this world derive from God, Who is the Source of all joy, and are only hints and harbingers of the final and direct union with Him at "Whose right hand there are pleasures forevermore." There is an almost terrifying ecstasy, a fearful joy, in the thought of union with the Creator, in fact the Inventor, of galaxies and pine trees, sunsets and smiles, babies and giraffes, angels and the Alps.

The darker side of human nature and history cannot be downplayed. Human history is simultaneously a history of savagery of every kind and degree and every man is Dr. Jekyll and Mr. Hyde. In the Word of God man learns of one called Lucifer who was the most powerful of created beings — who was nevertheless infinitely inferior to the Most High — a pure spirit with a mind incomparably more virile and vibrant than any human intellect and a will capable of destroying the entire universe if it were not restrained by God. In the most tragic and terrible decision in the history of created reality, Lucifer, motivated by pride of a kind that limited human minds can never fully comprehend, refused to acknowledge the supremacy of the Source of Life and rejected the Divine offer of love. Instantly, inevitably, Lucifer was transformed into Satan, the Adversary, and the creature closest to God became the one most distant. Plunged into a never-ending nightmare of evil his only goal became one of destroying God's creation. But, because his will and his intellect were fixed in rejection of his Maker, all his powers were mockeries of what might have been and he could never infringe in any ultimate manner on God's plan for reality.

Satan's attitude to man, made in the image of God, could only be one of utter and undying hatred. Were it not for the infinite love and patience of the "jealous" Jehovah, the sinister Satanic scheme, which began to unfold at Eden and culminated in the Fall and in death, would surely have resulted in final frustration of the divine plan for mankind and in the victory of the hordes of Hell.

Death is, in a dreadful sense, diabolic, for it was the Devil who brought it about and more powerfully than any other experience it manifests his malefic will and reflects the negation of his nature. But the death-dealing tree of the knowledge of good and evil was replaced by the life-giving tree of the Cross for "the reason the Son of God appeared was to destroy the works of the devil" (I John 3:8). The diabolic dragon that had for millenia preyed on pilgrims progressing towards the Celestial City was slain by the King Himself. Through the death and resurrection of Jesus Christ death itself was "swallowed up in victory." Though it is, like every fruit of sin, ugly and unnatural, death has been transformed into the means of eternal life by Christ ("This day you shall be with me in Paradise"). Once he is through the Valley of the Shadow of Death, man shall dwell forever in the House of the Lord.

Though death was dethroned *de jure* on Calvary it still retained *de facto* power in the hearts of those who faced it in terror and despair. In modern society, for instance, death has replaced sex as the great taboo because death is the dread nemesis that stalks its dreams of constant progress and turns them into nightmares. Whereas the Victorians, who talked of sex in "hushed tones," discussed death quite cheerfully, the average moderner revels in talk about sex but is mortally afraid of reflecting on human mortality. Modern attempts to evade the reality of death are reflected in such funeral practices as that of preserving embalmed corpses in moisture-proof coffins.

Admittedly there has been some modern interest in thanatology, the psychology and sociology of dying. Books on thanatology have minutely mapped the mechanics of death and dying and have been of great value on the practical level. But the value of such contributions has been limited by the fact that the thanatologist's perspective rarely transcended the horizon of this life. In his concern with technical medico-ethical problems, the modern thanatologist saw little need for relating death to man's ultimate destiny. And he was addicted to the naive notion that man could give meaning and significance to his life even if there is no God and even if he did not survive death. But the futility of life in an atheistic universe makes it clear that it can have meaning and significance only if it has an ultimate goal ordained by God and not by any amount of human manipulation. Thanatology tells man to accept death. Christianity tells him to accept life everlasting and death in the light of that life.

Predictably the non-Christian response to death has, in varying degrees, distorted Christian attitudes and, in general, Christians have not manifested a living awareness of the link between death and the Enduring Ecstasy. For instance, many Christian funeral customs face the reality of death ("dust to dust") but ignore or only mention in passing the reality of everlasting life. Again, Christian thanatologists are almost solely preoccupied with technical problems of coping with grief and make very few, if any, references to the after-life. Finally, Christian theologians who write on death and bereavement do not often wax eloquent on the definitive nature of the victory over death and the Devil on Calvary or on the overwhelming difference that the revelation of man's eternal destiny should make to the Christian, intellectually and psychologically.

Perhaps the pre-Christian sorrow and horror in the face of death has continued to condition Christian attitudes. Undoubtedly many Christians have been confused by death because they had never received a clear or credible exposition of Christian teachings on the life to come or because they had been so intensely involved in the affairs of the here-and-now that they had never taken the hereafter seriously. Concerning the latter it must be pointed out that the question of man's everlasting destiny is of the most practical possible relevance: only in the context of such a destiny can all or any of his activities in this world make sense.

The authentic Christian response to bereavement is possible only if a person has grounded himself in the Christian perspective on life and death. The Christian will see death not as the end of the story but as its beginning and will face death with joy and faith in Christ Who has gone to prepare a place for him. Christians rarely realize the full extent of what is offered man by God: they are to have FOREVER. In the most fantastic, and yet the most realistic, of fairy tales, they are to "live happily ever after." Mere reflection on this tremendous truth will change their perspectives, attitudes, views, totally. In the expectation of their eternal destiny they will find joy for, as benign Jane Austen wrote in a letter, "the expectation of happiness is happiness" or, as Shakespeare (in *Richard II*, Act II:ii) put it, "And hope to joy is little less in joy/Than hope enjoyed."

The vital insight that "the expectation of happiness is happiness" can be best explained and illustrated by means of an analogy — imagine a schoolboy whose school will close in a week, and who will then be going on a vacation to a place he has yearned to go to all his life, the Swiss Alps. The knowledge, the anticipation of the forthcoming vacation will inevitably color his emotions, attitudes, thoughts, in the preceding week. He will be joyous in the expectation of the joys to come. Far from diminishing it, annoyances and afflictions in the week before will excite his enthusiasm all the more. And if the vacation is a complete gift from someone who wishes him to work very hard before it begins (not to earn it but to prepare himself for it) there is little doubt that he will enter into his daily tasks with fullest vigor. The vision of the week ahead will be a magnet drawing all his energies.

With some minor modifications we can apply the analogy to the Christian vision of life. The school is the world, the schoolboy a Christian. The week is the brief fragment of life between womb and tomb. The vacation is eternal happiness in union with the Creator of the cosmos. The Host, who wants us to do our best while on earth, is God. As Christians our awareness of the upcoming "vacation" should flood our perspectives, priorities, thoughts, emotions, feelings, attitudes, while we are in "school"; we should be literally joyful in the expectation of the joy without end which will follow. No annoyance, no affliction, should dim our expectant ecstasy. The schoolboy vacationing in the Alps may find his vacation not to be as enjoyable as he expected, may even find it positively disappointing. But the vacation of eternal happiness in Heaven will, when experienced, exceed our most extravagant expectations. Again the schoolboy may find that he had been deceived or had deceived himself in his hope of a vacation. The Christian, however, knows that his vacation is not a vain hope, that the Host keeps all His promises. Any number of major catastrophes and tragedies during the last week in school could ruin the schoolboy's "joy in expectation" as well as the possibility of joy during the actual vacation. But, as far as we are concerned, no earthly tragedy or catastrophe can dim the joy that "no man taketh" from us: what we are offered is infinite, eternal happiness and no number of finite mishaps can affect infinite joy, or the joy in expectation of this infinite joy. To be sure, a life which lasts fifty to eighty years will not seem like a week. The crucial word here is "seem." It may not seem to be just a "week" but in fact, in relation to eternity, it is infinitesimal, a bare milli-second, and one needs only to train one's thoughts and perceptions in an appropriate manner to make it "seem" what it really is. If we know that, in a milli-second, we will enjoy eternal ecstasy, we cannot but be joyful during that milli-second. Modifying the earlier analogy, we can think of someone who is told that he will live on earth for a day and that thereafter he will have a thousand years of perfect happiness in some other realm — if he accepts the offer. If his mind is not muddled up and if his sensibilities are sharp he will live his day on earth in the light of the thousand years to come and of the choice he must make.

The constant "joy in expectation," offered to all Christians, can be described as the Rejoice Response. The Rejoice Response, loosely defined, is happiness here and now in the knowledge and expectation of happiness hereafter: it means focusing on our destination and of gearing all our energies towards our transfinite, transtemporal "coming of age." Admittedly the bare outlines of the approach which has been briefly sketched will seem naive if not a mere jumble of irrelevant truisms and superficialities — some of the objections to it must be faced and its claims must be carefully qualified.

Philosophically and psychologically the Rejoice Response is dependent on certain fundamental insights. For one thing it is rooted in the Christian revelation of reality and it can be fully effective only if we begin to live in the Christian cosmos which is Reality, i.e., only if we are conscious of the true goal of our lives, God. We must know where we are going and why: only then are we truly sane, intelligent, practical, normal. (Unfortunately in modern society you are not normal if you are normal.) A psychology of endless happiness on earth can be built only on the foundation of the Christian revelation. Optimism which is founded on anything but this foundation is self-condemned.

The Rejoice Response is also rooted in the perception that "being is good." All that exists has been created — made from nothing — by God and is therefore good in itself and to be reverenced. ("Every creature of God is good"; I Timothy 4:4.) God's purpose in creating everything was one of sharing His perfect goodness with His creation, of manifesting His infinite glory through finite being. The material universe is neither illusory nor evil and is in no way to be despised. That there is evil in the universe we cannot deny. But nothing is evil in itself. Evil is a corruption or privation of what is good. At the same time the Christian knows that he lives in a world in which evil is not the victor in any ultimate sense. After Easter the forces of evil can never again do any permanent damage to those who seek the living God and who live in Christ Who conquered the Kingdom of Darkness. And the redemptive death literally had cosmic effects, "having made peace through the blood of His cross, by Him to reconcile all things unto Himself ... whether they be things in earth, or things in heaven" (Colossians 1:20). " ... in the dispensation of the fulness of times he might gather together in one all things in Christ, both which are in heaven, and which are on earth" (Ephesians 1:10).

Central to our experience of the Rejoice Response is an all-encompassing awareness of God's infinite love for us, His infinite mercy and of the salvation freely offered in Christ. In *Heaven the Heart's Deepest Longing*, Peter Kreeft writes, "Now suppose both death and hell were utterly defeated. Suppose the fight was fixed. Suppose God took you on a crystal ball trip into your future and you saw with indubitable certainty that despite everything — your sin, your smallness, your stupidity — you have free for the asking your whole crazy heart's deepest desire: heaven, eternal joy. Would you not return fearless and singing? What can earth do to you if you are guaranteed heaven? To fear the worst earthly loss would be like a millionaire fearing the loss of a penny — less, a scratch on a penny.

"But this is our true state, according to God's own word. This is the Gospel, the scandalously good news: that we are guaranteed Heaven by sheer gift. 'Let him who is thirsty come, let him who desires take the water of life without price.' The only qualification is thirst, desire; 'all who seek, find.' To this day millions of Christians simply can't believe it."[1]

Too often we forget that God is a Savior "who will have all men to be saved and to come unto the knowledge of truth" (I Timothy 2:4). In Titus 2:11, we read, "for the grace of God that bringeth salvation hath appeared to all men" and in II Peter 3:9, "The Lord is not slack concerning his promise, as some men count slackness; but is long-suffering to us-ward, not willing that any should perish, but that all should come to repentance." "Herein is love, not that we loved God, but that He loved us, and sent His Son to be the propitation for our sins," says I John 4:10.

Dr. Norman Geisler sums up the situation thus, "From the perspective of biblical theism, God never intended hell for man. God is holy and loving and wishes that every person would come to repentance (Exodus 34:6,7; Jonah 4:10,11; 2 Peter 3:9). Though the God of biblical theism is a God of justice and righteousness, He is also portrayed as a God of love. Second, the very nature of God prevents Him from being unfair. Third, we see from biblical theism the claim that men are not in total spiritual darkness. Fourth, biblical theism is very clear in its statement that anyone who wishes to establish a relationship with God will receive the necessary information on which to make a decision ... Fifth, the responsibility for a decision concerning salvation is in the hands of each person. Each of us is ultimately responsible for the course he chooses."[2]

There are some Christians who are, unfortunately, obsessed with and terrified by the danger of damnation. This frame of mind definitely does not seem to be warranted by Christ's teachings. While Christ warned that damnation was an available option, He revealed and manifested the incredible and infinite love of God, a love which seeks the salvation of all mankind. Our Lord did not encourage agnosticism and fear about one's eternal destiny but rather a loving trust in God's infinite love for every one of us and utter confidence that He will do all He can to lead us to salvation. He encouraged joyful expectation of Heaven rather than an obsessive fear of damnation and Hell. The dark night of the soul — experienced by the spiritual heroes of Christendom — was not induced by fears of damnation but by an awareness of their inherent creatureliness and sinfulness and of the need to overcome attachments to the world; all this balanced by joy that God should yet love them and want them.

We must realize that nothing can come between us and God's love. Paul assures us, "that neither death, nor life, nor angels, nor principalities, nor powers, nor things present, nor things to come, nor height, nor depth, nor any other creature, shall be able to separate us from the love of God, which is in Christ Jesus our Lord" (Romans 8:38,39).

The call to constant joy can make sense only when we have begun to experience God's infinite love acting in our lives, and this love can be experienced by all who open the doors of their hearts to the One who knocks there. We must also be aware of our true identities as sons or daughters of God destined for everlasting union with Him. And the Rejoice Response is not something we earn or force into being but something we are given: we have, however, to accept the gift.

Joy is what the Christian message, the Christian life, is all about (implicit in Christian joy is the love of God). The vast majority of mankind, on the other hand, seems to have been programmed to grieve and to be obsessed with the seamier side of life. We must try to understand why this has been and is the case and how exactly Christianity makes a difference. For the sake of clarity we can call man's penchant for pessimism and negativism the Melancholist Mentality. Faced with the menace of this mentality, the Rejoice Response seeks to "reprogram" man to a permanent state of joy, a joy undiminished even by the seamier side of life. Such reprogramming with the Rejoice Response is not an escape from reality but an escape *to* Reality. It is an effort to live in a Christian cosmos, to see joy as the most natural and normal mood in the redeemed world.

The Melancholist Mentality manifests itself in almost all the philosophies and ideologies and religions that have hurried through the history of human thought. Gnosticism, Manicheanism, etc., are all thought — tendencies which see Good and Evil, the powers of light and the demons of darkness, as equally powerful (and, sometimes, evil as more so) or matter as innately evil and malevolent or salvation as a privilege of the elite. It has expressed itself in ethical systems which condemn all pleasures and joys and the body as evil and which sees human beings as hopelessly evil.

It has been said that the basic difference between Christianity and all other religions is the Christian affirmation that being is good. In all other religions one finds that created being is feared or despised or regarded with suspicion or explained away. In Christianity alone, created being is reverenced and rejoiced in as a reflection of God Himself. Christianity is radically different also because it is fundamentally, and at all levels, optimism itself, the good news, joyful tidings; making sense of human life and revealing as it does a destiny of boundless bliss. In contrast, the Oriental religions have gloomy tales and tidings: earthly existence is seen as retribution for past sins, and nothing lies ahead but an endless series of rebirths which will, it is desired, end in non-existence. These religions are shot through with the despair of all do-it-yourself belief systems. Judaism and Islam too are basically "works" religions submerged in layers of legalism that barricade the believer from God (and in Islam there is no personal relationship with the Creator, no perception of God as Father). All the most influential atheistic philosophies of the modern age have been built on foundations of despair and have no place for joy: in Behaviorism man is seen as a complex kind of animal, in Marxism he is seen as a momentary manifestation of matter, in atheistic Existentialism he is "une passion inutile." All non-Christian philosophies and religions, then, are enemies of joy, embodiments of the Melancholist Mentality.

Only in the salvific soil of the Christian garden has (and could) joy take root and flower.

In his daily life it would seem that man is waging an endless war with the Melancholist Mentality and that any joys which manage to survive its assaults come guilt-coated. All the psychologists and the gurus of the modern age are more or less "reacting" to the depression-despair syndrome that results. But, as we have seen, only on the foundations of the Christian Faith can the fortress of Joy be built.

Increasingly, the primary health problem of the modern age seems to be stress. Researchers emphasize the fact that stress is most often caused not by the problem but the manner in which the subject copes with the problem. And the most effective remedy for stress is, apparently, relaxation. In both respects, the Rejoice Response has much to recommend it. The transformation of priorities and perspectives, thoughts and emotions, it entails, is of critical importance in the "age of anxiety."

To avoid any misconception we must remind ourselves that the ugliness of sin must not be minimized or explained away. If there is one thing in the world which should cause grief, it is this deliberate rejection of God — but even such grief must be tempered by the joy implicit in Christ's conquest of the empire of evil. And the Christian, whose life is rooted in and related to his eternal destiny, is not less involved in the affairs of this world; rather, emboldened by his eternity perspective, he embraces it all ecstatically, "baptizing" it, bringing it into "fullness of life." It is important to remember that although the Devil and damnation, evil and suffering, are realities which must not be ignored, the Christian is called to focus himself on the reality of God's love and of the joy found in Him here and hereafter. In fact, the Manichean temptation — of thinking of the powers of darkness as almost equals of God, of devaluing the goodness and glory of God's creation — is so strong that the Christian is well advised to think and talk of Satan and Hell only after thoroughly soaking himself in the Divine power and glory, in the Love and Joy that dwells at the Heart of the Christian cosmos.

The kind of psychologist who says, "All's well with the world and with ourselves — if only we learn to have any kind of fun we feel like and to not feel guilty about anything we do" is, we have seen, reacting to the Melancholist Mentality. Faced with the onslaught of despair and anguish, he clutches at such straws as human ingenuity can invent. This paranoid, hysterical reaction can aptly be called the Hedonist Heresy. In his search for a way out of the Valley of the Shadow of Death man has followed many substitutes for the true Shepherd. Thus, Eros and Epicurus are the gods of our generation, gods who are devils in disguise.

The only sane and balanced outlook on the pleasures and natural happiness of the world is the Christian mean, the clear-headed acceptance of the reality of both Original Sin and the Redemption. There is definitely a delicate balance between a joy in all things and an unabashed awareness of the evil that is in man. And self-denial and sacrifice, the way of the Cross, are part and parcel of Christian love though they are not sought as ends in themselves and are, in fact, vehicles of joy. Christians have no illusions about the frailty of human nature. At the same time, we must realize that evil is condemned in Christianity precisely because it is joyless and false love.

All Christian morality is founded on the laws of love, goodness and truth — only in following these laws can man find true freedom and joy. This is the delicate balance which must be maintained if man is not to plunge into the miasma of the Melancholist Mentality.

God's revelation of the everlasting happiness awaiting man should be a reality both in his life and in his attitude to death. This comes through practice not through mere intellectual knowledge. He should realize in his daily life that every one he meets is an immortal being. The great theological truths that have been revealed in Christianity should animate and guide all his activity. Not merely his intellect but his emotions, feelings, imagination, should be dominated by them. Only if his every thought and action is guided by these truths can his intellectual understanding be real, conscious and complete.

The Rejoice Response is not merely a conversion of the intellect but a conversion of the psyche, of the imagination. There should be a conversion not only of thoughts but also of emotions, so that one can *feel* joy — all the time — in expectation. And this "conversion" of the emotions comes through an act of the will for "practice makes perfect." (True, joy can be present even in the fact of external emotional depression; but emotional conversion of a fundamental and permanent nature is possible if the effort necessary is made, though, of course, it is an ongoing process.) Man must be constantly conscious of the knowledge that he is on his way to Heaven; this knowledge should permeate his being, transform his thoughts, his feelings, his will. As he becomes constantly conscious, at all levels of his being, of the eternal joy awaiting him, all melancholy thoughts and nameless fears will vanish and will be replaced by a constant, ever- increasing sense of joy. There need be no question of sorrow at death, for the only things which should cause sadness are those things which separate one from God. Christ wept at the tomb of Lazarus because death was still victor then; but, when He died, death was forever "swallowed up in victory" and became the means of eternal life; the death and Resurrection of Jesus Christ marked the transition from the pre-redeemed world to the Christian cosmos. The angel's question to Mary Magdalene at the tomb, "Woman, why do you weep?" is a question addressed to all those who weep at the deaths of their dear ones.

No one can be perfectly prepared in confronting or coping with the death of a dear one. But some general guidelines, which are "part and parcel" of the Christian revelation, could be useful in such a situation. It must be realized firstly, that death is inevitable and that it is pointless to wish it did not exist. Secondly, it should be realized that man lives in the world for only (in comparative terms) a milli-second and then, almost immediately, leaves it and is united forever (if this be his choice) with God and with his loved ones. Thirdly, the brevity of life on earth and the imminence of eternal union with God make it imperative that man focus all his attention on his God-given duties in this world; all else is secondary. If he is discouraged by the sufferings of this life; if the emotional burdens of facing his own death or the deaths of others seem unbearable; then he has only to remind himself to be conscious of what awaits him at the end of the journey of earthly life.

Emphasis on the "joyful and triumphant" nature of the Christian response to bereavement and to all other earthly afflictions should not be construed as callous disregard for the numbing grief which almost everyone feels in the face of the death of a dear one. This emphasis is, rather, an emphasis on that which is the only source of hope for the grief-stricken — the reality of the resurrection and of eternal life. And, while it may seem "natural" to grieve at such deaths, it is quite possible to have such a conversion of the emotions and the feelings that it would be just as natural to rejoice and to give thanks to the "God of the living." It is true that such factors as the suddenness or intensity of bereavement, the practical hardships that follow in its wake, the sense of physical separation from the dead person, will give rise to emotions which can be released through tears. But, again, the inevitability of death, the brevity of life in this world and the fact that it is preparation for endless ecstasy in union with God and His children, the Rejoice Response, are also facts to be considered — if "real" enough to the Christian, they will transform all his emotions.

It is easy to see how such notorious objections to the Christian Faith as the problem of suffering — how can pain and evil exist in a universe created by an infinitely good and loving God? — are seen in an entirely different light from the perspective of the Rejoice Response. Even the most heart-rending tragedy is reduced to infinite insignificance when the milli-second between womb and tomb is revealed to be a stepping-stone to an eternity of happiness.

The Rejoice Response is available to Christians of different denominational backgrounds regardless of doctrinal differences. For instance, the Catholic belief in purgatory does not affect it. This Catholic doctrine does not in any way reject the radical distinction between Heaven and Hell. It does not assume that man has a second chance after death. While the doctrine does claim that there is a process of purification after death, this process is not seen as anything less than the beginning of Heaven.

The Rejoice Response is offered to all Christians regardless of their moral caliber and is not restricted to the saintly. Of course those who come closer to God experience suffering but this is not the suffering of those grief-stricken by bereavement. It results, rather, from breaking loose from attachments to "things of the world" in order to enter the "Kingdom not of this world."

The call to joy is not a call to the indifference of the Stoics who rigorously restrained all expression of emotion. It is, rather, a call to the fullest possible expression of the emotions that are natural to the Christian cosmos; the chief of these are love and joy. Thus we are not in any way "chaining down" or suffocating emotions and feelings. All we are saying is that heart and mind should be guided by the Rejoice Response.

The arrogant assumptions and assertions of most modern psychologists have been mentioned. And since for many people the psychologist has now become prophet and priest, it will be useful to see the relation of modern psychology to the Rejoice Respose.

Such pop psychology books as *Your Erroneous Zones*, *Getting Divorced From Mother and Dad*, *You Can Cope* and *How to be Your Own Best Friend*, preach a frankly and fully self-centered "only-you-can-make-yourself-happy-and-you-can-do-it-if-you-like" philosophy of life. We have seen why such efforts can only result in final futility and despair. For one thing the "ye shall be as gods" philosophy of self-worship has a very poor track record as far as delivering the goods is concerned: the "best friend" promised Dr. Jekyll in his "erroneous zone" is Mr. Hyde and, by himself, Dr. Jekyll has never been able to cope with or "get divorced" from Mr. Hyde. For another, no narcissist has ever dared to look death, the ultimate "erroneous zone," in the face: in its lurid light the pursuit of "the pleasure principle," the frenzied efforts "to be your own best friend" turn out to be just "games people play" in a cosmos which does not care.

Though we cannot but puncture the more pompous pretensions of the selfist psychologists (if we wish to retain our sanity), we must not overlook what is positive and promising in their works. Surely at least some portion of the huge mansions they have constructed on such fragile foundations can be salvaged; fly swatters are useful even if they cannot kill dragons. In "From a Secular to a Christian Psychology," Paul Vitz says that, "the best defense is a good offense. In this instance that means the development of a powerful Christian alternative which can absorb and baptize the legitimate secular psychological material providing a second new framework and many new concepts and useful techniques."[3] We should, then, see whether and how the Rejoice Response can sit in the secular saddle.

Enduring ecstasy in everyday existence — that is the Rejoice Response, that is the possibility offered to all who are born and live in Christ. Every perspective, priority, thought, emotion, attitude, feeling — one's entire mind-set, mentality, outlook — must rejoice, be energized by ecstasy. Every instant and aspect of life, every memory, every experience, must be seen and felt as Joyfull, as a hint and echo and taste of God and heaven. The mind, the heart, must be baptized in joy, be reformed by the Rejoice Response — and here the methods of the selfist psychologists may be of some value.

When Wayne Dyer, author of *Your Erroneous Zones*, says that it is neurotic and not natural to feel unhappy and guilty, when he tells us that we must not let our happiness be hampered by ourselves, with problems of our past, or the external factors which formed us or relationships we have with others or our roles, he is partially right. All the principles he offers are valid and invaluable — if we are living in the Christian cosmos and if all that we could ever desire or dream of desiring is offered to us forever. To cap it all he says, "Your *own expectations* are the key to this whole business of mental health. If you *expect* to be happy, healthy and fulfilled in life, then most likely it will work out that way."[4] In a similar manner the insights of other self-help psychologists can be adopted as appropriate by the Christian who answers the call to constant joy.

At all times we must be aware that we should be utterly abandoned to the Divine Will, that there is nothing which is ours, that the "ultimate I" is now Christ Jesus: In accepting Him as our Lord and God we accept Him too as the Thinker of our every thought. And the Rejoice Response cannot be made unless it is Christ in us Who makes it.

From all that we have seen of the nature of the Rejoice Response, we can conclude with C.S. Lewis that, "All sadness which is not either arising from the repentance of a concrete sin and hastening towards concrete amendment or restitution, or else arising from pity and hastening to active assistance, is simply bad; and I think we all sin, by needlessly disobeying the apostolic injunction to 'rejoice' as much as by anything else."[5]

The atheistic existentialist Martin Heidegger saw human life as "being towards death."[6] The Christian, however, sees it as "being towards-the-Resurrection" and, hence, C.S. Lewis parted from his friend Sheldon Vanauken with the words, "Christians NEVER say goodbye."[7]

The joys of the world can, at their best, as prelude and promise, as vehicle and veil, help man long for the joy without end in the Direct Vision of God. Man cannot describe the joys of Heaven exhaustively for the same reason that the embryo in the womb cannot say anything about the world it is about to enter. But he knows that God will make Heaven the way He wants it to be, and that cannot but be the best for man. Once man is through the Valley of the Shadow of Death (with the Lord as his Shepherd) he enters the land of everlasting sunshine. At the end of the narrow, rocky path through this "vale of tears" is the summit of joy. Beyond the darkness of the world shine the lights of the Celestial City. Man lives in this sin-stained, sorrow-filled world for a milli-second. He lives in Paradise for all eternity.

NOTES

1 Peter Kreeft, *Heaven the Heart's Deepest Longing* (San Francisco: Harper and Row, 1980), p. 116.
2 Norman Geisler, *The Roots of Evil* (Grand Rapids: Zondervan Publishing House, 1982), pp. 83-4.
3 Paul Vitz, "From a Secular to a Christian Psychology," in *Christianity Confronts Modernity*, edited by Peter Williamson and Kevin Perotta (Ann Arbor, Michigan: Servant Books, 1981), pp. 147-8.
4 Wayne Dyer, "Happiness — It's Only Natural," *Family Circle*, March 8, 1977.
5 C.S. Lewis, *The Problem of Pain* (London: Fontana Books, 1957), p. 55.
6 Martin Heidegger, *Being and Time* (New York: Harper and Row, 1962) p. 296.
7 Sheldon Vanauken, *A Severe Mercy* (London: Hodder and Stoughton, 1977), p. 125.

25
GOD'S WILL
Reflections on the Problem of Pain
Sheldon Vanauken

"I still can't get over it, Jane, losing my baby. Just before her second birthday. But it was God's will." — "God must be testing Sue by giving her cancer." — "He broke his back when the tractor turned over. It was God's will, of course." — "God took both our children." — "How can a good God let the Cambodians starve? I refuse to believe in a God like that." — "All three of his sons, such fine boys, died when the cruiser was torpedoed. It was God's will." — "How can God make me suffer so? I hate God!"

It was God's will. Or, as Allah wills it. Is this, in truth, the way of it? Does God indeed award a cancer here, a car wreck there, all according to His high and mysterious purpose? Does He punish Mr and Mrs Smith by willing the death of their child when the drunken youth rams their car? Does God will the earth to quake? Did He will the deaths of millions, Christians as well as Jews, in the Nazi death camps, or at the murderous hands of Stalin?

It may be indeed that good men must sometimes suffer to learn that their only lasting joy — their only security — is in God. Some may be called upon individually to bear the weight of the cross for His sake, nor can we always see how their pain shall be to His glory. But in speaking of every disaster as God's will, we forget something essential to the Christian faith: the Fall and its consequences. The story in Genesis may be taken as literal truth or as myth; but *myth* implies an essential truth. Moreover, the Fall is not only affirmed by St. Paul, it is affirmed by redemption itself — redemption in Christ — for redemption is *from* sin. The sin that entered the world with the Fall.

Let us consider what the Fall was and is. It is man, a created being — a *creature* — in rebellion against his Creator. It is man in his pride seeking independence — autonomy — by choosing something other than God. By choosing *himself.* Self. Self-centeredness. Selfishness. Self-expression. Self-realization. Self-fulfillment. Some of these sound quite innocent, don't they? But Christ's command was to *die* to self. We are not roused to enthusiasm by the idea.

A question arises: Why did God let the Fall happen? Why didn't He give Eve a frightful slap and say in a voice of thunder: "*Stop* that!"? Why did He *let* us become infected with sin? We are so addicted to self, so infected, that our self-love doesn't even shock us, we hardly notice. But God allows us choice. That is the answer to the question of why He didn't slap Eve. A simple answer — and utterly astonishing. He not only made living, moving creatures. He made creatures capable of saying "No" to Him, of defying Him. Unlike the trees, we have free will. God's great experiment was to create us free to *choose* to love Him (the only love worth having) or to reject Him. We love Him and serve Him, or we love our self and serve that self. We don't admit we're self-serving, but we're often proud to say we're self-sufficient, without need for God.

But if we are fallen — infected with sin and addicted to sin — what hope is there for us? Perhaps God, not caring, has abandoned us? — He cares so much that He allowed us to drive the nails through His hands. My God! He loves us that much! The phrase has become so boring as to lose meaning: Christ came to save sinners. Awesome meaning, in fact.

He came down from heaven — God himself — and became man and died in agony as man, trusting forsaken (as He had to be to taste the whole of death). When we suffer, let us remember the Son trusting the Father — and the validation of the trust in the Resurrection. Christ was, precisely, God's action to save us from the Fall. On our own we cannot conquer our addiction to self, but with Christ in us we are not on our own.

When the Fall occurred, it was not only man that fell. All creation (at least on earth) somehow fell too. We cannot know how it was before — whether it was only with the Fall that the lion learned to bite man. And we don't know whether there is indeed a Prince of this World, an archangel, himself fallen after "dubious battle on the plains of heaven." But we may remember that that ominous figure, however much not "in" among Christians these days, was spoken of with authority by our Lord. What we cannot know is what that fallen creation — and that prince — may have to do with the cancer that tries our trust.

The finite mind of man cannot comprehend the infinite mind of God. We can know only what God has revealed to us in Christ. We know that we have choice, for He told us. And we know, even with our finite minds, that if men can choose evil, other men will suffer. Three-quarters of the suffering is clearly traceable to man's own cruelty and greed. And we know — it is much — that He loves us and that we can trust Him. We cal hold to that.

It is the implications of free will that I wish to explore. That we were given choice is one of the things we know. But it was not Eve only making a choice, and choosing further to tempt Adam: consequently he was faced with *his* choice, and he made it. And we have been making choices ever since: the Nazis were men making choices, so is the fellow who snaps at his wife at breakfast.

But choice has consequences or it wouldn't be choice at all. If we pull the trigger, the bullet strikes, and our victim gasps and dies. If God gives us freedom, freedom to choose, He must allow us to have what we choose — the taste of the apple, the death of the man we shoot, or, if we insist, Hell — or it wouldn't be choice at all. He must allow the consequences. And the consequences of the consequences, going on endlessly, involving the innocent.

If a young man drinks too much (a choice) and pridefully decides to show his girl how fast he can drive (a choice), he may smash hideously into your car, killing his girl and leaving you paralyzed for life. Is this God's will (except in the sense of permitting the choosing)? It cannot be, for that would mean God forced the young man to choose evil (self). He chose; the consequences follow. The girl's family plunged in grief. You unable to send your son to college. The policeman who came to the wreck not being somewhere else to stop a crime.

But there may be good consequences, too — God will bring these about if possible. You and your wife may learn to trust God more deeply; the young man, haunted by grief, may become a Christian. But those would be bringing good out of evil, not bringing about the evil in hopes of the good. The *evil* was the consequences of a choice.

To say that because God is sovereign and all powerful He can simultaneously give us freedom to choose and compel our choice is not to say something profound about omnipotence but to speak nonsense. The glass is either transparent or opaque. The Holy Spirit urges us towards the good, not towards the evil. And, of course, our good choices — our prayer for strength to bear pain or for healing — also have consequences. The consequences of good acts also go on and on.

Millions of people choosing, millions upon millions of choices, choices at every second of the centuries. *One* choice is like a stone chucked into a still pond with the wave spreading out in all directions. But *all* the choices: imagine an ocean with a constant hail of stones plunging into it and a chaotic tumult of boiling waves in a patternless storm. Only God could comprehend it.

The murderer is making a choice. So is the monk praying in the night. The rapist is a monster of self-choosing, as is the woman who feeds on her children to bolster her ego. The man who rushes into a burning house to save a neighbor's child; the businessman who cuts his neighbor's financial throat; the child who tortures the cat. The choices are not in a vacuum: someone else is helped or harmed, including the cat.

Sometimes it is said about monstrous evils like the Nazi death camps that, if there were a God, He would stop them. Why *doesn't* God stop such human suffering? Let us, then, suppose He *does*. Let us imagine God looking down at the Nazi death camps: the squalid misery, the near starvation, the cold, the brutal guards, the firing squads, the skinny children herded into the gas chambers. God sees it all and hears the wailing and the prayers: "Help us, oh God! Let our cry come unto Thee!" — Suddenly the divine fist slams down upon the table, and thunder drowns out the guns below.

"By God!" He says. "It's too much. Eating an apple is one thing — but *this*! I never dreamt that my men could be this wicked. I *will* it to stop."

Well, of course it stops. A Nazi guard turns a handle to start the gas flowing in upon the huddled victims behind the heavy glass. He yawns, he's done this so many times. No thrill left. Then he notices that the people in the chamber are not clawing their throats. Odd. He gives the handle another push, just as the walls of the gas chamber dissolve. He and the other guards snatch out pistols and fire. God catches the bullets in His hand. In time the prisoners shuffle away, finding that the perimeter fences have vanished.

God has acted. Elsewhere, booted feet ascend the stairs, and a door is kicked in. Storm troopers enter, guns leveled, and the man they've come to get cowers. But the blow and the kick do not land; and the storm troopers, bewildered, go away.

Now that God is acting, He will have to act the next time the Russians purge a few million people. In the meantime, there is the Hitler war. Hundreds of Luftwaffe bombers are over London, bombs whistling down. But God's hand is in the way. Londoners go back to bed. The roar of the guns on the Russian front is stilled. A submarine fires a spread of torpedoes. It appears that two at least will strike the cruiser, and 800 men will die, including one family's three fine sons. God reaches into the water and seizes the torpedoes. The proud cruiser steams on.

But agony is not to be measured quantitatively. The 50 people in a gas chamber — a quick death, after all — or one man being hideously tortured, hour after hour, day after day, by the Secret Police. God stops that: no line can be drawn. And the woman in a hospital, her body eaten up with cancer: she is suffering almost as much or perhaps more — who can measure? God, committed now to action, acts. The woman draws a long breath, flinching. It doesn't hurt. She sits up and asks for lunch.

A rapist is leering down at his terrified victim. Then he finds an invisible wall between him and her. In a few moments she pulls her torn frock round her and goes, possibly sticking her tongue out at the shrunken man. A woman watches her husband drink the coffee she has put strychnine in. She turns pale when he gives her a kiss and goes off to work. Another woman screaming at her tired husband, as she has done for years, is suddenly voiceless. A boy's cruel epithet flung at a high school girl who would be scarred by it is heard by no one. The child's hands torturing the cat go limp. The cat goes away, tail in air.

All this — it's right nice, isn't it? This is the God we want, we think. We are ready to re-elect God, God. But let us look further. When all this begins to happen, people will be astonished and unbelieving, victims and predators alike. Of course many of the victims are predators in their own ways: the man in the death camp may be, in what he thinks of as better times, a rapist. People will go on for a while trying to find pistols that will work and have fun again.

But finally it will dawn upon mankind that God has stopped all victimizing. You cannot shoot anybody, but also — since God can't draw lines — you cannot bark at your wife or cheat on your income tax. The fist cannot connect. The cruel word cannot be said. Free will has been repealed. No one now chooses to be good; he *must* be.

Newspapers shrink. No more wars or rumours of war, no more corruption in Washington, no more murder trials, no more juicy scandals. Lions lie down with lambs, and capitalists with workers. Almost every novel ever written will soon come to seem unreal, for they were about a world where good guys strove with bad ones, and courage meant something. And goodness.

The gift God gave to man was the freedom to choose. If God acts to prevent the consequences of choice, the gift is withdrawn. No one will choose to shoot if the bullet cannot strike. No one will accept cancer with fortitude and prayer if there is no cancer. No one will wound with a cruel word if it is unheard. For awhile people will wistfully yearn to hurt somebody, but new generations will have forgotten choice. No longer will it be salvation through the redemptive sacrifice of Christ. Indeed, the Passion itself will seem meaningless to a world that has never known suffering, a world where wickedness is unknown.

But, also, a world where goodness is not chosen and is, therefore, unknown. To finite man, what meaning can *goodness* have if there is no badness? Is this, after all, the world we should like? As it is now, we are moved by valour and goodness because they shine in an evil world as stars shine in darkness.

No stars, so to speak, in our new world. God's grand experiment of creating people free to love and trust Him or to hate Him will be all over. We, compelled to be good without choice, shall sink into apathy. Perhaps our minds will decay. We shall not have achieved autonomy. We shall have become automatons. More and more like vegetables, merely existing. We who were created for the stars.

After all, perhaps it is as well that God is running the universe, not us.

When God became one of us in Christ, He never promised us an easy time or said that Christians would be spared. In fact, the lions in Rome were already looking forward to their first taste of raw Christian. What Jesus said was: "Take up your cross and follow me."

We shall suffer because of evil loosed into the world, most of it men's choices. Despite a shudder for what may lie ahead for me, I say thank God — imagining a world without choice. Pain may seem an unmitigated evil — and, unless it draws us or others to deeper trust in God, it is. But would we escape it by rejecting God's grand gift of freedom? We must indeed use that freedom to lessen the suffering in the world: thus good comes from evil.

And if we must suffer, let us remember Jesus forsaken. And, like Him, trust in agony — remembering that God Himself in awesome compassion is suffering with us. In the end we shall have what we have chosen: we shall have Him: and in the light of His face all the suffering unto death — the bearing of our cross — will then have been less than a half-remembered dream.

Glossary

ANTHROPIC PRINCIPLE: If certain forces in the universe, such as those of elementary particles, electromagnetic forces or the force of gravity, were only slightly different, life could not have arisen. This suggests that the universe was made, designed, to lead to life, including human life.

APODICTIC REASONING: Reasoning about necessities.

COSMOLOGICAL ARGUMENT FOR GOD: Why does the universe exist? It could not have created itself or popped into existence. Its existence depends on a Being Who transcends it, Who is the Source of His Own Being, and that of the universe.

DETERMINISM: The general thesis that everything is determined; that is, that all events, including human choices, are such that they occur necessarily, given the relevant conditions and the laws of nature. Nothing that happens, including human choices, could have happened differently, unless the initial conditions had been different.

DUALISM: The thesis that human consciousness (or the soul, the mind) is distinct from the body, especially the brain. The mind is other than the brain it uses; thinking is other than the brain processes that accompany it, and is necessary for it.

EMPIRICISM: The general thesis that sense experience is the course of, and provides the justification for, all our knowledge.

ESOTERIC: That which is meant for, or understood by, only the select few.

EXOTERIC: That which is meant for the general public, as opposed to the select few.

FIDEISM: The thesis that religious belief is based ultimately on a faith that cannot be rationally justified.

MATERIALISM: The thesis that everything that exists is material; that there are no spiritual beings. Thus consciousness is said to be a form of material reality, or somehow reducible to it.

MECHANISM: The thesis that nature is to be explained in terms of mechanical action and material forces alone.

MONISM: The thesis that the many things that comprise reality are ultimately one, or of one kind. Materialism is a form of Monism: all things are material, or somehow reducible to matter. Monism is opposed to Pluralism: there are many kinds of reality, irreducible to each other.

ONTOLOGICAL ARGUMENT FOR GOD: The essence of God is absolute, definite perfection. He is the Being greater than which nothing can be conceived. Necessary existence must be part of the essence of God as absolute perfection, else that essence would lack a perfection. But if God's essence necessarily includes necessary existence, God must exist. God cannot not exist; His actual, necessary existence is part of His essence. Therefore God exists.

POSITIVISM, OR LOGICAL POSITIVISM: The thesis that science, mathematics and logic are the only sources of knowledge. It is the denial of a specifically philosophical kind of knowledge. Virtually identical to Scientism.

PRAGMATISM: As a theory of truth, the thesis that the test of truth is practical consequences, as opposed to what is viewed as mere abstractions. Roughly, truth is what works.

REDUCTIONISM: The tendency to reduce certain notions to allegedly simpler, or more basic, or more easily accessible notions. For example, consciousness to a brain process, moral values to the dictates of society, physical objects to patterns of sensations and mental images. Reductionism is often the attempt to reduce the "higher" (e.g., mind, spirit) to the "lower" (e.g., matter, physical forces).

SUPERNATURALISM: The thesis that, in addition to the natural order (studied by science, history, etc.), there is also another realm of being, transcending it (God, heaven and hell, angels and devils). Opposed to Naturalism, which acknowledges only the natural order.

TELEOLOGICAL ARGUMENT FOR GOD: The universe exhibits a marvelous order and pattern, which could not have come about by chance, but must have been designed (e.g., the marvels of the human eye). Design requires a Designer, and so God must exist as the Great Designer of the universe. Also called the Design Argument. See Watchmaker Argument.

THEISM: Belief in God, the assertion that God is; as opposed to Atheism, the denial of God; and Agnosticism, skepticism or doubt about God's existence.

VERIFICATIONIST: One who adheres to the Verificationist Principle of Logical Positivism, that all meaningful statements (other than expressions of emotion, questions, etc.) must be verifiable or falsifiable by science, mathematics or logic. An adherent of Positivism, or the positivistic method.

WATCHMAKER ARGUMENT FOR GOD: A form of the Teleological or Design Argument. If you see a watch you know there must be a watchmaker, it could not have come into being by chance. The universe is like a watch, only much more wonderful in its design, so it too needs a "Watchmaker," that is, God.